AFRICAN
WARS

ADST-DACOR DIPLOMATS AND DIPLOMACY SERIES
Series Editor: Margery Boichel Thompson

Since 1776, extraordinary men and women have represented the United States abroad under all sorts of circumstances. What they did and how and why they did it remain little known to their compatriots. In 1995 the Association for Diplomatic Studies and Training (ADST) and DACOR, an organization of foreign affairs professionals created the Diplomats and Diplomacy book series to increase public knowledge and appreciation of the role of American foreign affairs officers in world history.

OTHER TITLES IN THE SERIES

Herman J. Cohen, *Intervening in Africa: Superpower Peacemaking in a Troubled Continent*

Charles T. Cross, *Born a Foreigner: A Memoir of the American Presence in Asia*

Brandon Grove, *Behind Embassy Walls: The Life and Times of an American Diplomat*

Parker T. Hart, *Saudi Arabia and the United States: Birth of a Security Partnership*

Michael P. E. Hoyt, *Captive in the Congo: A Consul's Return to the Heart of Darkness*

Cameron R. Hume, *Mission to Algiers: Diplomacy by Engagement*

Dennis Kux, *The United States and Pakistan, 1947–2000: Disenchanted Allies*

Jane C. Loeffler, *The Architecture of Diplomacy: Building America's Embassies*

William B. Milam, *Bangladesh and Pakistan: Flirting with Failure in Muslim South Asia*

Robert H. Miller, *Vietnam and Beyond: A Diplomat's Cold War Education*

David D. Newsom, *Witness to a Changing World*

Yale Richmond, *Practicing Public Diplomacy: A Cold War Odyssey*

Howard B. Schaffer, *The Limits of Influence: America's Role in Kashmir*

James W. Spain, *In Those Days: A Diplomat Remembers*

Ulrich Straus, *The Anguish of Surrender: Japanese POWs of World War II*

James Stephenson, *Losing the Golden Hour: An Insider's View of Iraq's Reconstruction*

AFRICA: MISSING VOICES SERIES

DONALD I. RAY, GENERAL EDITOR
ISSN 1703-1826

University of Calgary Press has a long history of publishing academic works on Africa. *Africa: Missing Voices* illuminates issues and topics concerning Africa that have been ignored or are missing from current global debates. This series will fill a gap in African scholarship by addressing concerns that have been long overlooked in political, social, and historical discussions about this continent.

No. 1 · **Grassroots Governance?: Chiefs in Africa and the Afro-Caribbean**
      Edited by D.I. Ray and P.S. Reddy · Copublished with the International Association of
      Schools and Institutes of Administration (IASIA)

No. 2 · **The African Diaspora in Canada: Negotiating Identity and Belonging**
      Edited by Wisdom Tettey and Korbla Puplampu

No. 3 · **A Common Hunger: Land Rights in Canada and South Africa**
      by Joan G. Fairweather

No. 4 · **New Directions in African Education: Challenges and Possibilities**
      Edited by S. Nombuso Dlamini

No. 5 · **Shrines in Africa: History, Politics, and Society**
      Edited by Allan Charles Dawson

No. 6 · **The Land Has Changed: History, Society and Gender in Colonial Eastern Nigeria**
      by Chima J. Korieh

No. 7 · **African Wars: A Defense Intelligence Perspective**
      by William G. Thom

AFRICAN WARS

A Defense Intelligence Perspective

WILLIAM G. THOM

UNIVERSITY OF
CALGARY
PRESS

University of Calgary Press
2500 University Drive NW
Calgary, Alberta
Canada T2N 1N4
www.uofcpress.com

The views expressed in this manuscript are those of the author and do not reflect the opinions, official policy, or positions of the Defense Intelligence Agency, Department of Defense, the U.S. Government, the Association for Diplomatic Studies and Training, or DACOR.

LIBRARY AND ARCHIVES CANADA CATALOGUING IN PUBLICATION

Thom, William G., 1945-
    African wars : a defense intelligence perspective / William G. Thom.

(Africa, missing voices series ; 7)
(The ADST-DACOR diplomats and diplomacy series)
Includes bibliographical references and index.
ISBN 978-1-55238-273-8

1. Civil war—Africa, Sub-Saharan. 2. Insurgency—Africa, Sub-Saharan. 3. Africa, Sub-Saharan—History, Military. 4. National security—Africa, Sub-Saharan. 5. Africa, Sub-Saharan—Politics and government—1960-. 6. Thom, William G., 1945-. 7. Intelligence officers—United States—Biography. I. Title. II. Series: Africa, missing voices series ; 7 III. Series: ADST-DACOR diplomats and diplomacy series

UA855.7.T56 2010   355'.033067   C2010-904441-X

The University of Calgary Press acknowledges the support of the Alberta Foundation for the Arts for our publications. We acknowledge the financial support of the Government of Canada through the Canada Book Fund for our publishing activities. We acknowledge the financial support of the Canada Council for the Arts for our publishing program.

Printed and bound in Canada by Marquis Book Printing Inc.
This book is printed on FSC Silva paper

Cover design by Melina Cusano
Page design and typesetting by Melina Cusano

To the late James L. Woods,
who understood the role of strategic intelligence,
and the legions of Africa analysts who fought over the years
to keep the region on the intelligence consumers' agenda

and to Dale and the boys

CONTENTS

PART TWO: AFRICAN WARS I HAVE KNOWN

LIST OF MAPS

FOREWORD

This book is a story of Bill Thom's personal and professional journey as a career intelligence analyst in the Defense Intelligence Agency (DIA). You will read about his life and career challenges from early childhood in the mid-twentieth century to the end of his government service in the early twenty-first century. But why read this book? His entire professional life was spent with DIA as an Africa specialist, and his career in intelligence generally parallels the emergence of independent African states and their struggles with insurgencies, internal strife, and civil wars. During his long career, he maintained a front row seat regarding sensitive information on African countries and, as he became more senior, he affected U.S. decision-making and policy implementation on key African issues and events. He also tended to notice things many people missed.

Bill journeys from a young boy interested in military maneuvers, to an African Studies student in college, to a new military analyst, to a wiser, more experienced advisor, to manager, and finally to a senior executive. His book contains all the bumps along the way on that winding road. Over time, he learned how to analyze, brief, and write critically about complex intelligence issues, and how to deal effectively with the myriad intelligence, policy, and military organizations at both the theater and national levels. These organizations had – and continue to have – different interests and agendas, and present potential minefields for an Africa specialist.

The reader will then venture into his personal and professional vision of what an analyst, advisor, and manager should be and, even more importantly, experience his challenges to maintain analytic integrity in the face of incredible pressures. He advocated on a regular basis to consumers of information at all levels of the government and military the importance of understanding the context of intelligence, especially with regard to military and political events in sub-Saharan Africa. He stressed the importance of laying out what information we knew, what data we could find out, and what we did not know. Intelligence consumers at all levels eventually asked us what we thought of it all. When Bill Thom wrote or briefed about what it meant, people with a need to know took notice.

He also mentored and counseled younger analysts how to think critically about intelligence and how it applied to both current and forward-looking analysis. This is how we first interacted in the early 1980s. He motivated me and other analysts to excel and was not hesitant to put one or more of us in front of senior military officers or executives if he knew we had the best information and a command of the subject. He did this to me more than once! At the same time, his professional quest was to persuade policy experts and military operators about the need to grasp the complexities and subtleties of political and military situations in sub-Saharan countries. These issues needed to be understood within a global context of events. Africa, after all, was at center stage during the Cold War, not for years, but for decades. In addition, after the insurgencies continued, terrorism increased, and the need for accurate information on African countries was never greater.

Perhaps, as with all journeys and quests – especially in the intelligence business – they are destined to remain at least partially unfulfilled. Was he successful and did he complete the journey? I will let those who read this book debate that. However, I for one know that he did his professional best to achieve these goals and no one can really ask for more.

I recommend this book to students of African issues, military historians, intelligence professionals, and those schooled in the ways of bureaucrats. You will be treated to quite a few historical and military insights, experience bureaucratic dog fights, and engage in the various daily duties of an intelligence professional. Some readers may find aspects of this memoir unpleasant; so be it. The career of this intelligence officer spanned numerous unpleasant, even heinous, issues and events on the African continent: wars, genocide, and death. He explores most of these issues; appreciate his understanding of things African and maybe, you, the reader, will become a bit more enlightened about the complicated world of intelligence as seen through his eyes.

William T. Stoakley
Corrales, New Mexico

PREFACE

Everyone must have an ego to survive in today's corporate world, but that is not why I wrote this book. The main motivating factor was to share experiences and lessons learned. Do I have something to say, something of value? I hope so. After thirty-five years as an intelligence officer, I am strong on practical experience. In telling my story, I hope to entertain as well as educate. Truth is stranger than fiction as the following pages will once again illustrate. This book is not a tell-all exposé on the intelligence community. Where deficiencies are cited, it is to instruct on practical limitations, human frailties, bureaucratic intransigence, that is, how and why the system sometimes fails. This is not a documented history of the wars in sub-Saharan Africa (SSA). Many minor conflicts are not discussed at all, nor are a few major wars that escaped my scrutiny. This is also not a comprehensive treatment of the subject. Specialists who have devoted their lives to the study of one country or conflict do a much better job of that. Nor is this book a scholarly or theoretical work. All the research here was done during my career as an intelligence analyst, manager, senior expert, and executive.

This book is a personal journey through time from the mid-1960s to the early 2000s. The trip meanders from conflict to conflict, from war to war, through SSA. My career closely parallels this path. Thus, it is the thread that holds this story together. The book provides insight into the wars of this troubled continent, and into the lives of those Africa analysts who did their best to understand them. It also sheds light onto the intelligence process to see how information is gathered, analyzed, and made into products for consumers. Finally, it seeks to place African wars into perspective. How do they stack up against the tides of global history?

The journey begins in the first chapter, which outlines my family background and explains how early influences contributed to success as a military intelligence analyst. The following chapters address the various conflicts in SSA in rough chronological order based on when they started. Not all the chapters are about wars, however. Some discuss other factors that round out the experience, such as traveling in Africa, working at a U.S. military command headquarters overseas, bureaucratic battles over resources, and briefing VIPs. The objective is to give the reader a good sense of what working at various levels within the defense intelligence community is really like. This work is dedicated to all those people, military and civilian, who toiled away as Africa analysts enduring the stigma of working on the lowest priority region in the world. Under-staffed, under-funded, and at times under-appreciated, they made a gallant and important contribution to our knowledge of Africa and its people.

—William G. Thom

ACKNOWLEDGMENTS

Special thanks to Dr. William T. Stoakley for his encouragement and critical review and for contributing the foreword to this book.

Thanks also to Margery B. Thompson, Publishing Director and Series Editor of the Association for Diplomatic Studies and Training (ADST), for all her editorial help and for seeing the project through; and to ADST interns James MacHaffie and Anders Walløe for their helpful technical assistance.

And, thanks to Ambassador Robert Houdek for his most valuable insights on East Africa and enthusiasm for the project.

Other helpers included Dr. Harvey Clark Greisman, Colin Harding, Andrew Montgomery, Robert E. Fitzgerald, and Dr. William J. Foltz of Yale University.

Special gratitude for graphic support provided by Eric Pietrzak.

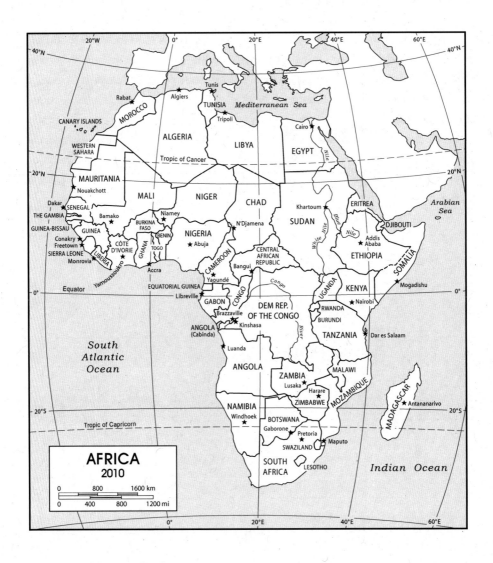

AFRICA
2010

PROLOGUE
The World of Defense Intelligence

It has always amazed me how little the general public knows about the U.S. intelligence community, even though its basic structure, organization, and functions are not classified. A brief primer on U.S. intelligence may thus be useful to readers with limited knowledge of the business and enable them to better interpret the text.

DIA AND THE INTELLIGENCE COMMUNITY

Since 1947, and until very recently, the basic structure of the U.S. intelligence community has remained essentially unchanged. The director of Central Intelligence (DCI) ruled the community and simultaneously served as director of the Central Intelligence Agency. For all practical purposes, this made the CIA the first among equals in the community. Other key players included the Defense Intelligence Agency (DIA), the National Security Agency (NSA), the State Department's Bureau of Intelligence and Research (INR), the National Geospatial–Intelligence Agency (NGA), and the Federal Bureau of Investigation (FBI). Today the new director of National Intelligence (DNI) supplants the DCI, and the CIA's special status is somewhat diminished.

The DIA was formed in 1961 to consolidate the views of the military services and serve as the focal point for Defense Department intelligence. DIA is primarily an analytic organization, although some oversight and management duties have been added over the years. Within the intelligence community, DIA represents military intelligence. The DIA director presides over his own defense intelligence community, but the services (Army, Navy, Air Force, and Marines) retain their own intelligence staffs in the Pentagon. The major military commands, such as the U.S. European Command, the U.S. Transportation Command, and others, also maintain intelligence staffs and control intelligence units assigned to them, mainly for tactical (i.e., battlefield-type) intelligence. The DIA director heads up the Military Intelligence Board, where all the military services and commands are represented.

THE INTELLIGENCE CYCLE

The production of intelligence assessments follows a cycle. First comes defining the target, the enemy, or simply the subject and what we need to know about it. After inventorying what we already know, we levy specific collection requirements to fill the gaps in our knowledge. Information may be obtained through human contacts (called HUMINT), which may be covert or overt. Signals intelligence (SIGINT) focuses on intercepted foreign communications. Imagery intelligence is known as IMINT. Scientific signatures, such as the profile of a missile launch, are measurement intelligence (MASINT). Regardless of the "INT," the information goes back to the analyst for evaluation.

Unlike police work where intelligence on a case is limited to its immediate investigators, the U.S. Intelligence Community shares information more widely. Thus, raw (unevaluated) intelligence reports collected by CIA case officers are shared with other agencies. The same goes for information reported by DIA's military attachés, embassy cables, and communications intercepts.

The heart of the cycle comes in the next step, analysis. The behind-the-scenes star of the show is the analyst who puts it all together. Analysts must use all their experience, training, and knowledge to arrive at the best, most accurate, assessment. The analyst must remain flexible, open to new information that may alter previously held analytical positions. The assessment – trimmed, refined, coordinated, and illustrated – becomes the product, the final stage and the object of the whole exercise.

The intelligence product comes in three primary flavors: current, basic, and estimative. In theory, the estimate should be the highest and most useful art form. In reality, however, it is the current intelligence assessment that drives the train. Policymakers are more interested in having the latest report on the latest development, the subject of that three o'clock meeting. Basic intelligence includes historical background material, order of battle information, military organization, and equipment, as well as the outlook for the next six months (e.g., are the insurgents winning or losing the war?). Estimative intelligence involves longer-term assessments usually two or three years into the future, but perhaps as many as ten years down the road.

THE DIA ANALYST

There is an old saying that intelligence is the second oldest profession, exceeding the first only in the number of amateurs wishing to participate. Another is that there are no good analysts, only good opportunities. Both sayings contain much truth. The analyst's first test, as in any other discipline, is to recognize what is important. Of the scores, perhaps hundreds, of pieces of raw intelligence moving from left to right across the analyst's desk (read, computer screen) daily, he or she must know what to discard, what to save for further study, and what to mark for immediate action.

As a manager, I looked for three things from aspiring defense intelligence analysts, beginning with area or technical knowledge. If you were going to work Africa, you had to know for example the region, its problems, its people, and cultures. An analyst for military aircraft production had to know the technical aspects of that business. For most DIA analysts, knowing the military is important. That is one reason so many former military personnel populate DIA's civilian ranks. But military expertise can be had in other ways as well. In the realm of strategic intelligence, which inhabits the national level in Washington and in the military commands, having studied the military, its history, and its culture can be equally useful. It helps to know the terminology and speak the language.

Learning the intelligence trade is another matter. Unless new analysts are recruited from the ranks of former military intelligence officers or from another intelligence agency, most of their learning is on the job. Back in the 1960s DIA was about equally divided between military and civilian employees. Today that ratio has slipped to about 70 per cent civilian and 30 per cent military. The all-volunteer military has made it more difficult for the armed services to staff defense agencies such as DIA.

Over the past forty years, management oversight of the analyst has changed with the times. Excessive management review characterized the early days. It was not unusual for a paper or briefing to be reviewed by senior analysts, supervisors, and managers a half dozen times or more. Today one or two reviews are often deemed sufficient. The result unfortunately can be thinner, more superficial analysis. From my post as Defense Intelligence Officer for Africa (DIO-AF) for fourteen years, I sometimes felt that I was the only really substantive senior reviewer of a product that might be going to a very high-level consumer.

THE PRINCES OF THE CHURCH: THE DIOS

The Defense Intelligence officers (DIOs) were created in the image of the National Intelligence officers who sit in the CIA building in Langley, Virginia, on the staff of the National Intelligence Council. The role of the DIOs was more circumscribed, however. Their responsibility was limited largely to defense intelligence and DIA, although the DIOs did sit at the right hand of their corresponding NIO and supported the NIOs on virtually all defense and military issues.

Most Defense Intelligence officers had a regional focus. They were broadly responsible for overseeing their slice of intelligence, including the quality and appropriateness of DIA products. But it was more than that. As senior staff practically immune from bureaucratic rebuke, the DIOs wielded significant power within DIA. They kept the director in the loop and had unfettered access to his staff, much like a cardinal with access to the Vatican Council and ultimately the Pope. While the DIOs nominally came under a senior manager (the deputy director for policy support), in reality they largely ran their own show. This extended to personal contacts with DIA's most important consumers in the Office of the Secretary of Defense, the State Department, the National Security Council, and the National Intelligence Council.

Within DIA, however, the DIOs were regarded with suspicion or outright disdain, as senior staff people who function largely outside the chain of command often are. A vital institution in DIA for more than two decades, they were eliminated in a 2003 reorganization. Senior DIA analysts were appointed in 2007 essentially to recreate the DIOs.

THE CONSUMERS: POLICYMAKERS AND OPERATORS

The customers for strategic intelligence fall into two categories: policymakers and operators. Most of the policymakers are members of the executive branch with responsibilities in foreign policy formulation and implementation. This not only includes the thousands of people in the departments of State and Defense, and the National Security Council (i.e., the White House), but also those in the departments of Commerce, Energy, Justice, Homeland Security, and other cabinet-level posts and their legions of foreign policy foot soldiers. They say that making foreign policy is like making sausage. If so, intelligence is a key ingredient in the mix.

The other group of customers, the operators, short for military operators, are the senior military leaders in the Pentagon, in the major commands, and elsewhere who monitor the world's trouble spots and work on contingency plans. In addition, a subgroup of long-term planners use intelligence information and estimates to determine what kind of weapons, equipment, and force structures we are likely to need decades into the future.

Requirements from consumers have changed with the times. During the Cold War – most of DIA's existence – the emphasis was on the communist threat, including areas of encroachment, such as Southeast Asia. Africa even got into the act when a communist challenge materialized in Angola and Ethiopia. Nevertheless, for the most part, intelligence managers gave short shrift to regions like Africa and Latin America, a practice that persists today with remarkable continuity. In the post-Cold War era, policymakers and operators were in a strange transition, dabbling in peacekeeping here and there. That all changed after the 9/11 disaster and the "Global War on Terrorism." The worldwide nature of the threat has changed how we look at places like Africa, although the lesson has been painfully slow to sink in.

CLOAK AND DAGGER: THE INDELIBLE IMAGE

When my college alumni magazine asked me to write a brief synopsis of my career in intelligence, I carefully spelled out what I had done in thirty-five years as an intelligence officer. They nevertheless titled my piece "Cloak and Dagger." About the time I was an undergraduate, Hollywood had come out with the first James Bond film, and the popular media spread the image of the spy versus spy view of intelligence that has obfuscated reality. While espionage does occur, and allegations of spying hit the media on occasion, 99 per cent of the people working in intelligence lead fairly ordinary lives. To exaggerate and distort their chosen profession and equate it with sensational exploits is to do them a disservice.

I remain optimistic about the future of intelligence. Funded better than at any time since 1947, we should be getting the best intelligence money can buy. Many artificial barriers once imbedded as problems in the Intelligence Community are melting away, albeit slowly. And we have a new generation of professionals coming on line, better educated and appreciated than their predecessors.

PART ONE
Non-Combat Realities

The Making of a Defense Intelligence Analyst

In the 1950s, I grew up on a farm in western Queens, New York City. That's right, if Barry Switzer was a bootlegger's son, then I was a flower farmer's son. Family patriarch Michael Thom arrived from Germany circa 1890. He bought land from a local farmer near Maspeth and got into the flower business. In 1847, New York State enacted the Rural Cemetery Act that created a commercial burial industry overnight. Cemeteries sprouted up in a semicircle from western Queens into eastern Brooklyn. These cemeteries, in still rural areas, were in easy range of day-trippers from Manhattan (a.k.a. "The City"). In those days, Sunday outings to visit interred relatives were a popular pastime.

Moreover, with the cemeteries came the need for flowers. An array of flower farms, florist shops, and monument companies popped up near the cemeteries. Most of the flower farmers were German immigrants.

When Michael Thom died in 1911, he divided his farm among three of his sons, one of whom was my grandfather William Frederick Thom. He, in turn, gave his farm to his three sons: my father George and his two older brothers, William (Bill) and Henry (Henny). Their lone sister, Margaret (Aunt Happy), got the house he built down the street, known in the family as "Happy's house."

Happy's house was important because it was the most frequent social gathering place for my father and his siblings, all of whom lived within two blocks. Uncle Bill – a bachelor – roomed in Happy's house. During long Sunday afternoons in Happy's yard, with the ball game on the radio, I was subjected to meandering conversations by the adults, complaining of everything and blaming everybody. They did not have a good word for any ethnic or religious group, including themselves! This really was not hatred; it was more ignorance and stupidity.

This is where I learned the family oral history, where we came from and how we got to America. My uncle Henny, the worldliest in the group, was certain that we came from Prussia, West Prussia to be exact. Years later, I found the family documents to prove him correct. And what are Prussians famous for? Militarism. As a kid, I thought this was something I should look into. I began reading military history. The civil war centennial in the early 1960s accelerated my interest in learning about armies and warfare. Toward the middle of my life I had an epiphany about how I had become hooked on the military at an early age – consciousness of my Prussian roots influenced me to pursue military studies.

The dramatic, romantic tales of the Thom family were, however, more than counterbalanced by their negativism and disregard for education. A strong shot of confidence was needed, and my mother provided that from the Polish side of my family. The Maliszewskis were from the Green Point section of Brooklyn, just across Newtown Creek from Maspeth. My mother, Helen, was a nurturing parent before that term was fashionable. She prided herself on how well she raised her two children. Possessed of a "can-do," the-sky's-the-limit attitude, Mom counteracted the Thom myopia. I believe that none of my career in intelligence would have happened without my mother's constant reassurance and conviction that I could become whatever I wanted to be, even though I had a childhood stuttering and stammering problem to overcome.

My uncle Henny. in a spiteful, envious rage one day, told my father that no Thom could make it through college and that sending me there would be a waste of money. My mother took that as a challenge and gave me the boost I would need to rise above my parent's station in life.

Actually, on my father's side the only immediate family member to serve in the military was Uncle Bill, my father's oldest brother. He joined the army in World War I, most likely to prove that the Thoms, who spoke German at home, were loyal Americans. He joined up with his best friend, another son of German immigrants, who was killed in action. Uncle Bill served in Company B, 102nd Regiment of Engineers, 27th Division. His unit was later designated a machine-gun company. He was recalled during World War II at the age of 46 to serve in the Pacific; he never got further than Washington State.

Our historical connection to the military was indeed real. The Thom family reportedly left Prussia to avoid conscription. Michael Thom hid his sons of military age across the border in nearby Poland whenever he learned that army conscription teams were in the area. Eventually they were caught. Salvation came when a young army officer named Johan Bloch fell in love with Michael's only daughter, the stately Johanna of the red tresses. Michael Thom struck a bargain with Captain Bloch: he could marry Bloch's daughter if he could get Bloch's sons out of the German Army and find the entire family safe passage to America. That he did, and the rest is history.

GROWING UP IN THE 1950s

The Cold War was blazing hot in my formative years. Air raid drills, fallout shelters, and nuclear nightmares haunted a generation. In the first grade at PS 73, I already had trouble getting my large frame beneath my tiny desk during "duck and cover" drills. My mother sat out in the hallway with her CD (Civil Defense) armband proudly displayed. On the way to Rockaway beach, we passed anti-aircraft guns, later Nike missile batteries, searching the skies for Russian bombers.

There was a steady diet of war movies in the theaters about how we won World War II, and then older vintage black-and-white flicks on TV, with everyone from John Wayne to William Bendix mowing down the Japanese and the Germans. It seemed the kids on every block were playing war, throwing dirt bombs, and building plastic models. I built scores of ships, planes, and tanks from kits.

I could play for hours with toy soldiers, wooden block fortresses, artillery, tanks, and the like all over the living room rug. But this was not just random play. Tactics and strategy were developed and played out. Concealment, fields of fire, flanking maneuvers, diversionary attacks, and artillery support were all carefully brought into play and tested. I was using Basil Liddell-Hart's indirect approach long before I read his classic book *Strategy* years later.

My father took a dim view of a twelve-year-old still playing with soldiers. After all, at that age he had already been pulled out of school to join his older brothers working in the family business. For Christmas that year, I asked for another set of toy soldiers. My dad was annoyed; but he realized how important they were to me, and on Christmas morning I wound up with two sets. My dad lived long enough to see that he had made a wise decision.

By the time I went to high school and college, I had discovered Avalon Hill war games. With a map board and tiny cardboard counters to represent military units, I was able to refight history's great battles, from Waterloo to Stalingrad. Once again, I was absorbing military concepts and terminology. As a kid with a stuttering problem, I was quiet and introspective, almost taciturn. I learned a lot about military concepts, issues, and terminology without ever having been in the service.

Another contributing phenomenon was the similarity between weather forecasting and military intelligence analysis. In farming, including flower farming, understanding the weather is essential to survival. At our house the weather was seemingly always on the radio or TV. Further, Uncle Henny – who knew the most about the subject – kept weather records. With six greenhouses full of geraniums heated by two boilers, an alarm was rigged to sound at Henny's house on the premises if the temperature in the hothouses fell below 36 degrees. In that case, we could have as little as an hour to hook up portable heaters borrowed from a Thom cousin also in the flower business.

The similarity with intelligence analysis is that in both cases one is forced to make daily judgments about the future with only partial information. One must face a daunting number of variables that, if ignored or misinterpreted, could lead to faulty assessments and possibly disaster. In both cases, you base your forecast on facts that must be verified. And, when you run out of data, you sometimes must make an analytical leap to arrive at a conclusion. Thus, the art of weather forecasting is a cousin of the art of intelligence analysis.

THE GREAT LEAP INTO SUB-SAHARAN AFRICA

At the State University College at New Paltz, New York, I had the good fortune to be introduced to African Studies. Everyone at New Paltz had to take a class on Africa and a class on Asia as part of the General Education battery of courses. I was a secondary education major, planning to teach social studies, until I bombed out of student teaching. My fascination with Africa led me to take other African Studies courses. When I left teaching and had to declare another major, African Studies looked good. I felt that, with such a specialty, there must be a job out there somewhere.

A more colorful version of the story is that with the big decision looming, I went to visit a classmate at his home in a more affluent section of eastern Queens. I met his father, a New York City police captain. He was a powerful figure in the community, and one demanding instant respect. He asked me what I was going to do now that I had left teaching.

I said, "Well sir, I am thinking of going into African Studies."

The captain, a short stocky fifty-something man with closely cropped white hair who resembled the late Carroll O'Connor of Archie Bunker fame on the TV show *All in the Family*, nearly inhaled his cigar. His face turned bright red, and then he burst out laughing. Finally, he said, "You silly boy, you don't have to go to college to learn about those people. I can show you the zenith of their culture in my precinct in Harlem."

My immediate conclusion was that if such an important man was so ignorant about Africa, there must be a place for me with a degree in African Studies. I went back to New Paltz the next day and changed my major.

One of the ironies of my thirty-five-year career in intelligence was that in actuality I spent much of my time teaching people about Africa, from the Secretary of Defense on down. Only I was paid much better than a schoolteacher.

TWO OUT OF THREE IS NOT BAD!

Much later during my career when I became a manager and had to hire prospective analysts, I discerned three areas of expertise required for success in defense intelligence. First, it was necessary to understand military things and how they work. If you lacked appropriate military experience, you must have studied the military and armed conflict as a civilian. Second, you must have a geographic or technical specialty. The latter might include electronic warfare, counter-narcotics, or terrorism. Third, one needed to know how the intelligence business at the national level worked. With the exception of active duty in military intelligence, this is the one thing that is next to impossible to learn beforehand.

My degree in African Studies and my fascination with military history allowed me to get in the door and learn about intelligence. But, to really be successful as an analyst you must also have well-developed communication skills. Good writing is essential. Intelligence writing demands clarity and brevity. It must be unambiguous. It cannot be interpreted any other way than as intended. I have seen many an analyst stymied at having to write a one-page assessment. I learned to write not in school but from mentors at DIA.

The oral briefing is the preferred way of conveying intelligence to consumers. People have less time to read in today's work environment. They want their intelligence quickly and well illustrated; we are in the video era. The trick to overcoming jitters when delivering a presentation is to know your topic thoroughly. Analytic competence breeds confidence. If you master your subject, you can overcome inhibitions. It is comforting to realize that you know more about the subject than anyone else in the room.

Thus, from a combination of happenstance and self-study, I was well prepared to begin a career in defense intelligence. When I graduated from New Paltz in 1967 with a shiny new B.S. in Africa Area Studies, I had three choices. Most of my haughty intellectual friends favored graduate school in African Studies at UCLA. A Peace Corps assignment teaching in Kenya seemed unwise, since I had washed out of student teaching. The final choice was an Africa analyst job with the little-known DIA. With the draft looming over my head, working for the Pentagon seemed like a good deal.

Assignment EUCOM J-2, 1977–1980

In January 1977, I arrived at the headquarters of the United States European Command (EUCOM) for what would be a three-and-a-half-year assignment as the resident Africa specialist in the J2 intelligence directorate. ("J2" also refers to the head of this directorate.) I had transferred from the DIA J2 current intelligence shop in the Pentagon. There was much similarity between the current intelligence job at DIA and at EUCOM J2. The only difference was that DIA was at the national level, where the morning briefing – the chief product of a current intelligence shop – went to the chairman of the Joint Chiefs of Staff and the secretary of defense. EUCOM was at the theater or unified command level, where the briefing went to the CINC (Commander in Chief) and DCINC (his deputy), both four-star generals.

While the CINC resided in Brussels, where he also wore the hat of NATO's Supreme Allied Commander Europe, the DCINC was stationed at Patch Barracks, where he presided over the day-to-day business of the EUCOM staff. Patch Barracks was a former German World War II facility in Vaihingen, a suburb of Stuttgart. It had been the home base of the 7th Panzer Regiment, part of the Afrika Korps under Stuttgarter Field Marshall Erwin Rommel. Allied forces in Tunisia captured the 7th Panzers in 1943. Ironically, the regiment's symbol was the American buffalo, a large statue of which was believed to have been buried some place on Patch Barracks. The J2 Warning and Analysis Division, where I worked, was housed in the J3 (operations) Command

Center, a windowless three-story cement cube right across the street from the J2 building. The Command Center building was later condemned because of asbestos and PVC (polyvinyl chloride) pollution, as well as electro-magnetic fields once caused by huge transformers in the basement.

The routine was similar to DIA. Monday through Friday there was a daily morning intelligence update briefing for the DCINC, who received the presentation at his Patch Barracks headquarters. The CINC also took the briefing when he was at Patch Barracks, which was not too often. Three professional military officers delivered the presentations derived from articles written by a small staff of a dozen or so analysts, half of whom worked on the Soviet Union. The briefers were more than just "talking dogs." They were a production team. The entire workday tended to revolve around the morning briefing.

The current shop at EUCOM was a one deep operation, with one analyst on each desk and no backup system such as we'd had at DIA. The J2 and his staff had to rely on a handful of experts in-house. He had to trust their judgment. As a result, his analysts were given a certain amount of "analytic license" – a two-edged sword. His analysts could be wrong. But, with the analysis from Washington just five hours behind, the risk was acceptable.

EUCOM covered Europe and the Middle East in addition to Africa. At that time, EUCOM had geographic responsibility only for North Africa. However, because sub-Saharan Africa was still not assigned to a major command, and because of EUCOM's proximity to the African continent, the headquarters was compelled to watch that area carefully. Any crisis in Africa would likely require EUCOM assets. The J2, an Air Force major general, took the briefing for final review before it went next door to the DCINC in the headquarters building. The analysts with items in the briefing sat along the right side of the room up front in what was known as the shooting gallery – hot seats – where they would answer the J2's questions.

One of the hidden advantages of working on Africa was that very few people knew anything about it. Thus, it was easier to get your assessments past middle-level managers and defend your analysis. There was only one drawback: you had to be right. As a coworker once said: "Make the analytical judgment. If you are wrong, they will forget about it; if you are right, don't let them forget about it."

Generally speaking, the DIA civilian analysts who sought to work a tour of duty at EUCOM were among the best the agency had. They had the experience of working at the national level, and overseas jobs in Europe – or anywhere for that matter – were scarce and selections very competitive. To DIA's credit, opportunities for field assignments have greatly increased over the past twenty years.

As analysts, we were allowed a lot of latitude. For example, I wrote an item on Libya's acquisition of MiG 25 FOXBAT jet fighters and called it "99 FOX-BATS." Although the Libyans had taken delivery of a modest number of aircraft, there were indications many more were in the pipeline. Despite criticism that Libya could not possibly absorb so many MiG 25s, the item went forward and served to alert consumers that scores of additional FOXBATs were on the way, which proved true. Sometimes we wrote shelf items, nonperishable intelligence that could be used in the briefing on a slow day. I prepared one on the reorganization of the Togolese armed forces. Many a time the item was set to go, only to be bumped at the last moment by another more important item. In that case, someone in the briefing presentation shop would yell, "It's a no go on Togo."

HITTING THE GROUND RUNNING AT EUCOM

When I arrived at Patch, my job had been vacant for months and the J2 staff were glad to see me. Almost immediately, I was thrown into the fray as things accelerated. In February 1977, Ugandan dictator Idi Amin rounded up U.S. and UK citizens in his country, menacing bodily harm. EUCOM set up a battle staff, and I was the J2 rep. Being the only civilian in the room when the group met was a new experience. In March 1977 the former Katangan Gendarmes based in Angola invaded southern Zaire (a.k.a. Congo Kinshasa) in a mini-war that became known as Shaba One. In May 1977 the new Marxist strongman in Ethiopia, Mengistu Haile Mariam, ordered Kagnew Station, a U.S. communications facility, closed on short notice and the American Embassy staff in Addis Ababa drastically cut back. By July 1977, war had broken out between Ethiopia and Somalia when the latter invaded the Ogaden region.

These events made me an instant celebrity of sorts at Patch Barracks. EUCOM differed from Washington in one obvious way. At home, there were numerous DIA analysts competing for attention, not to mention those at CIA, State, NSA, and the military services. Consumers and senior intelligence officials could call on a multitude of experts – even on Africa. At EUCOM the leadership depended largely on the small J2 analytical staff; they needed to be able to reach out and touch an analyst, not call the Pentagon in the middle of the night in Washington.

The evacuation of Kagnew and the Embassy drawdown in Addis Ababa were tense times. The United States arranged for chartered airliners to do most of the work on the assumption that the mission would be unopposed. During the critical twenty-four hours of the operation, the J2 would ask me the same questions every hour or so: "Do we still believe the operation will be unopposed, and what if it's not?" The first answer was always a yes, and the second was that there would be no evacuation, because Mengistu had 40,000 troops to stop it.

According to legend, Mengistu hated the United States because he encountered racial prejudice while in the States for training. He allegedly got into a fistfight with some rednecks and was thrown in the brig. But the story is deeper than that. Mengistu had racial identity problems. He was raised in the household of an Amhara nobleman, Azaz Kebbede Tessema, the illegitimate son of a lady of the court and an army sergeant of Oromo extraction. He called himself Amhara, but his complexion was much darker than most highland Ethiopians.

THE EUCOM EXPERIENCE PAYS DIVIDENDS

One of the rewards of serving in EUCOM was working for three outstanding Air Force generals. The first was Maj. Gen. James Brown, followed by Maj. Gen. Lincoln D. Faurer, and the late Maj. Gen. Billy B. Forsman. In 1978, I got to coach the J2 team for the annual touch football game with NCEUR, the NSA contingent at Patch Barracks. To my surprise, General Faurer wanted to play. In my offensive scheme, I had the audacity to assign the general the job of blocking back. He never said a word and put some serious blocks on the opposition. We had one play where we threw a pass to him; it worked like a charm. Oh yes, we won that game.

There was camaraderie at EUCOM J2 that was very different from anything in Washington. It extended to the NSA contingent that I worked closely with, and to a lesser extent to the small CIA office as well. One remarkable character was the late Alan Danahy, who went by "Danny." An NSA analyst and an authority on the Middle East, his rendition of Danny Boy could melt your heart. It could also transfix the Germans on a midnight streetcar ride back from a beer tent downtown.

For the most part, I was the only Africa analyst in the J2, but I was at times joined by others, notably Captain (later Colonel) Michael Ferguson who went on to become a legendary defense attaché in Africa. At one point, a navy commander was assigned to work with me. The first thing he said was, "Don't mind my rank; I know nothing about Africa, so I am really working for you."

During a weeklong Defense Department-wide military exercise, the J2 analysts were divided into two shifts: twelve hours on and twelve hours off. One daring young naval officer assigned to my shift discovered how to insert phony messages into the exercise and tried to get EUCOM out of the game prematurely. His first phony message reported that Russian paratroopers had landed near Patch Barracks and that EUCOM headquarters should be assumed to be in enemy hands (and out of the exercise).

A second message said that aerial reconnaissance indicated that the EUCOM Command Center (where we were sitting) had been reduced to smoldering ruins by a Soviet air strike. Exercise controllers caught these phony messages and we soldiered on; in the end, I think we won the war.

GENERALS HAIG AND HUYSER AND THE SOFT UNDERBELLY OF NATO

One thing that certainly kept Africa in the news at EUCOM was the perception by the command element that NATO was vulnerable on its southern flank. Blocked in Europe, the Soviet Union was attempting to penetrate the politically unstable Middle East and Africa. Remember, this was the 1970s, not long after the fall of South Vietnam.

Like many of the VIP visitors to the Command, a member of the House Armed Services Committee received the Africa Hot Spots briefing along with other material. Hot Spots was a flashy presentation I put together, highlighting all the security problems in sub-Saharan Africa (SSA). He was so taken by the presentation that he declared his whole committee ought to hear it. Sure enough, EUCOM was invited to Washington to brief the committee. The DCINC, the late General Robert "Dutch" Huyser, briefer Major Colin Harding, and I headed for Washington.

When we arrived, a staffer said that the committee wanted us to cover Iraq as well as Africa. General Huyser asked me if I could handle it. When I said no, recognizing that I had worked in DIA, he told me to see Major General Forsman at my former agency and ask him to provide an analyst to back us up on Iraq.

I had no trouble at all getting in to see General Forsman, who was most obliging. He gave me a personal tour of the "Africa Room," a show-and-tell facility lined with DIA products and displays. The room was a prop to fend off criticism that DIA was not doing enough Third World analysis, especially on Africa south of the Sahara, after the turbulence created by "communist victories" in Angola and Ethiopia.

At EUCOM, I was frozen in time as a GS-13 while my contemporaries marched on to higher grades. But what I gained in practical experience, especially living and working in a military community, was a wise career investment. It was also a confidence builder. Allowed to think and write with minimal constraints and test one's analytical mettle were all part of a maturing process. Today the intelligence community encourages such rotational assignments to give analysts a better grasp of the inner workings of the system.

One afternoon in the spring of 1977, I was posting order of battle (OB) data on large sliding map boards in my office in EUCOM J2's Warning and Analysis Division. A voice from behind asked what I was doing; it was the Marine Corps colonel in charge of the division. I replied, "Getting ready for the next war, sir." At the time I had no idea how prophetic my reply was. The information I was posting was for Ethiopia and Somalia.

TRAVELING THROUGH AFRICA

As a deskbound analyst in Washington, Stuttgart, or elsewhere, it is not enough to read the intelligence reports crossing your desk. You need to travel in the area you are responsible for, to soak up those local sights, sounds, and smells that rarely come across in a cable from the field. You cannot understand a region like sub-Saharan Africa without traveling to your countries of responsibility on a regular basis.

As a junior defense intelligence analyst in the 1960s and early 1970s, however, getting a trip to SSA was a monumental task. When the budget belt tightened as it did once a year, travel was always one of the first casualties. And, if you were an Africa analyst, the low priority of the continent made it even more difficult. Travel to Africa was also relatively more expensive than to some other regions.

Above all, however, traveling to your countries was a matter of credibility. Young conscientious analysts who thirsted for information but never set foot in Africa were capable of giving excellent performances. They often prompted the senior official receiving their briefing to ask, "How recently have you been to Zambia?" This usually sent managerial hosts scurrying for excuses, "Well, he hasn't actually been there yet, but we are working on it."

Ironically, one of the things you learn by traveling to the field is what shapes embassy thinking. Most information that embassies report is obtained in the capital where the diplomatic mission is located. The cocktail circuit can be brutal even in SSA, with five or six diplomatic social functions a week. The embassy usually has a good handle on what is going on in the capital and hence what is going on in the host nation government.

This often does not extend too far beyond city limits, though. To find out what is going on in the hinterland ("the bush" in Africa) one needs to consult the people who live there. Missionaries, relief and aid workers, and contractors all have a good sense of what is actually happening out there. They are "passive collectors" of information, learning things simply as a by-product of their jobs. Embassy personnel frequently do not talk to these people enough for fear of "compromising" them, although the host government often assumes anyway that they are spying for Washington. African governments are often super-sensitive about spies and intelligence operatives. (Africa analysts used to say the less there was to protect the more fanatical the security regimen.)

My First Trip to Africa

Travel in Africa is difficult. Many a book has been written about the almost unbelievable stories of travail in sub-Saharan Africa. From battling through chaotic African airports and being held up to pay bribes to shabby hotels and numerous immunizations, in the view of the average American traveling there entails one horror after another. In my early days, the venting stories I heard at embassy gatherings were about snakes and airports; more recently, they concerned violent crime, terrible diseases, and personal safety. I got my chance in 1974 and became a "beentu." Traditionally in the former British colonies a member of the fictitious "beentu tribe" was someone who had *been to* England. Among Africa analysts, it meant someone who had been to Africa.

In the mid-1970s, I was the military capabilities analyst at DIA for southern Africa and jumped at the chance of visiting the continent. I accompanied the late Commander Winston W. Cornelius on a trek through west, central, and southern Africa. Cornelius described himself as an old broken-down navy com-mander, and no one could argue with that. Overweight, fatigued, and a chain smoker, Cornelius was in charge of our defense attaché offices in Africa. Defense attachés are military officers assigned to U.S. embassies whose mission is liaison with the host nation military. In 1974, we had about ten defense attaché offices (DAOs) in SSA; today we have about 28! Back in the mid-1970s, we had DAOs in Chad, Congo-Kinshasa, Ethiopia, Ivory Coast, Liberia, Madagascar, Malawi, Nigeria, Senegal, South Africa, and Sudan.

Cornelius and I boarded a Pan Am B-707 at JFK Airport in New York for Monrovia, Liberia. The pilot told us that we were at maximum fuel, so do not be alarmed if we bounced a few times before take off; bounce we did, but only after taxiing back to the terminal to rearrange some misloaded livestock. Days later on a flight to South Africa, our jetliner flew into a thunderstorm cruising over Angola. We dropped like a stone down a well. When we hit bottom, I thought the wings would fall off. Cornelius told me not to worry but later back in Washington confessed he had been frightened too.

I was prepared for culture shock in SSA but not for culture shock in reverse in South Africa. On the approach to Jan Smuts International Airport in Johannesburg, the scene below looked like a wealthy section of southern California, red-tiled roofs and swimming pools, but everyone was driving on the wrong side of the freeways. Bustling downtown Johannesburg with its tall buildings looked like the New York of Africa.

On the way back to Washington I was smuggled onto a Pan Am flight at Accra, Ghana, by the station agent, a ringer for Colonel Harland Sanders. I expected him to hand me a bag of chicken as I boarded. Instead when I thanked him he said, "We love your business." During my early career I managed to visit Africa twice during major wars. In 1975 I visited South Africa during the Angolan civil war. The defense attaché had me talk at the South African Army Staff College. As I described the situation in Angola, the CIA chief bolted from the room in obvious distress. He got on the phone to Washington to find out who I was.

A couple of years later I was in Mogadishu, Somalia, during the Ogaden war. I was the first regular official visitor to the tiny U.S. Embassy since the Somalis had thrown the Russians out several weeks before. My host was the consular officer, a short white guy married to a statuesque Congolese woman at least six feet tall.

The Big Trip

In 1978 while at EUCOM J2 I was given the opportunity to travel on my own schedule. I proposed and the J2 approved a thirty-two-day eleven-country circumnavigation of the continent – a clockwise unaccompanied tour through Sudan, Somalia, Kenya, Zambia, Mozambique, South Africa, the Congo (Zaire), Nigeria, Ivory Coast, Senegal, and Morocco.

Among the highlights of this trip were: being met at the airport by an enraged attaché who dumped me in a third-rate hotel that had a door and window that would not close, meeting an American father and son driving the length of Africa who had already been robbed four times but were enjoying their adventure, staying at the Polana Hotel in Maputo before it was refurbished (i.e., no electricity, almost no plumbing), in Durban meeting a woman in a bikini who wanted to go into my room allegedly to hide from some hoodlums, walking through mounds of burning garbage in a Kinshasa street to get to an elegant French restaurant, landing in Lagos's airport in the middle of the night when my plane was eight hours late and the embassy had no one to meet me (I could write a chapter just on this stop alone), flying on an African airliner where the cabin was filled with hundreds of plastic balls, many out of control of their owners, being met by an attaché with the greeting "I've just come from a dinner in your honor," or "I hope you have had your meningitis booster," and, finally, getting a two-day tour of Morocco with good food, good hotels, and lots of things to see. Miraculously, the only flight I missed was the result of a snowstorm in New York where the Pan Am plane was grounded!

Traveling with VIPs

During the later stages of my career I was fortunate enough to travel to Africa with VIPs. In the case of the three directors of DIA I accompanied to Africa, I was the key organizer, the cruise director. VIPs usually travel with their own aircraft, obviating the need to go through airport customs; access to the serenity of the VIP lounge was assured.

My first VIP was the late Rear Admiral Ronald Marriott, who in 1989 was the deputy director of DIA. We picked up a USAF C-21 (a Lear jet also known as the flying cigar) in Germany then proceeded to Africa. The only glitch was having a return flight canceled on us in Germany, which nearly made the admiral miss the next day's Army-Navy football game. All of the DIA VIPs either flew commercial to Germany and picked up their executive jet there or went commercial all the way to Africa where they would meet up with a C-12 (two-engine turboprop Beech King Air) operated by a DAO in the region.

In 1994 Lt. Gen. James Clapper made history by becoming the first serving director of DIA to visit sub-Saharan Africa. While still a boy after World War II his family had lived in Eritrea, where his father (an army officer) was assigned to Kagnew station. In the late 1990s LTG (Lt. Gen.) Patrick Hughes set a record for DIA directors by making three trips to SSA, visiting a total of eight countries.

In 2001 Vice Admiral Thomas Wilson was the last director to visit SSA on my watch.

Illness is a constant concern in SSA. My greatest fear was getting sick when traveling through Africa. Once, a director sleeping in the next room got so violently ill that I feared my career was at end. Twelve hours later he was up and running. Later on that trip I picked up a parasite and was sick for six months. It is all part of the experience.

If you really had the horsepower in the U.S. government, you did not have to worry about C-12 support or long hours on a flying cigar without a head (toilet). Such was the case with General Colin Powell's 1992 visit to West Africa. I had the opportunity to accompany him aboard a USAF C-135 VIP jet that had served as Air Force One for many years and was only recently retired to the Air and Space Museum. This was the military version of the B-707 intercontinental jetliner.

Traveling with General Powell, chairman of the Joint Chiefs of Staff, and his wife, Alma, was quite a privilege. I sat toward the back of the aircraft with various staff officers. The general sat in the VIP suite closer to the communications panel. Shortly after take-off Powell came by to greet all of us in the back of the plane. Elegant and charming even in a lounging suit, Colin Powell possessed star quality. We visited Senegal, Sierra Leone, and Nigeria in that order, all countries that had contributed troops to the recently concluded 1992 Persian Gulf War. In Freetown, Sierra Leone, the Powell party was hosted by President Momoh, who would be ousted in a military coup a month later. The purpose of Powell's trip was to thank those countries in SSA that had participated with the United States in the Gulf War and to expose the chairman to Africa south of the Sahara, expanding his worldview.

Nigeria was a bit chaotic, to no one's surprise. A huge throng of officials turned out at the Lagos airport for the arrival, including the massed bands of the Nigerian armed forces. As Powell deplaned and followed the red carpet to a podium set up on the tarmac, the bands played on. Off to the right in a patch of weeds between two hangars was a battery of Nigerian Army Artillery, apparently not seen by some security men. Moments after Powell stepped up to the podium, the first salute rang out causing a few seconds of panic in which American security people rushed to protect the chairman.

Whether traveling on a VIP jet or an embassy truck through the bush, one simply must get to see the real Africa and meet everyday Africans. Imagery, communications intercepts, and all the wonderfully written reports in the world will not fill the void left by the lack of on-the-ground experience. There is nothing like the intelligence officer who can gather instant respect by simply saying, "I was there, sir, and that road was passable during the rainy season." The analyst who does not have field experience is at a severe disadvantage.

Analysts traveling to their area of responsibility have long been a bone of contention. Traveling to sub-Saharan Africa is expensive, and the funding for it is usually the first thing to go when the budget is cut. Because opportunities are scarce, who gets to go and when too often becomes politicized. It is management's investment in the analyst, not rewarding the boss's favorite, that must be the primary consideration.

The War for Resources – and Briefing VIPs

Aside from the battles in Africa itself, Africa managers, supervisors, and analysts fought other wars as well – wars over resources. Sub-Saharan Africa had the lowest priority and was the region least understood by most senior-level managers and consumers. It was the only area of the world we (the United States) could write off as a backwater not worthy of full intelligence coverage. As an analyst, a manager, and later an executive in defense intelligence, I fought against this prevailing attitude for years with little success. Like the late Rodney Dangerfield, Africa analysts too often felt as if they got no respect.

I was occasionally called upon to address the General Defense Intelligence Plan (GDIP) to reassess Africa. The GDIP would determine the funding made available for intelligence programs with regard to SSA. One factor influencing the African assessment was the assumption that no major U.S. troop deployment would ever be made to sub-Saharan Africa. I made Africa's case to the GDIP staff, and they enjoyed my recounting of the region's problems and conflicts. While warning of changes to come in Africa, enhancing its long-term importance to the United States, I usually wound up endorsing the GDIP assessment. There would be no U.S. deployments to SSA, and no significantly increased funding for that region. Even I had been brainwashed into accepting the inevitable. In December 1992, however, the White House sent 28,000 U.S. troops into Somalia. It was never supposed to happen.

Detractors called the Somali intervention a freak incident, a one-time wild guess. Two years later, the Rwanda crisis made believers of some in high places. Even though no U.S. troops went into Rwanda, there was again a sizable deployment to neighboring Uganda and the Democratic Republic of the Congo (DRC) in a humanitarian role. Africa gained a few more adherents, but old attitudes still prevailed.

UNFAVORABLE PAIRINGS

For most of my career there were two Africa shops at DIA: a current intelligence office in the Pentagon, and a military capabilities (mil cap) shop at Arlington Hall Station (AHS) or, after 1984, the Defense Intelligence Analysis Center (DIAC) at Bolling Air Force Base just across the Potomac from Reagan National Airport. For a time in the 1970s and 1980s, there was also a small Africa team in the Directorate for Estimates that worked exclusively on forward-looking assessments.

Organizational structures that paired the Africa shop with a Middle East shop, a West European shop, or a Latin America shop under a common manager always worked to Africa's disadvantage. This is simply common sense: Africa could not compete with these other higher-priority regions for resources – people, floor space, computers, funding for travel to the continent, and so on.

It was tough on the Africa analysts' morale and made retention of bright, up-and-coming analysts difficult. Routinely, the Africa military capabilities shop was expected to produce on par with other geographic offices, although it never had the personnel and equipment to get the job done or even be realistically competitive. How do you maintain a healthy database with fewer analysts, fewer tools, the weakest collection effort, and the most countries of any geographic region? If there ever was an uneven playing field, this was it.

Part of the problem was the ignorance of senior managers who knew little about the forty-eight sub-Saharan countries. African states had small, unsophisticated armies. How difficult could it be doing political-military analysis on a Chad or a Botswana? Simply having to answer for the sheer number of sub-Saharan countries was a challenge not fully understood either. Requirements that began with "For each of your countries please provide …" were dreaded. There were at least twice as many countries in SSA as in the Middle East, Latin America, or free Europe. Meanwhile, someone had to brief the new U.S. ambassador to Swaziland!

Additionally, severe political instability erupted into many hot spots in SSA. Crisis support was becoming more common as Africa analysts were snatched away to supplement numerous crisis support teams run by the J2 in the Pentagon. Operational support to the war fighter from defense intelligence was becoming commonplace.

And, we must factor in the lack of intelligence collection that went along with Africa's low strategic priority. Those more important regions always had the edge in competing for collection assets. The Africa analyst had to be creative in gathering and piecing together spurious bits of information. At times, finding the simplest information proved difficult. Further, collection environments were often hostile. A colleague once remarked, "The fewer secrets they (African countries) have to protect, the more zealous their security efforts."

The Africa current shop in J2 (a semi-autonomous part of DIA) fared better than their mil cap counterparts. Located in the Pentagon, the general or admiral assigned as the J2 wears two hats: the head of crisis intelligence management for the director of DIA and the top intelligence officer for the chairman of the Joint Chief's of Staff. The J2's mission includes current, crisis, and indications and warning (I&W) intelligence. It has to cover the world daily – including Africa. If there was a coup in Togo, somebody in J2 had to know its significance!

There was also rivalry between the mil cap shop and the current shop. The latter (working grade GS-13) was regarded as the first team, while the former (working grade up to GS-12) was seen as the second team. Mil cap analysts had to prove their mettle when stepping up to the first team in the Pentagon. While this competition could be constructive, it also contributed to an often unhealthy "us versus them" mentality.

OUT OF AFRICA

Crises outside of Africa led to the temporary assignment of Africa analysts to the Middle East or other intelligence task forces. Africa mil cap analysts in the 1960s through 1990s felt like DIA's internal foreign legion. Africanists all did their turn serving on task forces that could have scores of people assigned. Some times their talents would be recognized and they would never return to work on Africa. Such an analyst would be deemed "too good to work on Africa," a phenomenon that exists to this day. I myself at an early age was warned by my military mentors to "get out of Africa."

There were also African crisis working groups within Africa. Whether called a task force, working group, or a cell, these were teams of analysts dedicated to expanded coverage of a crisis country. They seemed to reach a high-water mark in the 1990s. When analysts from the mil cap shop were dragooned to the Pentagon for weeks or months of task force duty, their desks remained empty and their accounts uncovered, a concept that managers never fully seemed to grasp. This was just another reason why sub-Saharan databases were not generally robust, and were often uneven.

Signs in the J2 alert center in the Pentagon were fastened to the ceiling to indicate the location of various task forces or working groups. Signs read "Somalia," "Liberia," and "Rwanda." After a while they were replaced with one sign simply saying "Africa." Many of us felt that we had made the big time at last. At the core of these working groups were knowledgeable, veteran Africa analysts from both J2 and the mil cap shop. They were scarce and much appreciated when this or that crisis was unfolding.

As a mil cap analyst, I served on the 1974 Cyprus Task Force. I got the opportunity to write a military analysis of the Turkish invasion for CIA's *National Intelligence Daily*, a slick publication that looked like a colorful brochure and went only to the high rollers from the president on down. West European analysts responsible for Cyprus failed twice to get the job done, and CIA bounced their paper back. Having the experience of writing broadly on military subjects in Africa, I was able to write a truly military analysis of the conflict that was greatly appreciated by CIA. This was a side of the SSA analyst few people saw.

The briefers on the Task Force used a map of Cyprus showing various lines depicting areas of control, treaty lines, the forward edge of the battle area, and the like. One of the lines was in the color magenta; others were green, red, yellow, and so forth. The briefers got in the habit of referring to the "magenta line" in their update briefings. One day after a briefing, we received a request from a high Pentagon official wanting to know the background of the Magenta Line, when was the Treaty of Magenta, who ratified it, and so on. Over a beer one night, a colleague commented, "You can't make this stuff up, no one would believe it."

AFRICA JUST DOESN'T MAKE THE CUT

During various reorganizations and cutbacks at DIA, SSA did not fare well. Throughout my entire career, periodic downsizing victimized Africa south of the Sahara. A usual formulation would have a handful of countries worthy of continuing mil cap and other basic intelligence analysis. The rest of SSA could be placed on the shelf, in library status, caretaker status, or some other inane condition. This would only work for so long. When questions came in that had to be answered, the Malawis and Nigers were quickly removed from the shelf and dusted off. Sometimes a country such as Sudan would be removed from Africa and given to the Middle East office because it had become too important to remain in SSA, where it would get short shrift. (Middle East shops traditionally handled Egypt and the rest of the North African littoral.)

The diminution of Africa never lasted, however, and there were times when the momentum was reversed. After the Angola crisis in 1975, for example, congressional investigations concluded that there were not enough Third World analysts in the intelligence community. This led to some modest beefing up of the effort on SSA. For example, the Smiley-Pickett billets (so named for the two members of Congress who sponsored the bill) of the late 1970s and early 1980s were mandated to be filled by Third World regional experts.

How do I know that some people did not take Africa seriously? Just listen to their off-color comments. Jokes about Africa by people not working SSA were common. A discussion of Africa's numerous security and other developmental problems often drew grins, chuckles, and snickers from those making light of the continent's failings. Africa was a mess and those poor bastards were stewing in their own juices. "We have real security issues to deal with, why waste our time on Africa?" Such comments were unprofessional, bordered on racism, and contributed to an unhealthy work environment. As a senior intelligence professional, I had to deal with these attitudes on a daily basis.

"SOMETHING NEW IS ALWAYS COMING OUT OF AFRICA" – PLINY THE ELDER

Why then would intelligence careerists stay with SSA? As mentioned earlier, there was a certain freedom that came with working on a low-priority region. Analysts had time to think through problems, test their intellectual mettle, and be imaginative. These things were harder to do under the weight of management scrutiny and overkill.

Then there were those bitten by the "Africa bug." Fascination with Africa and its long-suffering people led to career choices. For my military cohorts, it could be joining the Army's Foreign Area Officer program to specialize on Africa, or striving to get an appointment as a military attaché in a sub-Saharan country. For the civilians it simply meant sticking with Africa.

People DIA hired for analyst jobs in the late 1970s and 1980s tended to be highly educated and already career Africanists. They worked SSA because that was their choice. They were not necessarily the best analysts, but they were dedicated to Africa.

When I was the Africa Branch chief in the mid-1980s, we received a request to send over our expert on Liberia to brief a high-level official. He had to go alone. There was no further guidance; no one wanted to go back up the chain of command to clarify exactly what the requirement was (a frequent circumstance). I had this new guy with a PhD in African studies covering Liberia, so we saddled him with two bags stuffed with all conceivable information at our disposal on Liberia. When he arrived at the VIP's office in the Pentagon, the first question he had to answer was "Where the hell is Liberia? I can't find it on the map." More sophisticated discussion followed.

On another occasion there was a request by the director of DIA for information on Cameroon. A flurry of requirements went out to the analysts. When they got to the Pentagon, it turned out the boss wanted to know about Cam Ranh, as in Cam Ranh Bay in Southeast Asia!

WHAT WE HAVE LEARNED

Despite the obstacles listed here, SSA has been accepted as a legitimate focus for defense intelligence. Africanists are no longer singled out for task force duties; these honors are now shared more broadly. The stigma of working Africa appears to have diminished.

Many of the things we in defense intelligence have been reporting for more than ten years now are influencing policymakers and military operators. The war on global terrorism has helped place Africa more conspicuously on the policymaker's map of the world. Collapsed states, spreading civil wars, competition over resources (water and food as well as oil), and humanitarian crises exacerbated by conflict have all been predicted for years, perhaps decades, by the intelligence community.

One of the greatest lessons is that no place on earth is immune from hosting potential threats to the United States. Lawlessness in Africa constitutes a threat to the United States in terms of terrorist breeding grounds, organized crime, drug trafficking, small arms proliferation, severe political instability, and global health issues. These are no longer theoretical problems but the realities of today and tomorrow. And, they cannot be defeated with main battle tanks, aircraft carriers, and nuclear missiles.

We need a robust contingent of analysts dedicated to studying the myriad of political and military problems around the continent. These human databases will be essential if we are to stay on top of events in SSA. To place African countries in some manner of reserve status where they get minimal national intelligence coverage would be a tragic mistake.

Reserve status will ultimately result in insufficient information on countries and issues, to the peril of policymakers and war fighters alike. As we continue to be aware of the many reasons to be concerned about SSA, today's Africa analysts must fare better in the internal wars for resources. Peeling back ignorance about Africa is still a mighty and continuous chore!

BRIEFING PEOPLE IN HIGH PLACES

The intelligence briefing is part of the military culture in the United States, and DIA was about as close to being in the military as you could get. In short, DIA is a military organization steeped in that culture. The briefing is the preferred way of delivering your product – your analysis. There are two basic types of briefings, routine and special. Routine briefings are usually regularly scheduled early-morning affairs written by an analyst but presented by professional briefers. A special briefing is for presentation to a visitor or senior staff person and is usually presented by the analyst who wrote it, or maybe his boss.

My first VIP briefings as a junior military capabilities analyst were for outgoing U.S. ambassadors, one going to Zambia, the other to Mauritius. In those late 1960s days, the director of DIA – a three-star army general – occasionally hosted the briefing. He was at the Zambia presentation and patted me on the back afterward.

The briefing was an art form all its own. The graphics were plastic viewgraphs laid on an overhead projector. Before the age of automation and computers, viewgraphs were virtually homemade from paper mock-ups done by the analyst. There was always a concern that they would not be ready in time for the presentation. A lesson I learned from an army colleague was that support people (like the graphics shop) were there to support you, and you must demand their cooperation.

Another thing that has changed for the better during my career is the diminishing need for dry runs or pre-briefs. Early on it was not unusual for an analyst to run the gauntlet of five or six different dry runs for various staff elements. They all recommended changes that had to be made, in their view, to improve the product.

As the southern Africa analyst in the 1960s and 1970s, I had a canned briefing on the insurgencies in my area that was occasionally offered up for special audiences or as a supplement to the scheduled briefing. At times I would go to the Pentagon to do my supplemental "special" briefing, only to be sent home because they ran out of time or something more important came along.

As a youngster I did fairly well. An exception was a presentation at an air attaché conference in Germany – my first overseas trip – in the early 1970s. This was at the height of the anti-war movement and I was sporting hair that went over my collar. I received hostile looks from attendees who were 99 per cent uniformed air force. My shaky presentation was on the last day, just before happy hour at the officers' club. The highlight for me came upon leaving the building, when the DIA director saw me, walked over to shake my hand, and said: "How are you today, Mr. Thom?" It was clearly done to show that the boss thought I was one of his guys, my appearance notwithstanding.

Peculiarities: Is the Water Blue or Green?

The briefing review process always involved dickering over the viewgraphs (yes, we were a video culture even then). One flag officer at DIA liked his water blue; perhaps he was a navy man. Another liked it green. Most Pentagon conference rooms used by DIA for high-profile presentations were elaborate affairs with rear screen projectors. It took two people to operate: one behind the screen in a back room, the other at the podium facing the audience. The backroom operator frequently had little experience dealing with the battery of buttons and switches that controlled everything from the lights, the curtains, the sound system, and the podium. The likelihood for screw-ups was high. On one occasion the operator kept pushing the wrong button, and instead of advancing the slides kept raising and lowering the speaker's podium.

Despite all the pre-briefing reviews, occasionally a mistake on a viewgraph would get by. Once during a briefing on the Middle East for a high-profile audience at the Pentagon, a viewgraph map came up. Over the Sinai desert were the words "Is Really Occupied." When one of the VIPs asked what exactly that meant, a colonel from the preparing office stood up and said it means the Sinai is really occupied! A big laugh was reportedly had by all.

Donald Rumsfeld, the First Time Around

In early 1976 just before I made the move up to the so-called "first team," the current intelligence office at the Pentagon, I was selected for a special mission: brief Secretary of Defense Rumsfeld on Africa. I was to cover Africa's history, geography, economy, and politics – all in twenty minutes. Viewgraphs were not allowed; I had to use butcher paper attached to an easel. Only one person would accompany me into the SECDEF's office, a civilian from Rumsfeld's staff who knew zero about Africa.

Amazingly, I had to do only one dry run for a general in DIA. To this day I do not know why I was selected for this assignment, but I think that general had something to do with it. Six times I went to the Pentagon with my paper and easel, and five times I sat in Rumsfeld's outer office only to be dismissed. The sixth time was the charm.

On entering the secretary's office, I remember seeing a gold telephone behind his desk; it looked to be twelve feet long. I set up my easel and paper and ran through the presentation without interruption. Rumsfeld stared intently at the graphics with the glare of an enraged dentist.

I finished only a couple of minutes overtime and girded myself for his first question: "What is the population of Mauritania?" I was floored.

I answered: "About three million, sir." From there it went into a productive dialogue that lasted over an hour with surprisingly little interruption. With the Angola crisis just concluded, Rumsfeld probably felt he needed to know more about Africa.

Secretary Dick Cheney and Somalia

In December 1992, Somalia was super-hot. One morning after the briefings were concluded, a J2 Task Force analyst called me up with a strange message. Secretary Cheney's office had called requesting an informal briefing on Somalia at 1100. The analyst was going along with a colonel who worked for the J2, who could not go himself for some reason. The funny thing was that the J2 did not want me, the DIO for Africa, to go. I checked with my immediate boss, the deputy director of DIA for Policy Support. He said I did not work for the J2; I worked for him, and he wanted me to go.

I arrived down at the Task Force just before the colonel arrived. When he did he informed me of the J2's decision, I could not go along. I told him of my boss's decision. The three of us walked out together. As we approached the SECDEF's office, the colonel said: "You are six foot four. I guess I cannot really keep you out of there." At the door to Cheney's inner office, the colonel went in, followed by the analyst, then me. I got one foot in and was grabbed by the doorkeeper, a sergeant. We were expecting only two he said. Luckily Cheney was already walking toward the door and made eye contact; swish I was in.

We settled down for an informal chat. I held back until the J2 analyst was stuck for an answer. Gradually, I took over the conversation, answering about half the SECDEF's questions. He wanted to know about the place and its people. He asked if any of us had been to Somalia; I was the only one who had. We were a big success. Upon exiting into the hall, the colonel said to me: "Do not ever tell the J2 but I was damn glad you were in there with us."

Postscript

I briefed other VIPs during my career, mostly Americans, some foreigners. As my career progressed, I more often set analysts up to do the actual briefing, while I sat back as director and senior expert. One thing still has not changed, though. To be effective, you must get into the room. Too often the people with the expertise we pay them for are not in the room. Policymakers frequently rely on the intelligence briefings they received before the meeting. I can find no noble reason for excluding intelligence from the inner sanctum of policy, only vanity and the perception of power.

Threats to Internal Security: Optimists versus Pessimists

When it comes to sub-Saharan Africa and its many problems, opinions about the reasons for the continent's plight are sharply divided. Those who see the glass half full are the so-called Afro-optimists. They foresee a brighter future for Africa once the damage of the past – the colonial legacy, Cold War distortion, wrong-headed Western policies – is corrected.

The optimists lean heavily on the sins of the past to explain away SSA's failings, and in this they are largely correct. From the Berlin Conference of the late nineteenth century that forced arbitrary collections of peoples into discordant territorial units, to today's World Bank controversies, the optimists see Africa's salvation in escaping the yoke of external exploitation.

The Afro-pessimists, on the other hand, see the glass half empty and Africans as bearing the greater responsibility for the continent's failings. If external influences are part of the reason SSA is suffering, then African collaboration with the outsiders makes them culpable as well. The pessimists see things getting only worse in Africa. They call the optimists dreamers and themselves realists; the optimists have been known to accuse the pessimists of racism.

THE OPTIMISTS

Among the groups that tend to be optimistic are diplomats, academics, liberals, NGOs (especially relief organizations), the clergy, the media, and the United Nations. Diplomats have a vested interest in plying their craft in an environment conducive to positive growth and improvement. Academics and liberal politicians are quick to see the perceived evil behind Africa's troubles. The UN sees Africa as a huge continent in need of their varied services, and other relief-oriented NGOs stake their existence on the clients they find in SSA.

The media are a two-edged sword here. While their coverage of disasters often reinforces negative stereotypes of Africa, they do focus attention on African issues and tend to validate the victimization of the continent by outsiders. Diplomats, academics, relief workers, and others are sometimes more reticent about Africa's problems in private than they are in public. For example, when optimists participate in closed government-sponsored conferences with nonattribution polices in force, they are more likely to take a realistic approach to analyzing African problems. In an extreme example of this change of spots on the leopard, I was surprised to see an outspoken academic critic of U.S. intelligence activities in SSA apply for a grant to do research work for the intelligence community.

THE PESSIMISTS

The list of Afro-pessimists includes the military, defense and intelligence communities, political conservatives, investors, the ex-colonial powers, and the so-called "K Street racists" – the Washington insiders in and out of government who employ impeccable logic to dismiss Africa as a strategic nonentity but whose position really reflects racial attitudes. The defense complex generally opposes U.S. involvement in SSA because of its deserved (in their view) low strategic priority; whatever preconceived ideas may have existed, they are reinforced by almost invariably negative intelligence assessments. And, the negative intelligence is almost always right. Realistic, unbiased assessments based on reliable raw reporting reinforce pessimism among intelligence analysts.

Afro-pessimism itself does not equal racism, but it can reflect a deep lack of understanding of Africa and Africans and lingering stereotypes, even among top officials. I have been dismayed from time to time by racist attitudes expressed by fairly senior officials. The reference to the K Street crowd reflects a more benign assessment of SSA as a hopeless place where significant improvement is not possible. As they would say, Africa has never been important and that is not likely to change.

Near the end of my career, an Office of the Secretary of Defense (OSD) staffer told me that for every geographic region of the world except SSA, in official documents oil was listed as a justification for the region's strategic importance. Shouldn't SSA be included? A quick check showed that 15 per cent of America's imported oil was coming from two West Africa countries (Nigeria and Angola). The oil companies anticipated a dramatic increase in that number. This fact was largely unknown or unappreciated, prompting my office to convene a conference on African oil.

THE BOTTOM LINE

Afro-optimists tend to look at SSA as a continent chained by outside forces, unable to compete fairly because of what history has done to it. The corollary is that if the chains could be removed, Africa could thrive. This will require a lot of remedial work, but we owe it to Africa to accomplish it.

The Afro-pessimists see fatal flaws in Africa. They are not convinced that corrective surgery or any other help will lead to significant progress. They oppose what they see as throwing good money after bad. They are blinded by the cloud of negativity that surrounds Africa and cannot see what is possible.

Many large problems beset the region regardless of the cause. These include: crushing and pervasive poverty, ethnic strife and other discord, HIV/AIDS and other deadly diseases, natural disasters such as drought and famine, exacerbated by military conflicts, a population bulge of alienated youth without prospects, negative effects of the communications revolution that enable Africans to realize the depths of their own poverty, growing criminal activity that destabilizes weak governments, and a variety of internal and other wars. Additional overarching factors are the lack of effective governments on the continent, pervasive corruption at all levels, and the "brain drain" of educated Africans who seek employment outside the continent.

In spite of all of the above, Africa is not without prospects. While it would take huge amounts of money to attack and ameliorate Africa's problems, sub-Saharan Africa is a region where small amounts of aid can go a long way. Further, in the age of the war on global terrorism and America's growing need for more oil, the pessimists ignore Africa at their peril.

DOMESTIC ANALOGIES

Some years ago, I was speaking to a CIA class on the causes of conflict in Africa south of the Sahara, a familiar theme. When I finished and took questions, a woman commented that these causes sounded very much like what she heard on the evening news about violence in our own country. She was quite perceptive, and correct.

The following ten conditions (at least) apply to violence in our inner cities and elsewhere and in weak African states. First is the gap between rich and poor. More than the gap itself is the perception that there is no peaceful way to close it. Thus, to some, the resort to violence and crime seems justified. Feeding this inequity is the large pool of alienated youth, the so-called population bulge. Found both in our inner cities and among disillusioned African youths who go to the cities in search of opportunity, these twelve- to twenty-four-year-olds can easily become criminals.

The easy availability of firearms in both cases is making crime more deadly and opportune. In the United States, the criminals frequently outgun the police. In Africa, military weapons can turn even minor criminal transgressions into mass casualty situations. In the old West, they said that God created men differently but Mr. Colt made them equal. In Africa, one could say that poor governance usurped the power of the peasants, but the AK-47 made them equal. Both here and there, the case can be made that state and local government has difficulty protecting its own citizens. In Africa, it could be from armed insurgency or sectarian violence. In the United States, it is from violent street crime.

In both conditions, we see the breakdown of traditional society. In Africa, it is the village, the elders, the very fabric of the belief system. In America, it is the family unit, broken with nothing constructive to replace it. The collapse of traditional institutions gives rise to violent substitutes: gangs, warlords, and organized crime. In Africa, it is often armed bandits, economic insurgents that fill the void. Child soldiers look to criminal leaders as their substitute families. In America, criminal gangs serve the same purpose.

In Africa, broken infrastructure on a national scale imperils peaceful development. On the continent, infrastructures are meager and fragile, easily disrupted or destroyed, with little prospect of renewal. In America, the equivalent is urban decay and rural poverty. Some parallels also exist in group hatreds. In Africa, these are the three horsemen of the sub-Saharan apocalypse: ethnic, religious, and regional differences, fanned by outbreaks of violence. In the United States, the counterpart is the legacy of slavery and racism and, increasingly, regional differences such as red states and blue states.

The communications revolution has certainly affected Africa. The message is getting even to rural Africa that the continent lags far behind the rest of the world. (It seems that every other country is labeled by someone as the world's poorest.) While Africans are learning how poor they really are, their American counterparts already know. Finally, corruption and ineffective government (bad governance) are still a major problem in sub-Saharan Africa, undermining development and playing into the hands of the criminal elites, whether they are in the bush or in parliament. Again, while many would argue this is not such a big problem in the United States, others would probably beg to differ.

Back in the office at DIA and elsewhere in the intelligence community, half-facetious comparisons were made between the District of Columbia and a small, downtrodden, corrupt West African country. This was especially true when Marion Barry was the mayor. Corruption and incompetence in running our nation's capital was complicated by the Congress's playing the role of colonial overseer. The point here is that the problems of Africa are not so far removed from problems we face right here at home. As Americans, we should not be so quick to belittle Africa and Africans when many American communities have similar unmet challenges.

PART TWO
African Wars I Have Known

Counter-insurgency in Southern Africa, 1961–1974

In 1967 when I joined the Defense Intelligence Agency (DIA) as a green college recruit, Portugal had been fighting nationalist insurgencies in its African possessions for seven years. These little wars were of some marginal significance to the United States. First, Portugal was a NATO ally, and as such eligible for U.S. training and equipment. The equipment was not to be used in Lisbon's African wars, but this proviso was impractical. Second, the communist powers supported the rebels, tainting them in Western eyes. Third, Portugal's African territories – "overseas provinces," according to Lisbon, that were more than twenty-two times the size of metropolitan Portugal – were of potential strategic significance in the global contest with communism. Finally, the United States enjoyed access to Portugal's Azores Islands in the eastern Atlantic. An airbase with long runways, the Azores would serve as a logistical air hub for any contingency in Europe or the Middle East.

The two largest colonies – Angola and Mozambique – formed the northern-most flanks of the white-minority-ruled bastion in southern Africa that included South Africa, South West Africa (Namibia), and Southern Rhodesia (Zimbabwe). Thus, Portugal was in the front rank of white-ruled southern Africa, and as such was in the most vulnerable position. Portuguese Guinea (Guinea-Bissau), a small province on the bulge of West Africa wedged between

Senegal and Guinea, was especially troublesome for Lisbon. The swampy terrain made fighting a counter-insurgency campaign extremely difficult. The remaining two African possessions, Cape Verde and São Tomé & Principe, were tiny island states remote from the conflict on the mainland.

It was not until the late 1960s, however, soon after I arrived on the southern Africa military capabilities desk at DIA, that Portugal began to show signs of stress. The conventional wisdom at the time was that Portugal would retain control of its African Overseas Provinces for ten years, perhaps twenty. By the early 1970s indicators of trouble had begun to persist, especially in Portuguese Guinea and Mozambique. Lisbon's control of parts of these territories was becoming tenuous. Much ballyhooed counter-guerrilla campaigns were largely unsuccessful.

Senior intelligence officials were difficult to convince, however. One afternoon at a coordination meeting of an intelligence estimate – a long-term assessment – on the future of Portuguese Africa, a colleague and I brought along a briefcase full of raw, unanalyzed reports of serious and growing problems in Mozambique. The hard-headed person running the meeting rejected the evidence out of hand and declared that nothing we showed him had changed his thinking at all. It was Lisbon forever in Africa, putting up the good fight against the communist guerrillas.

During the Cold War there was a penchant to label guerrilla fighters "communists" simply because they were armed with communist-origin weapons and received training from communist countries. This simplicity ignored the fact that these insurgents were fighting to overthrow oppressive minority governments and that no one else would provide them with military assistance. Did these groups become Marxist by necessity?

A few years later, the government of Portuguese dictator Marcelino Caetano collapsed, and so did Portugal's African empire. And how did the naysayers interpret this? The Caetano regime had been undermined at home; the African wars had nothing to do with it! Surely maintaining an army of over 100,000 troops in Africa must have had something to do with it.

The point here is that the system, in this case the defense intelligence community and one well-placed senior officer, prevented forward thinking that challenged the prevailing belief system from seeing the light of day. Policy-makers were not warned and hence were not aware of changes about to come. This is what happens when senior officers develop a stake in the outcome of the analysis.

PORTUGAL'S COUNTER-INSURGENCY IN AFRICA

Compared to the large-scale U.S. operations in Southeast Asia during the 1960s, Lisbon's campaign in Africa was war on a shoestring. Portugal boasted that there was no place in any of its overseas provinces that it could not go and that there were no rebel safe havens in its colonies. This may have been literally true, but still it was a vacuous claim.

There were essentially three parts to Portugal's counter-insurgency (COIN) program. First, its elite force (called the "intervention force") mounted search-and-destroy operations. These forces comprised the army commandos, air force paratroopers, paramilitary special groups, and the *flechas* or arrows – retrained former guerrillas. The special groups and the *flechas* were local Africans, while the commandos and paratroopers were Portuguese military. Second, the program used regular army units containing conscripts from Portugal to man garrisons and backfill areas seized by the intervention forces. Third, it used *aldeamentos,* fortified villages, to control the population in contested areas.

For the most part combat was small-scale and occasional. But the trend lines ran against Lisbon. The insurgencies began to spread, Portuguese movement became more difficult, casualties slowly rose, and more troops were deployed to Africa. The rebels began to employ heavier weapons, including artillery rockets and shoulder-fired surface-to-air missiles. Our military attachés based in Lisbon covered the Portuguese colonies and made infrequent trips to visit them. As the guests of Portugal, they were shown what Lisbon wanted them to see. On one trip to Mozambique, the aircraft in which the American attachés were flying was hit by an SA-7 surface-to-air missile. Luckily the warhead did not explode and the plane made a safe landing, but this was definitely something the Portuguese did not want as part of the tour! These wars were becoming more serious, the price of a poor man's empire more expensive, and the writing on the wall more obvious. Lisbon's days in Africa were numbered.

Angola's Three-Ring Circus

The revolt against Portuguese rule in Africa began in Angola in 1961. Called the "jewel" of Lisbon's African Empire, Angola had oil, diamonds, iron, and good farmland. Portugal was more successful in containing the insurgency in Angola, where it faced a fractured rebel front. At the time of the collapse of the regime in Lisbon, the Portuguese military held the initiative in Angola.

The opposition evolved into three guerrilla army movements. The Popular Movement for the Liberation of Angola (MPLA) was the most sophisticated. A group led by "boulevard Marxists," many of whom were mulattos, the MPLA was firmly in the Soviet camp. Che Guevara was an advisor, and a special unit was trained in Cuba – the "Cienfuegos Detachment." This group benefited from Portuguese culpability during the transition to independence in the mid-1970s. The coup in Lisbon brought many closet Marxists out into the open, where they participated in the revolution. People such as the "Red Admiral" (Rosa Coutinho) were sympathetic to the MPLA and surreptitiously assisted that group.

The National Union for the Total Independence of Angola (UNITA) was the second strongest during the pre-independence period. Led by Jonas Savimbi, a charismatic figure who evolved into a demagogue, UNITA had grassroots support from the Ovimbundu people, Angola's largest ethnic group. Savimbi and UNITA during this period were backed by Communist China. They went on to become capable guerrilla fighters.

The third insurgent group, the National Front for the Liberation of Angola (FNLA), was an anomaly. Led by Holden Roberto, the brother-in-law of Zairean (Congolese) dictator Mobutu Sese Seko, the FNLA was a largely artificial movement supported by the West, including the United States. Based in neighboring Zaire, the FNLA mostly fought the other rebel groups, especially the MPLA.

African Wars – William G. Thom

Mozambique: A Weak Link in Portugal's Colonial Chain?

In the Front for the Liberation of Mozambique (FRELIMO) Portugal had a singular and capable opponent, one that could learn from early mistakes. The story of the war in Mozambique is about the spread of insurgency from north to south, the largest single military offensive ever launched by Portugal in Africa, and the breeding-ground for insurrection in Lisbon's ranks. FRELIMO combined Chinese tactics and Soviet weaponry to threaten Portugal's hold.

When hostilities began in 1964, insurgent attacks were ineffectual, confined to the two northernmost and rural districts bordering on Tanzania: Cabo Delgado and Niassa. By 1969 the guerrillas began infiltrating into Tete District and attacked power lines from the strategically important Cabora Bassa Dam. From that time on, there was a steady progression into central Mozambique threatening key lines of communication, such as the Beira Corridor, Southern Rhodesia's nearest access to the sea. The effectiveness of FRELIMO fighters improved as they were cycled through the Chinese training base "Farm 17 Nachingwea" across the border in Tanzania.

In 1970 Portugal undertook its largest military campaign in Africa. Lisbon's best general, Kaulza de Arriaga, was appointed commander of all forces in Mozambique with the writ to organize a large-scale offensive against the rebels. Operation "Gordian Knot" lasted three months and involved as many as 35,000 troops – the number committed to actual combat may have been no more than half that amount. All targeted FRELIMO bases were captured and it was believed to have been a great success, knocking the rebels out of the war. A year later, however, FRELIMO guerrillas were back in business in the same areas.

Ironically, Operation Gordian Knot had a positive effect on FRELIMO, as the insurgents abandoned large base camps for smaller ones. They reduced the size of guerrilla units and emphasized their infiltration south through Tete District. They became a more elusive target, spreading the Portuguese ever thinner. And the offensive had a negative impact on the Portuguese. Lisbon had given it its best shot and failed. Portugal reverted to a more passive defense strategy, and a kind of fatalism set in. The war was unwinnable and the future was bleak.

Portuguese Guinea: Lisbon's Hell Hole

Portuguese Guinea (Guinea Bissau) was a swampy, remote wasteland bereft of any minerals, gems, or important transport links. Yet it was Portugal, and Lisbon did not want a domino effect to start in Bissau. The Portuguese army was an occupation force in a land said to be half underwater at high tide. There was an effective liberation movement in Bissau: the African Party for the Independence of Guinea and Cape Verde (PAIGC). By 1974 it controlled most of the territory, tied down over 25,000 Portuguese troops, and declared unilateral independence.

The PAIGC was led by a brilliant man, Amilcar Cabral, who was later assassinated and never saw his life's work – Bissau's Independence – achieved. My first Temporary Duty (TDY) trip as an Africa analyst was to attend the first Eduardo Mondlane Memorial Lecture at Syracuse University, featuring an address by Cabral. Syracuse in February was far from conducive to studying Africa. A highly respected former Portuguese commander in Bissau, General Antonio de Spinola, wrote a book published in early 1974 that helped put a nail in Caetano's coffin. In *Portugal and the Future*, he said Portugal had no future in Africa.

The Empire Dissolves

Mozambique in the early 1970s spawned a group of young Portuguese officers who called themselves the "Captain's Movement." I did not hear much about the movement until April 1974, when a military coup in Lisbon ousted Caetano. The instrument of his dismissal was the Armed Forces Movement – formerly the Captain's Movement. The war in Mozambique put more strain on Lisbon than the other wars. Troop strength in Mozambique jumped from 25,000 in 1964 to 80,000 in 1974.

In 1974 Washington was buzzing with concerns for multiple communist victories in Southeast Asia, Europe, and Africa. People were less concerned about the African colonies, but Africa watchers in town still had a groundswell of interested clients. While Mozambique and Portuguese Guinea had been the colonial war hot spots, Angola was about to take center stage.

LEARNING ON THE JOB

From 1968 to 1976 I worked the southern Africa military capabilities desk at Arlington Hall Station (AHS), an army post since World War II a few miles west of the Pentagon. This posting proved to be an important opportunity to analyze ongoing military conflicts, not only in Angola and Mozambique, but also in Southern Rhodesia, South-West Africa, and South Africa, and enabled me to practice the craft of a strategic military intelligence analyst.

Working essentially alone, I plotted military movements on a map, counted up and analyzed incidents such as guerrilla attacks, and worked closely with my counterparts at CIA and the State Department. The grunt work (plotting, counting, and evaluating) is the only way to determine the ebb and flow of a conflict, especially an insurgency without front lines, major troop formations, or large numbers of heavy weapons. I learned how to read and evaluate raw intelligence traffic to determine the basics: what is important and what is not. Reading and interpreting raw intelligence is an art form one learns through experience.

My contacts at State included young Foreign Service officers in the Bureau of Intelligence and Research (INR) who went on to become ambassadors and assistant secretaries. I provided them with insightful military analysis; they educated me in the ways of diplomacy. Military officers I worked with at AHS also helped me learn the ropes of military intelligence. Most of them had first-hand military experience in Africa. For example, the late Colonel Donald O. Clark served with the United Nations in the Congo crisis in the early 1960s and had the distinction of having been in a helicopter shot down with a bow and arrow. (An arrow pierced a hydraulic line on the low-flying aircraft, causing it to make a forced landing.)

Responsibility for Angola and Mozambique also brought me into contact with civilian analysts in the Western Europe shop. They were responsible for the Portuguese forces in Africa; I was in charge of the guerrillas. These Western Europe analysts had a definite bias toward Portugal, making coordination of assessments difficult. They tended to overvalue rosy reports coming in from our embassy in Lisbon that downplayed the seriousness of the African insurgencies.

When I signed on with DIA and went through security processing, I was youthfully impressed by the thoroughness of the exercise. For example, if you had any relatives or friends in foreign countries, your security clearance could be denied. I was worried that investigators might find some long-lost relative in East Germany or Poland: communist countries!

Reality struck when as a trainee I was temporarily assigned to a DIA office that featured a Hungarian, a Swede, an Austrian (was he really a German?), a mental patient suffering from deep depression, and the guy who sat in front of me chain-smoking celery cigarettes! Some twenty years after World War II ended, DIA still had leftovers on its payroll from the Crusade in Europe. The staff included people who had been helpful to the United States during and after the war, and some of the young women who flocked to Washington to support the war as described in the late David Brinkley's book *Washington Goes to War*. Some of these women worked in DIA's Western Europe shop that covered Portugal and, hence, a piece of the African wars.

Working with them was another kind of learning experience. Analysts in the Europe shop were accustomed to receiving detailed reports from the military attachés based in their countries of responsibility. These raw intelligence reports so closely paralleled the studies the Europe analysts were scheduled to produce that it was largely a matter of copying the attaché's report. And, with perhaps a little editing, you would have the scheduled product such as an order of battle study, or a more comprehensive ground forces study that would evaluate all aspects of an army.

In the Africa office, quite the reverse was true. Analysts there had to piece together a picture of their subject from scores if not hundreds of fragments of information. With SSA being such a low priority for defense intelligence collection, analysts had to make mental leaps in their assessments to fill out the subject. That is why so many of DIA's best analysts learned their trade working in low-priority Third World regions where they were not spoon-fed information. They learned how to shake the tree to get those fruits of knowledge to fall.

The collapse of Portugal's African empire in the mid-1970s was the beginning of the end of white rule in southern Africa, although at the time South Africa itself still looked impregnable. Apartheid South Africa would not stand by and watch the high tide of militant black African nationalism wash up against its shores. The struggle would continue and even intensify in southern Africa after Portugal's departure.

INSURGENCY IN SOUTHERN RHODESIA, 1965–1980

In 1965 when I was still an undergraduate and two years before I joined DIA, the British self-governing colony of Southern Rhodesia, or simply Rhodesia, became the latest addition to the white minority bastion coalescing in southern Africa. Named for the great imperialist Cecil Rhodes, Rhodesia had a population of about 10 million people, only some 250,000 of whom were white. In 1964 Great Britain granted independence to two other colonies in south-central Africa: Northern Rhodesia became Zambia, and Nyasaland became Malawi. Equipped with borrowed British democratic institutions, they were both ruled by African majorities. The same fate awaited Southern Rhodesia, but that was not yet to be, at least not without a struggle.

Southern Rhodesia, arguably the richest of the three colonies, with the largest white population, refused to go along and on November 11, 1965, announced a Unilateral Declaration of Independence (UDI). London threatened to send in troops and even deployed forces to Zambia, but the ruling Rhodesian Front party led by Ian Smith, a steely-eyed former World War II fighter pilot, stood firm. Illegally independent, Rhodesia became a pariah state facing economic sanctions and international isolation.

The Great Chimurenga (Struggle)

The African nationalist opposition was divided between two major groups. The Zimbabwe African People's Union (ZAPU) and its armed wing, the Zimbabwe People's Revolutionary Army (ZIPRA). ZAPU drew its support from the Ndebele tribe, a sizable minority; its chief military backer was the Soviet Union. Their rival was the Zimbabwe African National Union (ZANU) and its armed wing, the Zimbabwe African National Liberation Army (ZANLA). ZANU was backed by the Shona ethnic majority and supported militarily by the People's Republic of China. The rivalry between ZANU and ZAPU was so intense that, when not fighting against the white minority government, they fought each other.

The two guerrilla armies differed, reflecting the military philosophies of their supporters. ZIPRA was more of a regular, conventional force. Toward the end of the war, it even created a heavily equipped army in exile with armor and artillery supplied by Moscow. The idea was for ZAPU to have "an army in waiting" across the border in Zambia that could march in and become the de facto state army of an independent Zimbabwe. If necessary, this force could seize power by besting its rival ZANU. The Chinese-trained ZANLA became an effective unconventional guerrilla army that eventually applied enough pressure on the Rhodesians to force a negotiated end to UDI after fifteen years. ZANLA insurgents were indeed the fish that swam in the sea of the Shona people, who comprised over 70 per cent of the population.

The war began in 1966. The rebels, especially ZAPU, launched incursions from Zambia into Rhodesia. In company- and platoon-sized formations (i.e., from 30 to over 100 men) the rebels were easily intercepted by the small but mobile and efficient Rhodesian security forces. Clashes in the 1960s and early 1970s were mostly one-sided encounters that bred a sense of overconfidence in the capital, Salisbury (now Harare). It also reinforced American and British notions that Rhodesia's white minority could not be defeated militarily by rag-tag African rebels posing as a nationalist liberation army.

The heart of the Rhodesian military establishment was the 4,500-man regular army. Its principal units were two 1,000-strong regiments: the Rhodesian Light Infantry (RLI) and the Rhodesian African Rifles (RAR). The RAR was composed of black African soldiers and NCOs, with white officers, and was expanded during the final years of the conflict. The RLI was an all-white force. The elite of the elite was "C Squadron, Special Air Services (SAS) Regiment." This Rhodesian unit was actually a part of the famed British SAS regiment, an unparalleled special operations unit the equivalent of today's U.S. Army Special Forces and Navy Seals.

The regular military were backed by 8,000 paramilitary British South African Police (BSAP), a force that was neither British nor South African but somewhat akin to the Royal Canadian Mounted Police. The most controversial forces, however, were the Selous Scouts, retrained former guerrillas sent back to infiltrate the insurgent organizations and wreak havoc on their internal security.

The Rhodesian Air Force employed Canberra Light Bombers, a squadron of Hawker Hunter jet fighter-bombers, Alouette II and III helicopters, and "Linx" light counter-insurgency aircraft (Cessna push-pull propeller planes modified to fire rockets and machine-guns). The Canberras and Hunters were ill-suited for counter-insurgency tasks but did figure in some spectacular missions, including a Canberra bombing raid on a suspected guerrilla training base deep into Angola. During the early years of the war, it is easy to see how the Rhodesians managed to project a romantic image of highly trained professionals hunting down incompetent communist-trained insurgents. Slowly, almost without perception, that would all change.

In Washington, with the focus on our growing commitment in Southeast Asia, there was scant interest in the Rhodesian problem; it was just another building block solidifying white minority rule at the southern end of the continent. What was a little worrying was communist support for the armed opposition. Officially there was condemnation for Rhodesia's defiance of the UK and its denial of basic freedoms to its black majority. Unofficially there was a sense of affinity with the valiant little band of men led by Ian Smith who dared to stare down the British and stand in the way of African nationalism sweeping the continent. I went to meetings where the principal often asked, "How is Smith doing?" as if he were some distant cousin.

Rarely Have So Few Fought So Hard to Disenfranchise So Many

The Rhodesian war can be divided into two phases. In the 1966–71 phase, the Rhodesians rather easily contained guerrilla incursions. The second phase, 1972–79, saw the stretching of the Rhodesian forces as the insurgents spread their attacks, employing classic and more ruthless guerrilla tactics. Gradually a sense of denial took hold of the white population. Toward the end, white Rhodesians, called "Rhodies," found taking submachine guns to the tennis court with them quite normal. Golf courses had signs for mortar hazards and warnings for land mines as if to say "Play through, old chum, and don't lose your leg in the process." Unwilling to give up privilege in paradise, many Rhodies refused to see the truth: the rag-tag guerrillas were slowly winning the war – it's the numbers, stupid!

This was a vicious war. Rural farmsteads were a prime insurgent objective, as were other soft targets. Two Rhodesian airliners were shot down by ZIPRA SA-7 shoulder-fired anti-aircraft missiles. The Rhodesian use of "pseudo-operations" – black Rhodesians posing as nationalist insurgents – to infiltrate the guerrilla groups led to the slaughter of thousands of nationalist combatants and civilian camp followers. Hundreds more were poisoned. The African rebels were "Ters" (terrorists) or "CTs" (communist terrorists), which fit the U.S. security lexicon of the 1960s perfectly.

Rhodesia had solidarity with its neighboring pariahs Portuguese Africa, South Africa, and South West Africa, but this was not all that helpful. South Africa allowed Rhodesia access to the sea, as did Portuguese Mozambique (the Beira Corridor being a more direct route). Pretoria also rotated companies of paramilitary police to patrol the border with Zambia where South African ANC (Nelson Mandela's African National Congress) guerrillas – unable to access South Africa more directly – joined in the attacks into Rhodesia.

The Smith regime's security apparatus had as its overseers the Operations Coordinating Committee, which in turn garnered support from the Joint Planning Staff. The Joint Operations Centers (JOC), established in areas heavily infested with insurgents, managed tactical control of the counter-guerrilla campaign. As the war progressed, more JOCs were established. The Central Intelligence Organization (CIO) headed by Kenneth Flower, provided intelligence assessments to all components. These organizations, like the conflict in general, were models of simplicity and efficiency.

Mozambique was the weak link. In the early 1970s, as the Portuguese began to lose control of their side of the border with Rhodesia, ZANU in particular began infiltrating via Mozambique. At first this was in cooperation with the Front for the Liberation of Mozambique (FRELIMO) guerrillas; by 1975 it was with the help of the FRELIMO government of an independent Mozambique. Infiltration routes expanded southward along the 765-mile border with Mozambique, exposing more of Rhodesia to guerrilla activity. The Rhodesians simply began to be overwhelmed by guerrillas operating in small groups. The turkey shoot had become a stranglehold.

A frequent theme in African conflicts is that groups (substate actors) out of power always repay their supporters once they gain power. This occurred when ZANLA fighters assisted FRELIMO fighters in northwestern Mozambique. Upon independence, FRELIMO closed its border with Rhodesia in solidarity with ZANLA.

Up until the end, the Rhodesians showed panache. Counter-guerrilla raids into Zambia and Mozambique grew more numerous. The infamous "Green Leader" raid of October 1978 had Rhodesian combat aircraft orbiting Lusaka, the Zambian capital, radioing instructions to the airport tower not to interfere with the heliborne raids on insurgent bases now underway around the city. The Rhodesians also created a counterforce to the FRELIMO regime in Mozambique that became the infamous Mozambique National Resistance (RENAMO).

By 1979, Rhodesia had a maximum strength of 16,000 under arms, facing an enemy with over 50,000 armed guerrillas in a country as large as Texas. Despite this human equation, the U.S. National Security/Decision Study Memorandum (NSSM) 39, issued in the early 1970s, foresaw no change in the dominance of the white minority regimes, including Rhodesia.

Years ago I penned in the margin of a book: "They (policymakers) didn't listen to the people who knew; they took the advice of old hacks out of touch, and fell victim to their own ignorance and prejudices." The established analytical elite in the intelligence community could not conceive of emergent black rule in southern Africa, and their "tomorrow will be much like today" approach held sway. Policymakers were uncomfortable with the notion of a new reality; they were more comfortable with what they knew: white regimes prevailing in the struggle against the communist insurgencies. It was a combination of discounting the African nationalists, denial, and wishful thinking.

Colin Powell has said, "Don't always trust what the 'experts' have to say." By the same token, however, you ignore expert opinion at your peril. The way the system works is that the higher up a policy meeting goes, the less likely there is to be a real intelligence expert on the subject in the room. The impact of the intelligence assessment is on the lower-level policy moguls, usually at the deputy assistant secretary level. It's often up to them to carry the intelligence input forward. Sometimes senior intelligence officers are invited to attend a policy forum, but their knowledge of the country or problem under policy review varies widely.

Some Career Lessons

During my formative years as an analyst at AHS, only a few people recognized that I had any potential. I was content with following the conflicts in southern Africa in splendid semi-isolation. At the time two colonels headed the Western Area Division in which I worked; the senior colonel was located in the Pentagon with the division's current intelligence shop. The current intelligence office reported on daily events, somewhat like a classified media outlet, and it was regarded as the analytical first team, close to the big wheels in the Pentagon.

The other colonel sat at AHS with the rest of the outfit – military capabilities, transportation, and biographics. The latter had the noble idea to upgrade the Division's biographic shop, long a dead end for analysts and a dumping ground for poor performers. Unfortunately, he pegged me to be his Africa bio-analyst. I immediately sensed career danger and resisted his pressure to comply. Eventually, I appealed to his senior in the Pentagon, who knew nothing of the plan to make me a bio-analyst and flatly set the other colonel straight. I had violated the sacred chain of command, but saved my career.

LANCASTER HOUSE MARKS A NEW BEGINNING

Toward the end of 1979, with 95 per cent of the country under martial law, the British-sponsored Lancaster House talks to end the war came to fruition. The way was paved for a temporary British administration, national elections, and legal independence set for the following year. This audacious war had come to its logical end. Robert Mugabe, the leader of the party now called the ZANU-Patriotic Front (PF), became president, sounded a moderate note, and marched into history. If the Rhodesian story started with Cecil Rhodes, it ended with Robert Mugabe.

For me the Rhodesian war was yet another example of how the West played into the hands of the communist powers. About the only thing Moscow had going for it in Africa was support for the various armed insurrections against white minority rule. The communists proclaimed conflicts like Rhodesia "just wars" and themselves as the "natural allies" of the African masses yearning for freedom from white oppression. Terms like "neocolonialist" and "anti-imperialist" were in vogue.

The war was like a boxing match in which the smaller weaker man opens up with a series of snappy jabs to the face that disorients his opponent. But, inevitably, the larger, stronger man finds the range and pounds his opponent into submission. The initial belief that the smaller man would win was in part due to psycho-emotional baggage from a bygone era. The belief that black Africans might have served as cannon fodder in World War II if not for their white officers was still popular in many circles. It is instructive to remember that UDI in 1965 came the year after the Civil Rights Act was enacted in the United States and the Tonkin Gulf incident occurred in Vietnam.

Soon after Zimbabwean independence in 1980, I visited the country. There was a sense of militancy in the air. But I was in time for the Harare Show (formerly the Salisbury Show), a kind of national state fair. I saw displays of weapons used during the war, the integrated army band, and lots of agricultural displays. The oddest thing, however, was Tanzanian president Julius Nyerere standing at a podium giving away blue ribbons to white farmers for prize-winning livestock. Welcome to comrade Bob Mugabe's new paradise.

(For further reading, see Ken Flower, *Serving Secretly: Rhodesia's CIO Chief on Record* [London: Galago Press, September 1987]; and, David Martin and Phyllis Johnson, *The Struggle for Zimbabwe* [Harare: Zimbabwe Publishing House, 1981]. References to NSSM 39 are taken from this book.)

Civil War in Angola

THE ANGOLAN CIVIL WAR, PHASE ONE, 1975–1976

One of the best things about working sub-Saharan Africa (SSA) in the U.S. intelligence community was that you had more freedom than your colleagues covering higher-priority regions. In the days of the old Soviet menace, committees formed to decide whether to upgrade a Red Army division from readiness category three to category two. Meanwhile an Africa analyst could totally reorganize the armed forces of one of his countries with only the slightest review or interest by anyone above him in the chain of command. It was "academic freedom" of sorts.

Early in 1975 the Armed Forces Ruling Council in Portugal was preparing the way for independence of Portugal's African colonies. The situation was most chaotic in Angola, where three separate nationalist groups vied for control of the country. Clashes between these groups became more common, and gradually the three groups became dominant in the homelands of the three major ethnic groups they represented. The MPLA was Kimbundu and mulatto, in the northwest and urban coastal areas. The FNLA was Bakongo, in the north along and across the border with Zaire. UNITA was Ovimbundu, in the central highlands and parts of the east.

I was watching developments in Angola with increasing interest at the expense of my other nine countries: South Africa, Namibia, Botswana, Zimbabwe, Zambia, Malawi, Mozambique, Swaziland, and Lesotho. A civil war seemed to be brewing, pitting the Marxist-Soviet-backed MPLA against the Western-backed FNLA, and the Chinese- and later Western-backed UNITA, comprised of the largest ethnic group in the country, the Ovimbundu, some 37 per cent of the total population.

All three factions had small arms left over from their guerrilla campaigns against Portugal. But by March 1975, arms deliveries to the MPLA from the East bloc began to increase significantly. These shipments really caught my attention, as arms came in by sea to ports controlled by the MPLA, notably Luanda, Lobito, and Benguella. Aside from small arms, there were crew-served heavy machine guns, mortars, recoilless rifles, and the ubiquitous individually operated rocket-propelled grenades (RPGs).

If the raw reporting could be believed, hundreds, perhaps thousands, of these weapons poured in, all brand-new in crates direct from the factory, not used hand-me-downs more typical of Soviet bloc aid to African guerrilla fighters. In addition, there were reports of heavier weaponry – armored cars, multiple rocket launchers, and artillery, with which the MPLA were not experienced. Thus foreign instructors could not be far behind. The battle for Angola had begun.

With scant interest, local management in the sub-Saharan Africa military capabilities shop at DIA let me forget about my other nine countries and focus on Angola. I developed a one-to-one-million-scale wall map that plotted which factions controlled which towns, where the bases for each group were, and their estimated strengths where available. In short, it laid out the order of battle for all three movements. Covered by an acetate sheet, the information was color-coded: red for the MPLA, blue for the FNLA, and green for UNITA. I began working on a DIA appraisal entitled "Angola Drifts Toward Civil War."

Technically, there could be no civil war in Angola until the Portuguese hauled down their flag on November 11, 1975. In reality, what developed into a conflict for control of postcolonial Angola had begun almost a year before. By the summer of 1975, the contest was well underway.

Suddenly the Powers That Be Awaken

Africa watchers in the intelligence community are fond of saying that every few years the authorities – the policymakers, politicians, and military operators – rediscover Africa. In early August 1975, with fighting underway around Angola, my gray phone rang one afternoon. (The secure telephones were light gray in color so everyone called them "gray phones.") A woman on the other end identified herself as a CIA analyst. She had heard that I had a wonderful map of Angola and asked if she could come over to Arlington Hall to see it and make notes. A woman in her early twenties arrived about an hour later and began feverishly writing things down on a yellow legal pad, asking nonstop questions. She explained that her boss back at the Agency was preparing for a very important meeting the next afternoon.

She left with reams of notes late that afternoon, and I was glad that I could be helpful. Just before I left for the day, my gray phone rang again. It was the young woman sounding frazzled. There was a crisis: her boss could not understand her notes. She asked if I could take the acetate sheet off my map and bring it to CIA headquarters at 6 a.m. the next morning. They had a map of the same scale; could I help them transfer the information? I looked for my boss; he was gone. I looked for his boss; he was gone. So, as a GS-12 I made an executive decision: I would be at the CIA the next morning.

Arriving long before dawn at my office in Arlington Hall Station (AHS), I rolled up the acetate sheet and covered it with two large green trash bags, then drove off to the CIA. They had my name at the parkway gate and told me to drive around to the front of the building and park in one of the VIP spots. There on the steps I was met by the young woman, who whisked me through the door and past the guards to the CIA Operations side of the building. (Previously I had dealt with my CIA analyst counterparts, who worked for the deputy director for Intelligence; I was now dealing with the deputy director for Operations, the collection and paramilitary arm of the Agency.)

I have been out to the CIA hundreds of times during my career, but this was the only time I have ever been in the building without a badge of any kind. I was taken to the CIA Angola Intelligence Task Force, walking through a door that looked like a bank vault. At the far end were two desks separated from the rest of the long rectangular-shaped room by partitions with two large maps of Angola mounted on them.

I met the task force commander, John Stockwell, and his deputy, who refused to tell me anything about what they were doing. But it was obvious they were planning for Angola. As I updated their maps right behind where Stockwell sat, I overheard various comments related to planning, such as what airline to use and "How will we get those things to Roberto's people?" (referring to Holden Roberto, head of the FNLA). They referred so often to Southeast Asia that I thought Angola must have been transplanted on the other side of the world.

That afternoon the CIA briefed Secretary of State Henry Kissinger and the 40 Committee – the National Security Council entity that handled covert operations. The United States was off and running into Angola, and I had supplied the intelligence community with its initial military database for the Angolan War.

One might ask why the CIA had to go to the DIA for such basic intelligence information. Historically, in my experience, there were few good military analysts outside DIA to cover regions like sub-Saharan Africa. The CIA's chief analytical focus is on politics and economics, not the military. They do have some excellent military analysts, but in places like SSA they are rare. I have seen them take an analyst off a country that suddenly develops a military problem and replace him with a better military analyst from another part of the continent or from outside the Africa region. When it comes to military analysis, DIA carries the ball for the U.S. intelligence community on a daily basis, especially in areas like sub-Saharan Africa, something that is not widely appreciated.

Cubans or South Africans: The Chicken or the Egg?

Back on the battlefield, the MPLA was gaining the upper hand, having taken complete control of Luanda, the capital. The MPLA benefited the most from outside support, which included communists in the Portuguese interim regime that secretly facilitated the arrival of military aid. The Portuguese officer in nominal charge of Angola during the early phase of the transition was the aforementioned Admiral Rosa Coutinho, the "Red Admiral," who later admitted his role in arranging support for the Marxist MPLA, including the influx of Cuban troops.

Some support came via air shipments to Congo-Brazzaville, a Soviet client state in the region. From Brazzaville and Pointe-Noire, military supplies were shipped south to Angolan ports in unassuming coastal freighters. Cubans in Congo-B were reportedly involved in training the MPLA, and reports of Cuban advisors with the MPLA in Angola surfaced as early as June and July 1975. The South Africans cited the Cuban involvement to justify their own intervention later that year. Recent research, however, indicates that the arrival of the Cuban military may have been much later, perhaps after the South African invasion. In my view from the Angola desk, the Cubans came first, most likely as military advisors; combat troops may have come a bit later, in September. Nevertheless, by the fall of 1975 both Havana and Pretoria were militarily engaged in Angola.

I participated that year in a long series of interagency meetings on the Angolan crisis, chaired by the National Intelligence Officer (NIO) for Africa. The NIO is the most senior intelligence officer for his or her region or specialty and sits on the National Intelligence Council (NIC), chaired by the director of Central Intelligence. I was one of two analysts the NIO-AF considered real experts on the military situation; the other was a CIA operations officer. No meeting chaired by the NIO-AF could start unless one of us was there to give the opening situation report and monitor the discussion for reality checks.

The Agony of Defeat

In the fall of 1975, anti-MPLA forces began a counter-offensive. From the north a force of FNLA guerrillas, right-wing ex-Portuguese Army troops, and two battalions of Zairian soldiers backed by field artillery and armored cars advanced on Luanda. At the same time, a force composed mainly of Angolan troops trained and led by South Africans advanced from the south. Using bases in South African-controlled South West Africa (now Namibia), Pretoria molded a force of FNLA and later UNITA guerrillas into South African–equipped, battalion-sized, combined-arms task forces, commanded and partly staffed by white South Africans.

In the north, the anticommunist advance was stopped in one decisive November battle near Caxito, about forty miles northeast of the capital. MPLA and Cuban troops showered 122-mm rockets fired from Soviet BM-21 multiple rocket launchers on the advancing enemy. The ex-Portuguese soldiers held the center and kept advancing, but soon discovered the FNLA troops on their left and the Zairian troops on their right were in full retreat. After suffering heavy casualties, the Portuguese pulled back, too, in what became a rout, all the way to the Zairian border. The MPLA was never again threatened by the FNLA.

Soldiers who have never experienced heavy combat are apt to panic when subjected to shelling for the first time. The BM-21 was a hellacious weapon in Angola and later elsewhere in Africa. Dubbed the "Stalin Organ" because the forty tubes mounted on a truck resembled a pipe organ, its rockets scream through the sky, then hit with the punch of a 42-pound high explosive warhead. Its almost seven-mile range makes it an ideal standoff weapon.

Apartheid South Africa to the Rescue

To the south, the MPLA faced a more serious threat from South Africa. Pretoria's highly mobile task forces were racing through southern and central Angola, and regular South African Defense Force (SADF) troops were being added to the mix. Resistance from the MPLA's army (FAPLA – the Angolan People's Liberation Army) was mostly light in the face of the SADF mini-blitzkrieg.

The South Africans had more trouble with MPLA allies. A force of ex-Katanga gendarmes from Zaire (see chapter 12) held the town of Luena in eastern Angola. These professional fighters had fought for Portugal in its counter-insurgency campaign, but lately had been recruited by the MPLA. Fighting from inside a soccer stadium, the SADF needed reinforcements to cope with Katangan resistance.

The SADF's road to Luanda got increasingly bumpy once they encountered Cuban troops. By December 1975, blitzkrieg was becoming sitzkrieg (stalemate) as they encountered Cuban stiffeners in the FAPLA ranks – MPLA units that had Cubans assigned and probably in command, not just as advisors – and then purely Cuban units. In reality, the SADF and its allies, with UNITA playing a much more prominent role, more than held their own against the Cubans. However, the nature of the war was changing. It was becoming a war of attrition, with more white South African troops being committed to combat. The SADF also discovered that its training for counter-insurgency war was inadequate for the more conventional combat it now faced. Pretoria also realized that its museum-piece assortment of heavy weapons compared unfavorably with what the Soviets had supplied to the opposition (see chapter 7 on South Africa's defense industry).

Despite tactical victories against the Cuban/MPLA forces, by the end of 1975 the South Africans and their allies had lost the strategic initiative. With the prospect of an endless stream of white South African soldiers returning in body bags, Pretoria decided in early 1976 to cut its losses and fall back to South West Africa, where it could organize support for its UNITA and remnant FNLA allies. Without the SADF in the field, UNITA defenses crumbled in the face of the inevitable Cuban/MPLA counter-offensive. The game was up by March 1976.

Cold War Fears

For the U.S. government, Angola was perceived as a defeat at a time when communist forces were on the march in other parts of the world, such as Southeast Asia. Saigon had fallen to the North Vietnamese Army in April 1975. UNITA, with its charismatic leader Jonas Savimbi, replaced the FNLA as the main recipient of American support and became a leading Reagan-Doctrine "freedom fighter" in the 1980s. Following Mao's example, Savimbi began his own long march into far southeastern Angola, where he would establish his new capital, which he called Jamba. He also cemented his relations with Apartheid South Africa, which would help sustain his movement for the next twelve years. The Chinese-trained Savimbi was by now definitely seen as wearing a white hat.

It was always difficult for us to locate Jamba. That was because Jamba was not any one place, or you could say there were quite a few Jambas. A CIA operations officer who had been there for a number of months explained this best to me. Security was tight, and even our CIA man on the scene could not travel alone. He was isolated, kept in the dark. If the South Africans were at Jamba, they could be forty miles away and he would never see them. Jamba was a sprawling network of encampments, supply dumps, airstrips, and assorted facilities supporting UNITA. Planes could be heard at night landing and taking off, but whose aircraft or what cargo could not be learned. The terrain around Jamba in the far southeast was so harsh the Portuguese called it the end of the earth. It was not the kind of place where you just struck off on your own to see what was around; furthermore, you had UNITA "escorts" twenty-four hours a day. This explains why it was always so difficult to get a reading on UNITA's supply situation.

In Angola, South Africa demonstrated that a black African force that it trained, led, and equipped could be a formidable force in sub-Saharan Africa. The infamous "32nd Battalion" included former FNLA soldiers and other Angolans. Although nominally a battalion, this unit was expanded at times to a force of thousands. Through its operations behind enemy lines in Angola and elsewhere, it served as the eyes and ears of Pretoria for many years.

As for Havana, Fidel Castro demonstrated that he was willing to put his troops where his mouth was and that he would back up revolutionary rhetoric with cold steel. In addition, Moscow proved that it was willing to provide the military wherewithal to support a Marxist movement in Africa to attain power. The Soviet Union mounted the first strategic airlift in its history from Russia to Brazzaville and then, after November 11, 1975, directly into Angola, using its fleet of An-22 Cocks and An-12 Cubs to deliver priority supplies for the MPLA and the Cubans. In retrospect, this first stage of the lengthy Angolan Civil War was smaller in scale than what was to follow in the 1980s and 1990s. While shocking in its own right, it was only a taste of what was to come.

(For further reading on this phase of the Angola conflict, see William Thom, "Angola's 1975–76 Civil War: A Military Analysis," in *Low Intensity Conflict and Law Enforcement*, vol. 7, No. 2 (1998); and John Stockwell, *In Search of Enemies: A CIA Story* [New York: W. W. Norton, 1978].)

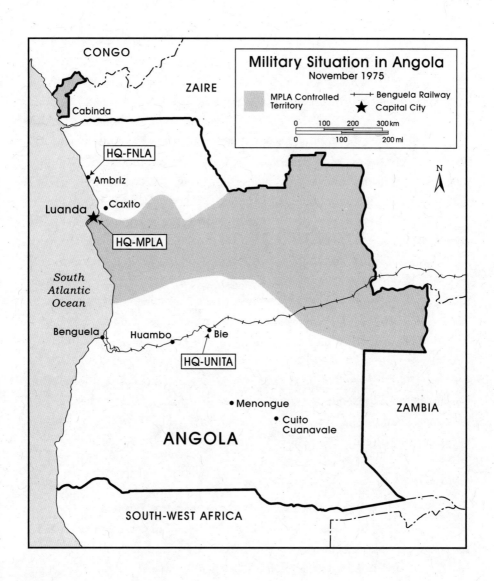

Military Situation in Angola
November 1975

MPLA Controlled Territory

Benguela Railway

Capital City

0   100   200   300 km
0   100   200 mi

CONGO

ZAIRE

Cabinda

HQ-FNLA

Ambriz

Caxito

Luanda

HQ-MPLA

South Atlantic Ocean

Benguela

Huambo

Bie

HQ-UNITA

Menongue

Cuito Cuanavale

ANGOLA

ZAMBIA

SOUTH-WEST AFRICA

N

THE ANGOLAN CIVIL WAR, PHASE TWO, 1980–1992

Jonas Savimbi's retreat to Jamba in 1976 was not the end of the war with the MPLA, but the beginning of a new phase in that war. UNITA was reorganized as a guerrilla army capable of operating countrywide, but it retained a smaller conventional capability to attack enemy bases and protect Savimbi's "free Angola" in the southeast. With American and South African support, and the ethnic backing of the nation's largest single ethnic group, the Ovimbundu, UNITA and its charismatic leader became a force to be reckoned with in Angola.

By 1980, UNITA was on the rebound, growing stronger, forcing FAPLA to abandon considerable territory to the insurgents. Simultaneously, links to South Africa were building. The SADF was still operating in southern Angola mainly to attack South-West Africa People's Organization (SWAPO) guerrilla bases, hitting the insurgents before they could infiltrate Namibia (South West Africa). Moreover, when the SADF attacked SWAPO – often collocated with FAPLA – it helped reduce the magnitude of the threat to UNITA.

However, Pretoria was also increasing its direct assistance. While UNITA was not totally dependent on South Africa, the Apartheid state afforded important help and provided Savimbi with an insurance policy in the face of a growing Cuban military presence in Angola. Meanwhile there was no shortage of military hardware arriving in FAPLA armories from the Soviet bloc.

Cold War Politics and Intelligence Analysis

This second phase of the Angolan civil war spanned two Republican administrations (Reagan and Bush I) and the ascendancy of my own career. In 1980, I was assigned to DIA's Directorate for Estimates (DE), that part of the agency that specialized in long-range intelligence assessments. As part of a two-man analytical team, I again covered SSA. With a European detour, I had covered the usual path of analyst advancement in DIA through the General Schedule (GS) ranks: from GS-12 military analyst, to GS-13 current analyst (in both DIA and EUCOM), to GS-14 estimates analyst. The rank of GS-14 was as far as one could go and still be considered an analyst. The GS is a federal pay grade synonymous with the rank structure.

The role of the estimator was to represent DIA on all national intelligence estimates (those requiring intelligence community review and approval) in his area of responsibility, to write intelligence estimates (either for DIA or the National Intelligence Council – NIC), and to coordinate all estimative judgments in DIA products.

Unburdened by heavy production responsibilities, DE was like a think tank within DIA. My esteemed colleague Walt Barrows and I were the Africa team and spent many hours dissecting all things African and fusing key judgments into DIA assessments.

In 1983, I was promoted to chief of the Africa Military Capabilities Branch, elevating me to the rank of GS-15, the equivalent of a full colonel. This made me the most senior Africanist in DIA. Four years later, I would advance to the position of Defense Intelligence Officer (DIO) for Africa, a job that had not been open to DIA civilians until 1986. As the DIO for Africa (DIO-AF), I was inducted into the Defense Intelligence Senior Executive Service, becoming the equivalent of a flag (i.e., general) officer.

All through this period, the war raged on in Angola. Jonas Savimbi, the son of a railroad stationmaster in central Angola, became a darling of the Reagan administration, and conservatives in the Office of the Secretary of Defense (OSD) adored him. His charm and wit made him a poster boy for the Reagan Doctrine – U.S. support for "freedom fighters" battling communist regimes around the globe. The clandestine but transparent U.S. aid program for UNITA was far more sophisticated than the mid-1970s program for the FNLA. Now Washington had a winner in Angola.

Savimbi visited the Pentagon often and was treated like a head of state. I briefed him several times on the situation in Angola, something that was tricky because, first, he presumably knew a lot more than we did, and, second, it was unacceptable to talk about what UNITA was doing. Savimbi was short, yet all his official photographs made him look like a giant. With his trademark beard and beret, in military uniform or a Mao suit, Savimbi was more than just charismatic; he was a demagogue, an "African big man" in the truest sense.

Who Is the Racist Here?

As the years rolled on, DIA had some analysts that were very pro-UNITA. This fit the powers in OSD well; from the deputy assistant secretaries on up to the secretary of defense himself, they liked being told their man was winning. The bruises of 1975 were still there. They did not, however, like being told that their man's success was largely dependent on help from racist South Africa. Once, as I explained UNITA's dependence on Pretoria, I was accused of being "racist" because I could not give Savimbi's forces full credit for battlefield victories won on their own. Ironically, the accuser always argued that FAPLA successes were the result of Cuban intervention. While many of the Cuban soldiers sent to Angola were black, their top commanders and many of their officers were white – not unlike the situation on the other side, where white South Africans often commanded black troops.

On to Mavinga!

UNITA was well suited for guerrilla operations and successful in operating against Soviet and Cuban-backed FAPLA troops that struggled with counterinsurgency. However, UNITA had one weakness: free Angola, an area in the southeast around its almost mythical capital Jamba, Savimbi's showplace. As long as it had ground to defend, it presented a target for FAPLA's conventional forces. Throughout most of the country, UNITA forced the MPLA to fight a guerrilla war; in the southeast FAPLA forced UNITA to fight a conventional war by mounting attacks on free Angola.

The gateway to Jamba was Mavinga, captured by Savimbi's troops in 1981. Beginning in the mid-1980s, Mavinga became the objective of repeated annual or biannual FAPLA offensives. The pattern was basically the same: a Soviet arms build-up, ponderous troop movements trying to beat the onset of the rainy season, treacherous river crossings, a force depleted by UNITA's harassing attacks, and the eventual fall back to Cuito Cuanavale, the usual jumping-off point. When these offensives became more ominous for UNITA, the SADF stepped in and punished FAPLA with artillery and air strikes.

The 1985 drive into UNITA territory prompted a significant SADF ground and air intervention. The FAPLA 1986 offensive was pre-empted by a UNITA attack on Cuito Cuanavale, but it did not deter Angola from launching its biggest effort to date the following year. The scale of combat had grown appreciably since 1976. An estimated 15,000 to 17,000 FAPLA troops had been amassed for the 1987 campaign. The Cubans usually did not participate in frontline operations; rather they garrisoned bases and major towns, freeing up Angolan troops for counter-insurgency operations or large-scale offensives. Cuban and Soviet advisors did frequent the front lines, however. The 1987 offensive would lead to rapid escalation of the war and a dangerous showdown between Havana and Pretoria.

Every FAPLA attempt to attack Mavinga featured a new wrinkle: new equipment, more troops, a secondary front, new tactical formations, more air defense equipment (why would they need this, UNITA had no air force?). It became more difficult to hide Pretoria's hand behind UNITA's defense, until South Africa would finally announce after the fact that the FAPLA/Cuban offensive posed a threat to its own national security.

In September 1987, FAPLA took troops from four or five brigades and organized them into six combat groups, marginally self-sustaining, reinforced battalion task forces. In late August, South African Special Forces blew up a bridge at Cuito Cuanavale complicating logistic support for government forces to the east. Nevertheless, FAPLA kept moving east and crossed the Lomba River in the face of heavy UNITA resistance, placing them in position to strike at Mavinga.

Then the SADF struck with long-range G-5 and G-6 155-mm artillery and waves of combat aircraft. Pretoria committed 3,000 to 4,000 ground forces, including the 32nd "Buffalo" Battalion, the 101st Battalion from the South-West Africa Territorial Force (SWATF), and the SADF's all-white 61st Mechanized Group. The SADF had fifty combat aircraft forward deployed to bases in northern Namibia at the time. The result was the complete devastation of the FAPLA offensive.

In early October 1987, the FAPLA 47th Brigade was caught exposed on the south bank of the Lomba River. Over a hundred vehicles were destroyed or abandoned amid thousands of bomb and shell craters. Although UNITA took credit for the devastation, imagery happened to catch a South African Air Force Buccaneer bomber in flight over the target area.

With every FAPLA formation in the attack suffering heavy casualties, Luanda's forces once again retreated toward Cuito Cuanavale. This time, however, UNITA and the SADF would follow. Pretoria hoped to bleed the FAPLA so severely that it would be incapable of launching another such offensive for years, if ever. It would perhaps open the way for a great UNITA victory. However, this violated one of the principles of negotiating a solution to the Angolan war: for talks to succeed, the military situation had to be in rough balance. One side could not hold the upper hand and dictate terms.

FAPLA and Cuban forces dug in around Cuito Cuanavale and resisted repeated attacks by UNITA and SADF troops. For months, government forces withstood attacks by South African armor and artillery, not to mention aerial bombing. The siege set off alarm bells in Moscow and Havana as well as Luanda. Washington rejoiced in Savimbi's battlefield success, not foreseeing the consequences. The communist powers feared that South Africa was back in the game big time. Pretoria had escalated the war and it was time for a response.

Castro's Strategic Masterstroke

By late 1987, of the 30,000 Cuban troops in Angola, about 1,000 were engaged at Cuito Cuanavale. Nevertheless, there were ominous rumblings in Havana. More Cubans were on the way. At first, this appeared to be just another incremental ratcheting up of the Cuban presence, as had occurred each time FAPLA suffered a major defeat. These were seen more as political gestures to mollify the MPLA than any intent to escalate the war. The Cubans were definitely augmenting their forces in Angola. But to what effect?

From the analyst's perspective, there was something different about this Cuban build-up from the beginning. The argument over how significant it was exposed an old weakness in the intelligence ranks. Africa analysts were responsible for African forces, but what about foreign forces in Africa? Frequently analysts covering the Soviet Union, Cuba, China, and other countries from different offices in DIA (and I suspect elsewhere) wrote assessments about their country's activities in Africa. This always seemed to lead to difficult coordinating sessions, sometimes holding up the publication of a paper for months.

This was mostly the result of not understanding the context in which foreign forces were operating. Further, the significance of the African role was denigrated. The Cubans were assumed to have more competence than the Angolans, and hence they had been in charge and dominated the relationship. At times, the self-importance and intellectual prowess assumed by analysts working higher priority accounts was stultifying. I once overheard an analyst working a higher priority area exclaim on the phone "What do you think this is, Cameroon or something." The inference here was: "Don't treat me as if I work some worthless African country."

At times, some analysts wore their country's or their region's higher priority as a badge of honor. Some lorded their prestige and self-importance over the lowlights working Africa or Latin America. This could cause problems when coordinating intelligence products, making management resource decisions, and maintaining good relations between analysts from different worlds of priority. For the most part, however, I believe DIA analysts, in conjunction with their managers, acted professionally to limit such behavior.

By early 1988, the menacing Cuban build-up was becoming obvious. Elements of the Cuban 50th Mechanized Division, based in Havana and regarded as a regime protection unit, were going to Angola. The Cubans flown into Angola would marry up with new Soviet-supplied equipment that replaced older weaponry left behind in Cuba. The combination of Cuban manpower and Russian arms was again on the loose in Africa. Soon Castro would have over 50,000 troops in Angola.

As the intelligence community watched with bated breath, Cuban forces began concentrating at Caconda in the central highlands. It was about halfway between the large government-held cities of Huambo and Lubango. The Cubans appeared poised to move southeast toward Menongue, relieve the siege of Cuito Cuanavale, and perhaps go on to Mavinga and Jamba! This was a force the likes of which Angola had never seen. The force around Caconda, which did not include Cuban forces elsewhere in Angola, eventually had 400 tanks, over 160 pieces of artillery and MRLs, and numerous light armored vehicles, backed by 45 MiGs.

Finally, in late March 1988, the Cubans at Caconda began to move, not southeast toward Cuito Cuanavale, but southwest toward Namibia. Along with FAPLA and SWAPO troops, the Cubans were marching south into the area where the SADF operated with impunity, a direct challenge to Pretoria's military dominance. It appeared that Havana was threatening to invade South African–controlled Namibia. The South Africans were slow to notice what was happening. During May, the SADF began to reinforce Sector 10, the command responsible for northern Namibia and cross-border operations into Angola. The Cubans were once again calling South Africa's bluff just as they did in 1975, only this time on a much larger scale with higher stakes.

Through the first half of 1988, significant fighting was taking place on several other fronts in central and southern Angola, but all eyes were on the Cuban move toward Namibia. Ongoing negotiations on Cuban troop withdrawal (CTW) involving the United States, Cuba, South Africa, Angola, and the USSR were continuing with renewed urgency. Inevitably, the Cubans encountered the SADF in southern Angola near the Namibian border. The events that nearly led to a major confrontation occurred on 27 June 1988. A Cuban unit (probably a battalion-sized tactical group) on a reconnaissance mission was ambushed by South Africa troops and suffered 200-plus casualties. The Cubans responded with an air attack on the Ruacana Dam just over the border from Namibia, and the source of that country's electric power. The Cubans launched a formation of eight MiG-23s, indicating they meant business.

The raid caused minor damage to the dam. One pilot missed the target by a wide margin, however. His bombs happened to make a direct hit on a South African armored personnel carrier parked under a tree, killing a dozen soldiers who had been watching the fireworks from what they thought was a safe distance. There was no response from the South African Air Force that had to contend with an in-depth Soviet-built air defense system in southern Angola.

Cooler Heads Prevail as Peace Talks Lead to Withdrawal

Later in 1988, the long series of troop withdrawal talks under the guidance of U.S. Assistant Secretary of State for African Affairs Chester Crocker, rotating among venues in Cuba, Angola, South Africa, and the United States, came to fruition in the form of the New York Accords. The SADF would pull out of Angola and eventually yield to an UN-supervised transition to Namibian independence. Havana would agree to a multi-year phased departure of its forces from Angola in what became known as CTW – Cuban Troop Withdrawal. Left out of the equation was the issue of national reconciliation between the MPLA government and UNITA. Absent this important detail, the war would go on but without foreign backing.

For the second time in twelve years, South Africa had backed down from a Cuban challenge. The SADF in theory had the capability to defeat the Cubans, but it would simply be too costly. There would be too many casualties and no certain end, with the war being bankrolled by Moscow. Castro seemed to recognize this and decided to gamble his expeditionary force on the belief that Pretoria would not commit its forces. This was Castro's masterstroke. He achieved strategic results with minimal casualties through an exercise in gamesmanship.

The Role of Strategic Military Intelligence at the National Level

U.S. intelligence, and in particular DIA, had an important role to play in this process. First was verifying CTW. There was considerable concern that the Cubans would cheat, leaving black Cuban troops behind, perhaps melded into FAPLA units. On monitoring South African activity the big question was, "How would the military balance be affected by the pullback of each side's key supporters?" If the Cubans were the only factor holding UNITA back, they should continue in the ascendancy. If the SADF was the backbone of UNITA, then FAPLA should have the upper hand. It was hoped some type of military equilibrium would lead to a negotiated settlement. Nevertheless, that would not occur without another FAPLA go at Mavinga.

Throughout this Angolan multi-decade passion play, DIA provided continuous military briefings for OSD and State Department officials, and at inter-agency meetings chaired by the NIO and other NIC officials. At times, desk-side updates for OSD officials ranging from desk officers to deputy assistant secretaries occurred daily. As the DIO for Africa beginning in the late 1980s, I was right in the middle of this. I spent many hours in analyst pre-briefings to insure that DIA had one position. It was difficult to accommodate all analyst views and retain a definitive product.

DIA Must Speak with One Voice

Having two different views of the situation was, and remains, a constant worry. For instance, the J2 in DIA operated semi-autonomously and was the intelligence officer for the Chairman of the Joint Chiefs of Staff (CJCS) in the Pentagon. The J2 briefed the SECDEF and the CJCS daily on world events. The DIO had to insure there were no conflicting opinions that, if exposed, could embarrass the agency. Although this rarely happened, critics of intelligence loved to cite two conflicted assessments coming out of DIA on the same day.

It was not unusual for senior intelligence people to assist policymakers in preparing briefings, policy papers, and the like. Some policy types viewed intelligence professionals as part of their team. While suggestions and other informal inputs were accepted, there was never any mention of intelligence's hand in the final policy product.

This was not a two-way street, however. On another occasion, I learned from a CIA colleague that there was a meeting in his building that afternoon to discuss Savimbi. The J2 was invited, and I was expected. A call down to the J2's office, however, indicated that only he was invited. My next call, to the DIA command element, resulted in DIA's deputy director telling the J2 to take me along. Such was the continuing struggle to be useful, and you can't be useful unless you are in the room.

The War Continues with Reduced Sponsorship

By mid-1989, the SADF was long out of Angola and a UN mission to supervise Namibia's transition to independence was on the ground. CTW was underway. The Angolan government could not resist the temptation of launching another grand offensive against UNITA, now without South African support. The first salvos of "Operation Final Assault" were not directed at Mavinga, but by December 1989 FAPLA had assembled 12,000 troops and supplies at Cuito Cuanavale for another attempt to pierce UNITA's "free Angola." Although Cuban troops were out of the equation, Luanda still had the services of Soviet and Cuban military advisors and logisticians. For its part, UNITA received a golden handshake from South Africa and Pretoria's sanction-busting little black book (i.e., – a list of contacts to procure arms and services on the black market.

The FAPLA advance on Mavinga once again met heavy UNITA resistance, but government troops made slow, steady progress. FAPLA employed more armor and more firepower than in previous offensives. Organized into Tactical Groups (combined arms, self-sustaining reinforced battalions) and Soviet-style motorized infantry brigades, FAPLA and its Soviet advisors assigned infantry brigades to escort large supply columns to the front. UNITA did its best to nibble away at advancing government forces using "gun jeeps," 4x4 light trucks armed with 106-mm recoilless rifles or heavy machine guns.

Where is Mavinga Anyway?

In early February 1990, FAPLA successfully crossed the Lomba River and approached within a few kilometers of Mavinga, establishing a large firebase. There was no doubt; there it was. The firebase made a beautiful blown-up picture from imagery. It was definitely FAPLA; look at all the artillery. Where was Mavinga? A few scattered bombed-out buildings lined what had been the main street. An abandoned dirt airstrip just out of town and some fields of maize were the only signs of habitation. For FAPLA it must have been like Napoleon's first view of Moscow in ashes.

There was no cry of "on to Jamba." In fact, the FAPLA base at Mavinga was under harassing attack, and its supply lines were vulnerable. An operative who had just returned from Angola where he had been observing the base from behind UNITA lines described a daily routine. At dawn UNITA gunners fired half a dozen rounds at the firebase. A few minutes later FAPLA replied in kind. It was quiet for the rest of the day, except maybe for an evening salute, although both sides kept talking about heavy fighting.

During this battle for Mavinga, in March 1990, I made the following note to myself:

> We [the intelligence community] failed to predict that South African withdrawal and Namibian independence would have an immediate negative impact on UNITA that would outweigh CTW. We didn't think the Soviets would hang in there either. We focused on how a weak and hapless FAPLA would come apart at the seams without the Cubans. It seems that we essentially bought the UNITA assessment of an inept FAPLA and Savimbi's boasting that if he could only get rid of the Cubans, he could handle FAPLA.

Back in the intelligence community, the significance of FAPLA's "breakthrough" at Mavinga was hotly debated. For those in the "UNITA can do no wrong" camp, FAPLA had not reached Mavinga at all. They had been stopped short by UNITA. Others were impressed with Luanda's accomplishment. As usual, the truth was somewhere in the middle. After a bit longer than two months at its Mavinga base, FAPLA began its pull-back. It was much like Napoleon's retreat from Moscow, only with the seasonal rains, not snow. FAPLA losses were estimated at 2,000 killed and some 400 pieces of equipment destroyed or captured.

The consequences were not entirely bad, however. UNITA had turned back a major FAPLA offensive once again, and its guerrilla forces were active all over the country. FAPLA did throw a scare into UNITA. Savimbi's troops came uncomfortably close to major defeat at Mavinga, and the Angolan Army showed it still had muscle without the Cubans. The looming independence of Namibia under MPLA ally SWAPO would expose UNITA's southern borders to attack. In a sense, the overall military situation was in rough balance.

The Bicesse Accords: Peace in Our Time?

The 1989–90 fighting led to renewed efforts at national reconciliation (NR) in Angola, to complete the diplomatic process by finally ending the war between the MPLA and UNITA. The effort was driven by the troika of the United States, the Soviet Union, and Portugal, and resulted in the Bicesse Accords signed in

May 1991 in the Portuguese town whose name it bears. The accords called for multi-party elections in eighteen months, demobilization by both sides, and the formation of a new national army, the Angolan Armed Forces (FAA). The UN would provide a monitoring team known as the UN Verification Mission in Angola (UNAVEM).

Again, DIA played a vital role in supporting OSD and State during the negotiations leading up to the Bicesse Accords and a monitoring function thereafter. UNITA and the MPLA needed a baseline of military information – order of battle intelligence – to agree on as a point of departure for military deliberations. Basic intelligence provided by DIA was declassified and became an annex to the Accord.

FAPLA was disbanded with some troops going into the FAA and some being hidden by the MPLA in the newly formed Emergency Police, a paramilitary force known as "Ninjas" because of their black uniforms. The bulk of the FAPLA troops withered away. The FAPLA had always been mostly a conscripted army with poor morale and terrible to non-existent troop support. Soldiers took every opportunity to run away. Aside from the Ninjas and a few thousand elite ex-FAPLA troops, the MPLA government had no army. UNITA's army (FALA – the Armed Force for the Liberation of Angola) had good morale and was much better disciplined. Savimbi kept 20,000 of his best troops under wraps. Throughout the transition period, UNITA held the military advantage.

Phase Two in Perspective

After many years of conflict, the Bicesse Accords offered a chance for peace in Angola. The inability to make good on that chance marks the transition between the second and third phases of the Angolan Civil War. Through years of escalating warfare, billions of dollars were spent by the MPLA alone on military equipment, supplies, and other services. Deep, unbridgeable distrust between the two parties and their respective leaders made a return to war seemingly inevitable.

In African wars, one never really wins a counter-insurgency, but has to settle for containing or minimizing the insurgent threat. That was certainly the case in Angola, but one could add another factor. From the insurgent's perspective, you must be able at some stage to transition to conventional war-fare, to take and hold major cities. UNITA was never good at this. It could bring Luanda to its knees but never strike the mortal blow.

THE ANGOLAN CIVIL WAR, PHASE THREE,
1992–2002

In the summer of 1992, I was in my fifth year as the Defense Intelligence Officer for Africa (DIO-AF). At my perch on the A (inside) ring in the Pentagon, I had progressed from being a one-man band sharing a secretary with another DIO to gaining a deputy and a military assistant. Apartheid was cracking in South Africa, civil war was sweeping West Africa, the Marxist regime was sinking in Ethiopia, and the United States was about to take a giant step into Africa in chaotic Somalia. As usual, many interesting security pots were boiling in Africa, and my little band was hard at work keeping track of them. One pot that always had to be watched was Angola.

La Luta Continua (The Struggle Continues)

The Bicesse Accords of 1991 that negotiated agreement to bring elections and an end to the war offered the best opportunity for a lasting peace in Angola since the Portuguese left in 1975. A cease-fire held, and Jonas Savimbi's National Union for Total Independence of Angola (UNITA) established a presence in Luanda. The charismatic Savimbi campaigned around the country confident of victory in the September 1992 elections. However, Savimbi's martial image dressed in fatigues did not go over well. In elections certified as "free and fair" by the UN, the ruling Popular Movement for the Liberation of Angola (MPLA) nosed out UNITA by less than 1 per cent of the vote. As expected, UNITA im-mediately called foul.

Tension rose in the capital, then on October 31 shooting broke out in Lu-anda. Who fired the first shot is irrelevant. For three days fighting raged in the capital until UNITA was forced out. The U.S. Embassy consisted of a series of trailers in a compound. Embassy personnel took cover under the trailers and watched as cars carrying UNITA officials sped by, heading out of town. U.S. defense attaché, Lt. Col. Richard Fritz, was at Angolan Army Headquarters when the shooting broke out. He was delivered back to the Embassy through the heavy fighting downtown in a Russian-built armored personnel carrier. Savimbi never returned to Luanda alive, but fighting would continue for nearly another ten years.

At that moment in time, the military balance heavily favored UNITA. Savimbi had encamped some of his troops in accordance with Bicesse, but was widely believed to have hidden 20,000 of his best men in the bush. The government's Popular Forces for the Liberation of Angola (FAPLA, the Angolan army at that time), however, had fallen apart due to the lack of pay and other support. FAPLA melted away during the cease-fire except for a few elite units, including the Ninjas hidden in the paramilitary police. The new Angolan Army called by the Portuguese acronym FAA, was mostly still on the drawing board.

Savimbi took the opportunity to seize the central highlands in the months following the Bicesse breakdown. By early 1993, UNITA occupied 75 per cent of the country, with government control limited to coastal areas, including the capital region, the oil-rich Cabinda enclave, and a few isolated garrisons in the interior. UNITA fought a fifty-six-day campaign to drive government forces out of Huambo, Angola's second largest city, and Savimbi's former capital. UNITA also partially occupied Kuito, an important government military center nearby. Both sides continued to prepare for another long war, buying weapons and acquiring advisors and technicians. The fighting had become more oriented toward control of urban areas, and casualties rose significantly.

The MPLA Turns the Tables on UNITA

By late 1993 the government's new Angolan Armed Forces (FAA) was rising from the ashes of the FAPLA with the help of hefty government spending (well over $1 billion), and the arrival of the South African private military company, Executive Outcomes. Foreigners, but especially the South Africans, were very effective in training the FAA, repairing and maintaining equipment, and leading offensive operations against UNITA.

In a supreme irony, South Africans, who used to assist UNITA, were now in Executive Outcomes fighting against UNITA. Executive Outcomes and other military contractors first made their African mark in Angola. Here an oil-rich country in desperate need of military assistance turned to private companies to provide rapid and lethal assistance to save the day. The FAA's fleet of transport aircraft was operated largely by foreign contractors from Eastern and Western Europe. Technicians brought the operationally ready rate for the FAA's combat aircraft up from a few to nearly forty airframes. A small army of technicians maintained new equipment purchased in Eastern Europe (mostly conventional equipment such as tanks, infantry fighting vehicles, trucks, and helicopters). South African personnel were also involved in planning and executing military operations.

WHAT WAS EXECUTIVE OUTCOMES?

Executive Outcomes (EO) was formed in the early 1990s by Eben Barlow, a former officer in the South African Army Special Forces. Many members of the Special Forces left the army as Apartheid was ending; few had marketable non-military skills. These experienced and highly professional white officers and non-commissioned officers had also effectively trained hundreds if not thousands of black soldiers to fight for South Africa during the Apartheid era. They also had ties to the 32nd battalion, a pool of highly skilled black soldiers. EO kept in sophisticated databases the names of military specialists who could be assembled for tailored assignments. These included technical specialists as well as combat personnel. Eventually, in the late 1990s, EO's role as a clearinghouse for militarily skilled professionals ended. It fell under increased scrutiny as a mercenary operation and faced a crackdown in South Africa, where it was headquartered, and personnel on its rolls could make their own deals with clients, cutting out the EO middleman. Ex-EO personnel began showing up in various trouble spots around sub-Saharan Africa.

By mid-1994, the FAA was once again on the offensive and beginning to roll back UNITA's advances. The army put together a large force, perhaps 15,000 to 20,000 strong, to attack Huambo. As the FAA crept to within artillery range, UNITA was forced to evacuate Huambo in November. The FAA victories restored the military balance and helped bring about the next chance for peace, the Lusaka Protocol of 1994. Peace accords like Lusaka amounted to a lull in the war, but fighting never stopped. Both sides violated the protocol, but no one wanted it terminated. For several years a condition of not war–not peace continued.

The year 1998, however, saw a return to full-scale combat. In April, the MPLA government declared Savimbi and the rest of the UNITA leadership "war criminals." Fighting gradually increased and, by the end of the year, the government was mounting an offensive against UNITA strongholds north of Huambo at Bialundo and Andulo.

UNITA's Last Hurrah

After the demise of the Lusaka Protocol in 1998, UNITA's actions surprised us in two ways. First, was their use of armor and other heavy ground equipment, an apparent effort to match FAA firepower. Second, was their selection of soft targets, mainly villages. The nature of UNITA's army (the Armed Forces for the Liberation of Angola or FALA) was changing too. The well-trained and disciplined guerrilla force was becoming a more typical African bush army. Volunteers gave way to conscripts and child soldiers. In short, FALA was starting to look and act like government forces!

In 1999, UNITA was eventually forced to evacuate its headquarters in the central highlands, trash its bid to become a conventional force, and go back to its guerrilla roots. The FAA took Bailundo and Andulo; Savimbi fled to the vast east of Angola as he had at times past when his star was waning. Losing access to important logistic bases in neighboring Congo-Kinshasa because of the civil war in that country and an unfriendly government in Kinshasa, UNITA was held together by the force of Savimbi's personality and his utter domination of the movement. In addition, diamond revenues, critical to UNITA's cash flow, declined.

The End

The MPLA had tried to kill Savimbi many times. A difficult task, it was a needle-in-a- haystack operation. However, by early 2002 UNITA was in such a weakened condition that it was as if the haystack had burned down. Finding that needle became much easier. In February, the FAA got lucky and ambushed Savimbi in eastern Angola. Shot numerous times, his bullet-riddled body was brought back to Luanda. Within a matter of weeks, Savimbi's number two, General Lukamba, signed a cease-fire with the government, bringing a hopeful end to twenty-six years of civil war.

During my long career, no other conflict challenged my senses as much as Angola. At times, especially during the 1980s, there was pressure on DIA to report what the policy people wanted to hear. Savimbi was their hero, their freedom fighter. News about his successes was warmly embraced with congratulatory smiles. Reports challenging his success were unwelcome. While no one in the Pentagon's policy cluster dictated what DIA should say about UNITA, there was subtle pressure to conform to the policymaker's expectations. In addition, no one enjoys bringing bad news to the customer.

The saga of Jonas Savimbi, from brilliant young revolutionary to fugitive in his own country, a man never destined to rule Angola but who made such a splash, parallels the course of late-twentieth-century history in southern Africa. Ultimately, Savimbi became a vestigial character on a shrinking stage. A Maoist-trained Cold Warrior, he didn't fit in the twenty-first century and exited on his shield.

Some years later while visiting a UNITA disarmament camp in Angola, I saw a former combatant wearing a DIA logo sweatshirt. I thought I might have found the "proof" of our assistance!

South Africa:
The White Redoubt

SOUTH AFRICA'S EVOLVING DEFENSE STRATEGY, 1960s–1980s

My first job as an Africa analyst at DIA was in the military capabilities shop. In the summer of 1968, there were several openings at the shop, and I was able to land the southern Africa desk. For the next seven years, I had the opportunity to study that subregion and its dominant actor, the Apartheid state of South Africa. I witnessed from a privileged position the evolution of South Africa's defense strategy. For most of that time, I covered not only South Africa but also a dozen other states, from Angola to Mauritius and from Zambia to Lesotho.

As a capabilities analyst, I was responsible for the military and paramilitary forces of the countries assigned to me. I maintained the database for orders of battle, military equipment inventories, training, and overall political-military developments. South Africa was, of course, my biggest account. My most challenging task was the assessment of military capabilities, that is, what these forces could actually do when called to military action.

Much of what I did was regarded as "bean counting," a semi-derogatory term in the intelligence community for basic military order of battle (OB) analysis – the tracking of military units and equipment and their overall, strength, organization, and deployment. Regarded by some analysts as tedious, simplistic work requiring little skill, OB analysis actually forms the basis of military analysis.

Far from "bean counting," capabilities analysis requires a thorough understanding of the forces under study and the confidence to make judgments based on incomplete information. For example, one day I set out to estimate the number of officers in the South African Navy (SAN). No estimate existed. I went through all the documents in my possession: classified, unclassified, U.S. defense attaché reporting, and more. Little information was available so I looked at all the places SAN officers would be assigned on ship or shore and found an estimated 400. A few months later, a manning chart showed 398 officers. This, and other incidents like it, gave this young analyst the confidence to estimate forces where no hard data were available.

From my cubicle in a putrid light green painted office in Arlington Hall Station's World War II temporary "A Building," I pounded out military assessments on the SADF. In the early 1970s, DIA established a new line of more in-depth force studies. I researched and wrote the initial Ground Forces Intelligence Study, Naval Forces Intelligence Study, and Air Forces Intelligence Study on South Africa, as well as scores of other assessments for DIA and intelligence community products.

These studies covered more than basic OB. They called for assessments of the force's logistic capabilities, training capabilities, and other components, not simply the combat forces. They comprised the most detailed information available to the U.S. intelligence community on the military forces of other countries. They took their place in the classified library we call the database. Because most SSA militaries were small and unsophisticated, these force studies were only done on the few that had sizable military establishments, such as South Africa, Nigeria, and Ethiopia.

South Africa was the dominant military and economic force in all of sub-Saharan Africa, and the keystone of white minority rule in southern Africa.

Pretoria exerted its influence throughout sub-Saharan Africa. In effect, the struggle of black nationalist insurgents against the white minority regimes in the south of the continent was a prolonged war against South Africa itself. Moreover, Pretoria enjoined that struggle by projecting force beyond its borders in an effort to keep the major fighting as far afield as possible.

At first, these projections were counter-insurgency operations, mostly in support of the other white minority regimes in the region, Rhodesia, and the Portuguese provinces of Angola and Mozambique. But, after the sobering 1975 intervention in Angola, where it encountered well-equipped Cuban combat forces, South Africa discovered that it would have to expand its conventional military forces to insure its ability to fend off foreign, namely non-African, forces and to fight conventional military campaigns to the north. Finally, the potential threat of growing white casualties led to a search for standoff capabilities to include weapons of mass destruction (WMD).

Apartheid South Africa

Apartheid, meaning separateness, or separate development, was a complex system of racial definition and separation engineered by the National Party after the white minority voted it into power in 1948. Apartheid enshrined whites at the top of an artificial socio-economic hierarchy, followed by coloureds (mixed race people mostly from the Cape Town area), Asians (Indians mostly from the Durban area), and finally black Africans, the overwhelming majority. Blacks, increasingly important to South Africa's growing economy, had to live in rural reserves called "Bantustans" or in townships that ringed the major cities to provide pools of manpower. Soweto (South West Township), just outside Johannesburg, was the largest and best known of these.

Apartheid was fraught with dehumanization and incongruity. At a downtown hotel early one jet-lagged morning, I observed a white supervisor instructing blacks on how to fold napkins and tablecloths. It was a typically demeaning experience for the blacks involved, with the overseer shouting insults and treating them like naughty children. At the same moment, across the street black construction workers were "hanging iron" on a high-rise building with no white superior in sight.

To illustrate the silliness of Apartheid, a colleague of mine, an African-American diplomat, was sent to South Africa. While there, he was given VIP status and escorted about town by white South African officials. When he stopped at a post office to mail some letters, he walked over to the "Non-Whites Only" window. His escorts signaled the clerk, who said he must go to the "Whites Only" window. When the diplomat walked over to that window, the same clerk came over to serve him. The black American had been given "honorary white" status! Everywhere I went in South Africa, whites had a rationale for apartheid that they felt compelled to offer foreigners like me. Every story was a little different but all justified separation of the races. Security was conspicuous; razor wire seemed to be everywhere. Fear and collective guilt stalked the land.

The South African Defense Force (SADF)

White South Africans fought for the allied cause in World War II and with the UN in Korea. They gained great respect as soldiers and airmen. I heard rumors, widely believed, that South African Jews flew Mirage III jet fighters for Israel in the 1967 war. The SADF was a quad-service (army, navy, air force, and medical) citizen-soldier organization. At its core was the Permanent Force, a full-time cadre that maintained the facilities and equipment during peacetime, ran the training program, and provided a few elite combat units. The bulk of the military comprised the Citizen Force, an active reserve that could be mobilized to flesh out the SADF as required. Citizen Force recruits or draftees served a year of active duty under the tutelage of the Permanent Force. Finally, the commandos were second-line home guard units designed to protect their local areas, but they could also serve active duty with the Permanent and Citizen Forces. The term "commando" originally referred to Afrikaner irregular forces in the Boer War and was picked up by the British to distinguish elite troops from regulars.

The SADF was almost completely white. Nevertheless, the South Africans were good at training black African troops. They knew how to handle and motivate them. This became an advantage when the SADF trained black guerrilla fighters from other countries in the region to go back and destabilize black governments actively opposing Apartheid. The SADF also trained Bantustan "home land defense forces" in South Africa, and the Southwest Africa Territorial Force in South African–controlled Namibia. Most successful and notorious was the "32nd Battalion," composed of Angolans that fought with the SADF in the 1975 intervention in Angola and became a mercenary force controlled by Pretoria.

White South Africa's Threat Perception

The vast majority of white South Africans were Afrikaners, mainly descendents of seventeenth century Dutch settlers, French Huguenots, and a sprinkling of Germans. Over the centuries, they forged their own identity, as Afrikaners, and feared being overwhelmed by the non-white majority. The Afrikaner elite built Apartheid and championed its cause. Defense of the republic and defense of Afrikanerdom were synonymous.

The Apartheid regime became increasingly concerned with non-white agitation for political rights and the scrapping of Apartheid. ("Non-white" was the term used by South Africa to bunch Black Africans, Coloureds, and Indians.) Two mileposts in this struggle were the 1961 Sharpeville massacre, when police fired on a crowd of black demonstrators, and the 1976 Soweto riots, a large-scale student demonstration that gained momentum, spread to other black townships, and took months to suppress. Pretoria's attention was clearly on internal security in the Republic of South Africa, but there was also concern that outside meddling – whether in the form of friendly persuasion from the West or an armed threat from the Communist bloc or a black nationalist state – could intervene to end Apartheid.

In the 1960s as pressures built on the white regimes to the north of the Republic, South Africa perceived a growing internal security threat from armed insurgents making their way south from bases in Zambia, Tanzania, and Congo-Brazzaville. Through the mid-1970s, the SADF focus was on counter-insurgency, with emphasis on small-unit operations, good tactical intelligence, and high mobility. These efforts could not be limited to the Republic and South-West Africa (Namibia) under direct South African control. They had to strike at guerrilla bases to the north to be effective. In addition, to be effective meant to keep this low-intensity war as far away from metropolitan South Africa as possible. Pretoria thus mounted a forward defense.

At first, prior to 1975, this meant assistance to the beleaguered Portuguese in Angola and Mozambique and to the Smith regime in Southern Rhodesia (Zimbabwe). It also meant raids into nearby independent states like Botswana, Lesotho, and Swaziland that were suspected of harboring infiltrators. Both major South African nationalist movements, the African National Congress (ANC) of the imprisoned Nelson Mandela and the Pan Africanist Congress (PAC), had armed wings that infiltrated agents into South Africa.

The 1970s also brought a new factor into the security equation. Independent states to the north, namely Tanzania and Zambia, soon to be joined by newly liberated Angola, Mozambique, and Zimbabwe, banded together under the banner of the Front Line States of southern Africa. They allowed the ANC, PAC, and SWAPO (the South-West Africa People's Organization, the main guerrilla group for Namibia) to maintain training camps and other military bases on their territory. The construction of the Tan-Zam Railway (1970–74) between Dar es Salaam, Tanzania, and Kapiri Mposhi, Zambia, with the assistance of some 10,000 Chinese, fed the growing fear in white South Africa of forceful intervention from the outside.

The railway was built to connect land-locked Zambia with ports in Tanzania, thereby, among other things, lessoning Lusaka's dependence on the South African railway system. As it turned out, port congestion in Tanzania limited the TAN-ZAM's effectiveness. Still, rumors ran rife that Beijing was using the project to hide the deployment of thousands of communist troops to support the black liberation struggle. While China deployed thousands of people for the project, including their own cooks, guards, and medical staff, and was involved in training African guerrilla fighters, this was not the feared communist invasion.

SURPRISE IN ANGOLA

The SADF maintained a small but regionally potent conventional force. Even before 1975, it began replacing its immediate post–World War II vintage weapon systems with newer models. A conventional force was believed necessary to dissuade any outside powers (read Western coalition, UN, or communist-backed force) from intervening in South Africa to end Apartheid. Such a force was also needed to defend against any coalition of black African states that might dream of marching on Pretoria. As my base assessment used to go, South Africa was capable of defeating any combination of black African states that might try to move against it.

When South Africa intervened in Angola's 1975–76 civil war, the conflict evolved quickly and unexpectedly into a conventional contest. For the first time the SADF faced Cuban troops, far more capable than MPLA guerrilla fighters. Further, the enemy deployed artillery that outranged South African guns and heavier armor that the SADF's wheeled armored cars could not match. Additionally, South Africa's air superiority was challenged for the first time by Cuban-piloted MiG aircraft. Ultimately, the SADF was not prepared to fight a more heavily armed force led by thousands of well-trained and well-equipped Cuban combat troops.

It was plain that to retain the capability to carry the fight to the north, South Africa would need to upgrade its conventional forces. The result was a commitment after 1975 to construct a larger and more modern defense force. South Africa built a variety of heavy weapon systems such as the G5 and G6 family of 155-mm artillery, 127-mm multiple rocket launchers, and Ratel infantry-fighting vehicles to replace the light Eland armored car. In addition, the SADF's old Centurion tanks were remanufactured into modern Oliphant main battle tanks.

THE SADF GROUND FORCES IN 1980:

60,000 Permanent Force and Citizen Force active duty.
100,000–150,000 Citizen Force reserves (in reserve status).
90,000 Commandos (local reserves).
35,000 paramilitary South African Police.

Source: *African Armed Forces Journal*, July 1996.

THE RECEDING WHITE REDOUBT

When Apartheid South Africa's buffer states, Angola, Mozambique, and Zimbabwe, fell to black majority rule between 1975 and 1980, the forward defense strategy entered a new phase. Instead of helping white minority regimes, Pretoria now sought to destabilize the newly independent black governments that replaced them. The SADF may have pulled out of Angola in 1976, but Pretoria's war against encroaching black nationalists was not over. Apartheid South Africa still faced insurgents infiltrating from the north.

Angola and Mozambique were hardest hit with Pretoria's backing of – and to some extent creating – anti-regime guerrilla forces. SADF raids into Angola were so frequent that they amounted to a nearly permanent military presence. A sizable triangular piece of southern Angola known as the "Area in Question" was the SADF's hunting ground for Namibian insurgents and whoever else, such as Angolans or Cubans, got in their way.

While practicing forward defense, mentally South Africa was circling the wagons, forming a *laager*. White South Africa believed it faced a communist menace, a "total onslaught" backed by Moscow and Havana. In the 1980s when I was briefing a senior political appointee in the Office of the Secretary of Defense, who later turned up in the Bush II administration, I said that Pretoria perceived a total onslaught backed by the communists. In what possibly may have been his only comment on my presentation, he interrupted with "What do you mean *perceived*? They do face a communist onslaught."

The official was evoking the Reagan Doctrine that called for supporting any regime or insurgency, no matter how flawed, that was willing to oppose communist expansion. Under this doctrine, Zaire's ultra-corrupt president, Mobutu, was a U.S. ally, forgiven all his faults, and Jonas Savimbi became a deserving freedom fighter. Moreover, Apartheid South Africa was tolerated through a policy of constructive engagement, on the idea that you can't influence the white regime to reform without talking with it.

Another facet of the return to the laager was the growing political influence of the SADF leadership, especially in the government of Pieter W. Botha (1978–89), an active defense minister from 1966. He was so well connected with the military that his nickname was "Piet Weapons" Botha. It was also during the 1980s that white South Africa reached the zenith of its military power. Concerned about getting involved in a protracted war with sizable troop commitments, the SADF searched for standoff weapons such as smart bombs, extended range artillery, and tactical missiles. This also led to research into WMDs and the subsequent construction of six deliverable nuclear bombs.

Late in the Apartheid era (which came to an end in the early 1990s), non-white participation in the defense force increased significantly because of the strain on white manpower caused by the continuing raids to the north, military involvements in Angola, and security duties in the black townships at home. Nevertheless, white casualties were still Pretoria's Achilles heal. Relatively few whites were killed in Angola in the mid-1970s, but the cumulative effect of carrying out a forward defense strategy over the years was becoming more expensive.

The real irony here is that South Africa built up its military into an impressive modern force but was never willing to use it to crush its enemies. Pretoria realized that its great destructive power was in the end self-defeating. There was no magic bullet to save Apartheid South Africa. Ultimately, white South Africa and the black opposition agreed that their struggle was not worth destroying their beloved country.

SOUTH AFRICA'S DEFENSE INDUSTRY

I have to admit that as an Africa analyst there was a certain amount of prestige that went with having South Africa in your flock of countries. South Africa not only had a sizable, modern defense force but was also a significant producer of military equipment. In addition, it had been an arms maker for a long time. For the allied effort during World War II, for example, it produced 11,000 mortar tubes, 5,570 armored cars, and 4.4 million artillery shells, among other things.

The growth of the arms industry from the 1960s onward can be attributed to the threat of outside interference, the fear of rising black nationalism, and the UN arms embargos. The first embargo, in 1963, was voluntary, an insignificant punishment of Apartheid. Several Western nations negotiated licensed production agreements with Pretoria, including the assembly of combat aircraft. The 1977 mandatory embargo was more crippling, but France for example continued its deliveries of Mirage F-1 jet fighters on a contract signed before November 1977.

Some nations (including the United States) continued with "gray area" sales of equipment that could be for either military or civilian use. The United States for example, approved the sale of diesel engines to South Africa for use in civilian mining vehicles. It just so happened that the exact same engine was used in the Israeli rebuild program for its Centurion tanks, a process that South Africa was emulating. Our embassy officials in Pretoria were assigned the nearly impossible task of verifying the proper use of the diesel engines by making periodic visits to the mines. "Now let's see, that's 400 engines, 250 Centurion tanks, and 150 diesels left over for spares?"

The South African Air Force had a squadron of early-model U.S. C-130B Hercules transport planes. The air force had a long-term maintenance contract with the U.S. manufacturer that resulted in having the aircraft flown to America, where each plane was virtually rebuilt from the tires up.

The Armaments Corporation of South Africa (ARMSCOR)

ARMSCOR, a parastatal corporation, was formed in the late 1960s and expanded in 1977 to provide centralized government control of South Africa's growing arms industry. It was to lead the effort to attain arms self-sufficiency to the extent possible and to develop foreign markets for South African equipment. Established defense firms such as Atlas Aircraft, Sandock-Austral, and Littleton Engineering were folded in under ARMSCOR.

What always amazed me was the array of products manufactured in South Africa. Aside from big-ticket items such as aircraft and armored vehicles, South Africa produced a full spectrum of light weapons and explosives, communications equipment, specialized military vehicles, and tactical missiles. At its height, ARMSCOR controlled fifteen major defense plants employing over 26,000 workers and hundreds of subcontractors.

ARMSCOR headquarters was in a modern space-age building on its own campus. A visit was like a trip to a James Bond 007 movie set. Aside from the usual car security procedures, individuals once out of their vehicles were screened through plastic body tubes that filled with a pleasant mist. This massive, ultramodern facility underscored South Africa's technical sophistication. If after a visit to ARMSCOR someone told you South Africa had a manned space program, you would probably believe it!

Some Major Weapons Systems Made in South Africa

G-5 and G-6 (self-propelled) 155-mm artillery

Ratel 20 Infantry Fighting Vehicle

Rooikat Heavy Armored Car with 76-mm gun

Olifant Main Battle Tank with 105-mm gun

Bateleur 127-mm Multiple Rocket Launcher

Twin 35-mm Air Defense Gun System

Casspir/Buffel/Mamba Light Mine Proof

Armored Personnel Carriers

Impala (MB-326) Jet Trainer and Light Attack Aircraft

Cheetah Multi-Role Jet Fighter (Based on Mirage III/V)

Rooivalk Attack Helicopter

Puma Medium Lift Helicopter

The Best of the Lot

The G-5 and G-6 155-mm artillery systems were, when introduced in 1982, among the best in the world. They could hurl extended range shells 39 kilometers and reportedly could fire nuclear rounds. The SADF left Angola in 1976 towing antiquated British 25-pounder (87-mm) field guns behind them, but returned in the 1980s with the world-class G-5/6. Some of these weapons benefited from the technology supplied by the late Canadian gun designer Gerald Bull, who was assassinated in 1990. Some of these South African–made artillery pieces found their way into the inventories of Persian Gulf armies, in time for the 1991 war.

The Rooikat armored car is actually a wheeled tank mounting a high-tech 76-mm main gun. It fits the market trend toward heavily armored wheeled rather than tracked vehicles. The Rooivalk attack helicopter is another weapon system that competes in the world market and is priced below most of the competition. South Africa also makes cruise missiles that supposedly are of short enough range to escape weapons convention scrutiny. Pretoria has also done some very good work in the area of "smart bombs," that is,, glide or self-powered bombs that can be released at high altitude and remotely guided to their target. This standoff weapon can be used to deliver conventional explosives or weapons of mass destruction (WMDs). However, South Africa has not had a breakthrough sale of any weapon system. In addition, sales slogans such as "battle-tested in southern Africa" are losing their appeal in the post-Apartheid era.

The Nuclear Question and Other WMDs

From my early days on the South African desk, there was mild concern – by analysts and policymakers alike – that the Apartheid state could develop nuclear weapons even though there was no viable strategic target for them. Nevertheless, Pretoria had a uranium enrichment plant at Valindaba, north of the capital, and a twin nuclear facility at Pelindaba a few kilometers away.

On my first trip to Africa with the late Navy Commander Winston Cornelius, who was responsible for the military attaché offices in SSA back at DIA, the South Africans offered him an aerial tour of Johannesburg and Pretoria in an SAAF helicopter. The weary Cornelius demurred but then agreed to take "the kid" (me) for the ride. We took off in an Allouete III from Pretoria and looped around Johannesburg. I got permission to take pictures with my borrowed DIA 35-mm camera and my own Super 8 home movie camera. On the return leg we passed to the north of the capital, crested a ridge and there below were the two nuclear sites. I don't think the pilots had any idea what they were showing me. I immediately knew what they were because I had seen them on imagery. Thanks to the pilots, I came away with a home movie of South Africa's most important nuclear sites.

In August 1977, the Soviet Union revealed that one of its reconnaissance satellites had discovered a nuclear weapons test site in the remote Kalahari Desert in South Africa. Pretoria immediately denounced the finding as communist propaganda. Soon everyone was looking at that hole in the ground. The experts could not confirm that it was a test site, but had no idea what other purpose it could serve. To confuse the world's analysts, the South Africans kept moving equipment in and out of the site, claiming it was for some kind of geological research. Hardly anyone in the intelligence business believed that.

Then in September 1979, the South African Navy posted a notice to mariners that military live-fire exercises were to be held in a large area off the coast of South Africa. During the period of the exercise, a U.S. Vela satellite recorded the telltale double flash of a nuclear explosion in the far southwest Indian Ocean. The verdict once again was that no conclusive evidence was found, but that there was no other logical explanation for what the satellite detected.

While I was not privy to unique or conclusive information on this, I believe the following is most likely what happened. Pretoria was planning an underground nuclear blast at the Kalahari site. When the site was discovered, plans were made for a nuclear test over the ocean, which was conducted two years later. The weakest part of this argument is that no proof such as radioactivity or other telltale indicator of a nuclear blast was ever collected to my knowledge.

It is possible that the test was a joint South African–Israeli venture. Weapon testing far from the Middle East would make sense for Israel. The six nuclear devices fabricated by South Africa were systematically destroyed in the early 1990s under the DeKlerk regime; international authorities verified the operation. South Africa is possibly the only country to build, test, weaponize, and voluntarily scrap its nuclear weapons. The "African Bomb" is no more.

The South African–Israeli Connection

Defense collaboration between Tel Aviv and Pretoria was well known among analysts, yet lacking in the specifics. There certainly was close cooperation between the two militaries in many technical and scientific fields. In the 1950s and 1960s, both countries found themselves surrounded by a sea of enemies, whether black nationalist insurgents or hostile Arabs. Termed "pariah states" by the international community, Israel and South Africa banded together to defeat economic sanctions and arms embargos. (Taiwan was also regarded as a pariah state during this period and linked with both Israel and South Africa.)

Cooperation was far from a one-way street. South African scientists contributed to Israel's technical knowledge as well. In the 1970s, I wrote a DIA intelligence assessment on South African–Israeli military cooperation that pasted together many of the scraps of information known to intelligence at that time. There were Israeli fingerprints on some South African weapon projects.

Meet "Doctor Death"

South Africa's nuclear program was the most advanced of its WMDs, but Pretoria did dabble in chemical and biological weapons as well. A prominent figure in this area was Dr. Wouter Bassoon, who worked on both chemical and biological programs. Bassoon was a Brigadier in the South African Army reserve and a bit of a loose cannon. After the fall of Apartheid, there was concern that Bassoon and other scientists that worked on WMDs might sell their services and their knowledge to the highest bidder. Bassoon made trips to Libya and other Middle Eastern locales. Overall, however, the WMD brain drain from South Africa appears to have been contained.

To summarize, there is a legacy here. Apartheid built an impressive arms industry, one that survives to this day in a truncated form under Denel, a user-friendly derivative of ARMSCOR that has had some sales success in niche markets. Pretoria's technological base in this area may be fading but will not disappear under majority rule. South Africa's black leaders won't let it. If South Africa has a manifest destiny on the continent, its military and defense industry will have a big part in it.

APARTHEID SOUTH AFRICA: A CHALLENGE FOR U.S. INTELLIGENCE

In the Reagan years, the U.S. policy toward South Africa was "constructive engagement" based on the premise that you cannot change Pretoria's odious policies if you don't talk to them. When bumps occurred on the diplomatic road between Washington and Pretoria, however, one of the first things liberal U.S. politicians called for was closing or cutting back our defense attaché office in

Pretoria. Our attaché's access to the South African government, not just the military, at times also caused tension within the U.S. embassy. For example, our attachés were invited to South African government functions that our diplomats were not. USDAO Pretoria was decremented at times but was never closed.

Heading a Delegation to Pretoria

In August 1985, I was chief of the Africa Military Capabilities Branch in the spanking new Defense Intelligence Analysis Center at Bolling Air Force Base. I was chosen to lead a mission to Pretoria at the behest of the South African government for three days of talks on topics of mutual interest, followed by a two-day sight-seeing tour. The conference itself was a disappointment to the SADF. Their delegation was headed by an army two-star general, who considerably outranked a GS-15 (colonel equivalent) branch chief. The briefings were quite general, and on the second day of the conference at a remote facility in the capital area, the general declared the meeting over.

Instead of going home early, the SADF would lengthen our tour by adding an extra day in Cape Town. When we landed at the Cape, the fun began. A plainclothes SADF VIP protection (secret service) detachment used us to practice their protective skills on. The leader, a six-foot-four ramrod-straight Afrikaner with shoulder-length black hair and dark piercing eyes, was called Long Johnny. The detachment – all youngsters in their twenties – used first names only except once when one of them addressed Long Johnny as "captain" and was quickly admonished. They whisked us around town in three sedans at breakneck speed. I had not been so frightened riding in a car since a high school friend demonstrated his new 1965 Plymouth with a 426 cubic inch Chrysler hemi-head engine.

A buffet breakfast was followed by a sumptuous lunch, capped by a full-course dinner, with sightseeing and shopping in between. Playing the role of the VIP, I was under guard at all times. Dropped at our five-star hotel for a pre-dinner rest, I fell fast asleep. The next thing I remember is Long Johnny and company breaking the door down! They said I hadn't responded to calls to my room.

As an aside, American officials were easily enamored of white South Africans; whites were about all you met and dealt with in official channels in the Apartheid state. They are a pioneering, God-fearing people that would make any TV evangelist happy. Fond as they are of cocktails, fine wines, and *Breis* (cookouts), hunting and fishing, shopping centers, and good restaurants, not to mention the beautiful scenery and excellent infrastructure, it was too easy for white Americans to feel at home with them.

Spy vs. Spy

Defense attachés, other embassy employees, and official visitors were under surveillance in South Africa. The hotels were bugged, and Americans were targeted for espionage. South Africa expelled the DAO aircraft and most of our attachés for spying, meaning flying over restricted areas. There was a reciprocal response from Washington. As a visitor, several times I heard people dressed as hotel employees discussing me in Afrikaans. In Durban, when the young bikini-clad woman ran up to me and demanded I take her up to my room because hoodlums were chasing her, I told her to ask the hotel desk to phone the police.

During a rare U.S. Navy transit around the Cape of Good Hope, the USS *California* Task Force was harassed by the South African Navy. Reshef attack craft armed with Gabriel missiles made a mock attack run against the task force. No harm was done, but this was an exercise in brinkmanship. In the 1980s, despite sometime tense relations with South Africa over its domestic and foreign policies, the U.S. Defense Department remained engaged with the SADF and maintained workable relations. The United States got what it needed most out of the relationship and that is all that counts.

Mozambique: The RENAMO War, 1978–1992

Angola was not the only ex-Portuguese colony to present challenges for the intelligence analyst. In the late 1970s, some thousand miles to the east, Mozambique was heading down the road of violence and mayhem, a precursor of what we would see later in West African trouble spots. In 1975, Portugal peacefully handed over power to the dominant liberation movement, the Front for the Liberation of Mozambique, known by the acronym FRELIMO. FRELIMO ruled over a vast and impoverished land trying to recover from a twelve-year guerrilla war with Portugal. Its leader, Samora Machel, began as a medic in the Portuguese army before he defected to FRELIMO. He rose rapidly in the ranks and became FRELIMO's leader in the mid-1960s.

Another group, the Mozambique National Resistance (RENAMO, or MNR) was controversial from its inception. Sired by the dying Smith regime in Rhodesia that used it as counterforce to attack its enemies, black nationalists based in Mozambique, the South Africans took over sponsorship of the group when white Rhodesia became black-ruled Zimbabwe in 1980. RENAMO continued to be seen as an artificial guerrilla movement, which now owed its existence to Apartheid South Africa and was merely an instrument of terror for the racists in Pretoria. In addition, sponsorship in the form of training, equipment, and advisory support under Pretoria was far more extensive than under Rhodesia.

RENAMO was not entirely an imported and foreign-directed movement. FRELIMO had enemies, those that were not backers of Samora Machel's movement, or worse, who supported other splinter liberation groups. Added to the mix were conservative Portuguese businessmen with extensive operations in Mozambique who had helped Lisbon with the counter-insurgency effort before independence. In 1975, tens of thousands of Portuguese settlers and other whites born in Mozambique protested the handover of power to the "communist" FRELIMO, then relocated to South Africa.

RENAMO: FROM AN INSURGENT SEED, A MONSTER GROWS

RENAMO took off as an insurgent group in the 1980s. With South African clandestine support, the movement spread rapidly and by the mid-1980s had some 20,000 fighters operating over the whole of the country. The capital, Maputo in the extreme south, was under virtual siege. RENAMO was doing much more than keeping the government off balance in accordance with Pretoria's forward defense policy. It was a genuine threat to the FRELIMO government, and its extreme brutality was becoming a matter of global concern.

Ironically, FRELIMO's army – a former guerrilla force itself – didn't have a clue as to how to combat RENAMO. Government leaders such as Defense Minister Alberto Chipande, a classic old warrior turned incompetent party official, preferred to talk about the glorious war against Portugal and ignore RENAMO's nightly harassing gunfire in Maputo. In SSA, it is easy to perpetrate insurgent attacks on soft targets and fragile infrastructure, but it is extremely difficult to generate the military efficiency necessary to curb an insurgency.

FRELIMO relied on its frontline state friends, namely, Tanzania, Zambia, and Zimbabwe, to keep it afloat and prevent the MNR stranglehold on the country from becoming fatal. Harare deployed 10,000 troops to guard the Beira Corridor's road, rail, and pipeline facilities that linked Zimbabwe to the sea. Tanzania sent 2,500 troops into Zambezia Province in central Mozambique to assist with counter-insurgency operations; even Malawi (not a frontline state, and an erstwhile ally of South Africa) sent a thousand troops into northern Mozambique to guard the Nacala rail line. The Zimbabwe National Army would on occasion mount "joint" offensives with FRELIMO against rebels menacing the Beira Corridor, but as soon as the Zimbabweans left a captured base, the rebels would return and rout the Mozambique army garrison. FRELIMO had one of the worst armies in Africa.

RENAMO was known for its brutality. Recruitment was often by coercion. RENAMO insurgents raided villages, killed the elders, kidnapped the children, made them participate in the murder of their parents, and turned them into child soldiers and slaves. FRELIMO's authority evaporated, especially in rural areas. Belief in magic and the use of drugs and alcohol were additional motivating factors. In one account of a RENAMO attack on a defended town, the rebels were described as marching like zombies wearing charms and apparently drugged.

U.S. POLICY SLIGHTLY OUT OF TUNE

During the critical stages of this war, from the mid-1980s to the early 1990s, U.S. policy appeared out of sync placing the intelligence community, and particularly DIA, in an awkward position. The Reagan Doctrine required support for insurgents fighting against communist regimes, as the United States was supporting UNITA in Angola. The logical extension of that doctrine would have been to back RENAMO in Mozambique. However, the United States recognized the socialist government of FRELIMO and sought to wean it away from communism with kindness and developmental aid. The RENAMO forces, according to policy spokesmen, were illegitimate butchers, and we don't talk to rebels, at least not in this ex-Portuguese colony! A senior official once said, "The best thing I can say about the MNR [RENAMO] is that at least some of them are Mozambicans." The implication here was that even the MNR combatants were largely outsiders.

Many in the Defense Department, however, along with conservative elements in the Congress, were sympathetic to the RENAMO. To obtain ground truth on the nature of the MNR, the State Department hired consultant Robert Gersony. He went to the region and collected empirical evidence that RENAMO was indeed responsible for the violence and terror in Mozambique. Gersony conducted extensive interviews with refugees and other victims of the violence that showed the RENAMO was, as suspected, the main culprit.

By the late 1980s, I was already the DIO for Africa, trying to ride herd on some strong-willed analysts who saw RENAMO as a legitimate movement. The analysts had a point but in my opinion seemed to go overboard. RENAMO boss Afonso Daklama was no boy scout and lacked many of the qualities of Jonas Savimbi. Without polish, charisma, or any real political agenda, he gave every indication of being either a puppet or a thug.

When the Gersony Report came out in April 1988, I was traveling overseas, and left an acting DIO at my desk. State sent Gersony to the Pentagon to brief his report. When Gersony called at my office, he was confronted by pro-RENAMO analysts who proceeded to tear his report apart. A bitter verbal confrontation ensued that resulted in Gersony storming out of the building and telling State officials that he was ambushed by DIA.

My agency was already tagged as "pro-RENAMO" when allegations surfaced in the media that DIA was clandestinely supporting the MNR! To my knowledge and belief, there was no basis for these charges. However, with DIA intelligence articles putting a pro-RENAMO spin on the events of the day, we were getting a reputation as having a bias. Nothing is more of a threat to an intelligence operation than attacks on its objectivity and integrity.

I spent many months trying to repair our relationship with State. Note that there were no strained relations with Defense. I conducted shuttle diplomacy between the Pentagon and Foggy Bottom (i.e., State), inviting officials to meet with the director of DIA, and conducting workshops on the situation in Mozambique, trying to convince State that we were not biased bad guys out to undermine U.S. foreign policy. We eventually found the middle ground – language acceptable to both parties to use in describing RENAMO – and bureaucratic peace was restored.

I had numerous meetings with Principal Deputy Assistant Secretary of State Chas Freeman, the number two man in State's Africa Bureau. DIA won a small victory by getting State to admit to a component of legitimacy in RENAMO. It was to some degree an education of Freeman's staff, but DIA promised to tone down its writings on RENAMO, conceding that Daklama was no Savimbi.

THE WAR WINDS DOWN: THE TIMES THEY WERE A-CHANGIN'

Exactly how much carnage RENAMO was responsible for is unknown. We can just say they did enough damage to Mozambique and its people to place it on the critical list for years to come. Eventually, in the early 1990s, the war in Mozambique petered out. Times were changing, and support and incentives were disappearing. First, RENAMO was incapable of taking Maputo, and if they had been, what would they do with it? They would certainly not be able to govern it – they lacked the expertise and the desire. Second, most everything of value in the country had already been looted, destroyed, or consumed. Third, several years of serious drought had debilitated everyone. Even the rebels stood in line for food handouts from the NGOs. Fourth, Soviet military assistance for the government was in sharp decline, and the same was true for South African aid to the MNR.

Enter the Sant'Egidio Community, a lay organization of the Roman Catholic Church with extensive experience in Africa. In the early 1990s, this group was able to foster peace talks between RENAMO and FRELIMO in Rome that eventually led to a peace accord in 1992. The UN deployed the United Nations Operation in Mozambique (UNOMOZ) peacekeeping force to monitor the transition from war to national elections. FRELIMO won the elections, and RENAMO, while not overjoyed at the prospect of being the loyal opposition, did remain pacified. Mozambique went on to become a modest success story in Africa by coming back from the brink of complete collapse.

In summary, here are some things we can learn from the RENAMO war. The RENAMO set a bloody record of violence against the population, something not seen in SSA since the Congo crisis of the 1960s. Its attacks against traditional leaders, village headmen, the very symbols of authority, led to a breakdown of law and order and petty terrorism on a national scale. Moreover, the inability of FRELIMO to cope with the RENAMO insurgency exposed its weakness. Despite communist bloc aid, the Mozambican army was inept and lacked motivation. One of the strange things about the peace accord, which, typically, called for the establishment of a new national army, was the lack of interest on both sides in joining the military. This was 180 degrees from the usual post-settlement condition, where most everyone wants to be part of the new army.

This conflict also shows how fickle U.S. policy can be. Not only did the policies toward Angola and Mozambique seem to contradict each other, but also State and Defense had differing policy views on Mozambique. While Defense has to follow State's lead on foreign policy, it need not be in lock step. There is room for negotiation and compromise. This places intelligence in a delicate position, under pressure to modify the analysis to avoid the policymaker's wrath. I am proud to say this did not happen, but I am disappointed by those who suspected foul play.

1. The late James L. Woods, Deputy Assistant Secretary of Defense for Africa, seen here on Gorée Island, Senegal. Woods was a demanding consumer of intelligence on Africa and a mentor for the author. (Bill Thom photo)

2. The author sits atop a Russian-built BRDM-2 armored reconnaissance vehicle, once again on the road to Addis Ababa in the final stages of the 1988–91 Ethiopian civil war. (DIO-AF photo)

3. Row upon row of T-55 tanks neatly lined up behind a chain link fence in Asmara, the Eritrean capital. The T-55 is known as the "battle queen of Africa" because of its wide use in a variety of tactical situations. (Bill Thom photo)

4. Dekemkare, Eritrea, was the site of the largest tank battle ever fought in sub-Saharan Africa. In February 1991, Ethiopian troops attempted to break the siege of Asmara by launching an attack on Dekemkare, the key to Asmara's southern defenses. U.S. Defense Attaché Colonel Mike Ferguson (standing) discusses the battle with DIA Director Lt. Gen. James Clapper (in car), the first serving director to visit Africa south of the Sahara. (Bill Thom photo)

5. The 1984 delegation to South Africa, led by the author (at far left), at the military museum in Pretoria. The mission turned into a holiday for the Americans. (DIO-AF photo)

6. South African forces captured this Russian T-34/85 tank in Angola. During the 1950s and through the 1970s, the Soviet Union was still giving its African clients T-34s, until the more capable T-55s replaced them. (Bill Thom photo)

7. The BM-21 multiple rocket launcher (MRL) was an extremely effective area-fire weapon in Africa's larger conflicts. Each truck mounts a rack that holds forty 122-mm rockets. The shrieking noise and 42 lb. high-explosive warhead unnerved many troops. (Bill Thom photo)

8. Somewhere in northern Namibia, the author and his party dismount from their Caspir armored personnel carrier. The Caspir was popular with South African and allied troops. Its V-shaped hull offered reasonable protection from land mines. (DIO-AF photo)

9. In March 1989 the author visited a South African forward base in northern Namibia. Flanking the three South African officers in uniform are the author on the right and longtime DIA Africanist Joseph C. Fenrick Jr. on the left. (DIO-AF photo)

10. Here is the real loser of Africa's wars: a student seeking education in the shadow of military encampments under adverse conditions. (Bill Thom photo)

11. The author sponsored a 1997 symposium on the Privatization of Security Functions in Africa. Experts from across the spectrum participated, including Eben Barlow, seen here at extreme right. Barlow was the former president of Executive Outcomes, a controversial security company that enjoyed success in Angola and Sierra Leone. Also on the rostrum were Deputy DIO-AF Dr. Bill Stoakley, at left, and the author. (DIO-AF photo)

12. At times DIA was accused of assisting the UNITA rebels in Angola. During a 1996 visit to a UNITA resettlement camp, we came across this former guerrilla fighter wearing a DIA sweatshirt! Assistant DIO for Africa Cmdr. Jeff Munson managed to get this grainy photo as we drove away.

13. The author rode in Malawi's presidential aircraft on more than one occasion. Malawi had a smart little army until its deployment to Mozambique during the RENAMO War exposed weaknesses. (DIO-AF photo)

14. LTG Patrick Hughes, DIA director from 1997 to 1999, was the most prolific traveler to Africa, visiting eight countries on three separate trips. Here General Hughes visits the Ghanaian military intelligence school in Accra. (Bill Thom photo)

Note: "Thom photos" were taken by the author personally. "DIO-AF photos" were taken by others on behalf of the author and are part of the Bill Thom photo collection.

Two Surprising East African Wars

THE OGADEN WAR, 1977–1978

President Mohammed Siad Barre, a dictator who came to power in a 1969 military coup, led Somalia. By 1974, he firmly aligned his country with the Soviet bloc, signing a treaty of friendship with Moscow. The following year, Siad Barre granted the Soviet Union air and naval base rights at Berbera in northern Somalia. This was an alarming development in the East-West context because it expanded the USSR's strategic reach into the Horn of Africa, the Arabian Peninsula, the Persian Gulf, and the Indian Ocean. For his trouble, he was rewarded with Soviet arms and amassed the largest fleet of tanks and field artillery between Cairo and Pretoria.

The irony of Somalia was that – while it was one of the few sub-Saharan countries composed entirely of one ethnic group – not all Somalis lived in Somalia. Further, clan and subclan divisions were as divisive as tribal distinctions elsewhere in Africa. The five points of the star on the Somali flag represent five territories, three of which – northeast Kenya, Djibouti, and the Ogaden region of Ethiopia – are under foreign control. The former colonies of British and Italian Somaliland comprise the internationally recognized state of Somalia. The hope of every Somali nationalist was one day to recover the three lost territories.

In 1974, the so-called "creeping coup" against aging Ethiopian Emperor Haile Selassie resulted in his ouster by a group of left-leaning army officers. Three years of violent rule by committee culminated with the installation of a new head of state, Mengistu Haile Mariam, a self-styled Marxist who literally shot his way into power. Mengistu, a lieutenant colonel in the Ethiopian Army, began a hot and heavy embrace with Moscow. Soviet military aid began flowing into Ethiopia, which had been a close U.S. ally in the days of Haile Selassie. Siad Barre saw the handwriting on the wall; the Soviet Union would favor powerful Ethiopia over threadbare Somalia. If Somalia were ever to regain the Ogaden region, it would have to be now.

Siad Barre and the Somali National Army (SNA) dominated by his Marehan clan had supported insurgency in the Ogaden for years. The strongest insurgent army belonged to the Western Somali Liberation Front (WSLF), which employed traditional guerrilla tactics against the Ethiopians. At times, regular SNA troops would take off their uniforms for civilian garb and join the WSLF. The insurgents lacked heavy weapons, however, in contrast to the SNA. The Ogaden was defended by the Ethiopian Army's 3rd Mechanized Division, well-trained and well-equipped by the United States in the pre-Mengistu years. Third Division brigades were deployed at key points in the Ogaden.

From Insurgency to Invasion

By June 1977, a WSLF offensive was underway and showing unusual resolve. Ethiopian units reported the enemy uncharacteristically using armored personnel carriers (APCs) and heavy field artillery in attacks on their positions. That summer there was a classic exchange of intercepted messages between a 3rd Division unit and Army headquarters in Addis Ababa. The field unit reported receiving artillery fire. Addis Ababa replied: "Don't you mean mortar fire?" The field countered: "I've got an unexploded 122-mm round impacted 50 feet from my position." This dud was from a Russian 122-mm howitzer not an 82-mm mortar, normally the heaviest weapon fielded by the guerrillas.

In early August 1977, a new EUCOM J2, Maj. Gen. Lincoln D. Faurer, arrived in Brussels. I had worked at DIA for General Faurer, a highly respected intelligence officer. At his first EUCOM pre-briefing, I began the piece with the by now usual "update of the Somali invasion of the Ogaden." Faurer listened for a minute and then asked when we decided the Somalis had invaded. Two days before, Washington was not yet ready to reach that conclusion. EUCOM J2 had made that call weeks earlier! After I answered all of his questions satisfactorily, Faurer let the update briefing go as written.

The intelligence community back in Washington either ignored EUCOM's analysis or discredited it as alarmist and exaggerated. It was partly a case of "group think" and partly shoddy analysis. On a visit to the Pentagon during this conflict, I found DIA's key analyst using a situation map that only covered the front lines. When I asked about troop movements behind the lines not shown on his map, the analyst dismissed them as unimportant. It is doubtful that this analyst could have picked up the military subtleties as the conflict unfolded.

One of the advantages of working as an intelligence analyst at EUCOM – the "theater level" as opposed to the "national level" – was a certain amount of journalistic license that went along with being at a command overseas five hours ahead of Washington. There were fewer supervisors and office chiefs to get your assessments through. In Washington, a briefing item would have to run the gauntlet of seemingly endless pre-briefs. At EUCOM if you got it by the J2, it was a go. There also was a sense that the command's job was to be provocative and analytically wander out in front of the assessments from Washington.

By September 1977, everyone knew what was happening in the Ogaden. Those analysts that had believed SNA tanks could not make it to the border without breaking down had to eat crow. The SNA – its strength increased from 23,000 to some 60,000 – went on to occupy most of the Ogaden region of Ethiopia. The capture of Jijiga in the northern Ogaden by SNA and WSLF forces in mid-September was the Somali high- water mark. The 3rd Division withdrew in good order, aerial photos showing its U.S. M-60 tanks firing to the rear while pulling back. However, the Ethiopian Army was in rapid transition to a Marxist mass army. The prewar Ethiopian Army numbered 70,000 soldiers, already almost twice the size of the force during Haile Selassie's day; it would grow to well over 200,000 by war's end.

Chairman Mengistu, acting like a traditional emperor, raised the militia for war against the hated Somalis. There is an old Ethiopian proverb that if you are in the desert and come upon a snake and a Somali, you kill the Somali first. The Somalis have the same old proverb, only it's kill the Ethiopian first. Oddly enough, the Russians were not expelled from Somalia until November 13th, and Soviet military aid continued flowing into Mogadishu even after hostilities with Russian-supported Ethiopia had begun. It was as if Moscow believed it could maintain good relations with both countries despite the hostilities, or perhaps it was the Soviet bureaucracy far out of sync with reality.

I was the first official visitor our skeleton crew embassy let into Somalia after the Soviets were thrown out. I was on an extensive tour of SSA and thought I might have a chance to get into Somalia at war. A car ride around Mogadishu revealed deserted military installations, an eerie sight. They had all gone into the Ogaden. Ethiopian air power played a significant role in the Ogaden war – a first for modern Africa. The squadron of U.S.-provided F-5 jet fighter bombers dominated the air from the start; the SNA's MiGs were taken out in the first few days. The Ethiopians retained control of Dire Dawa and its air base throughout the war. Twice the SNA tried to move an armored force in position to converge on Dire Dawa from the north. Once they were chewed up by the F-5s; the other time they ran out of fuel and abandoned their tanks.

Typical of the ignorance that at times affected judgments on military capabilities was the reaction of the EUCOM Soviet air analyst when he heard me brief that MiG-23s were on their way to Ethiopia. He was highly skeptical and argued that the MiG-23 was too sophisticated for a black African air force. He was unaware that Ethiopian Airlines had been flying with Ethiopian pilots since the 1930s, and that the Ethiopian Air Force had quickly mastered the U.S. F-5 supersonic jet fighter.

While the Ethiopians stabilized the front with Somalia, they had little success in taking lost ground. At one point, Mengistu massed several of his militia divisions in the southern Ogaden for an offensive. The Somalis evidently learned about it and, with the effective use of artillery, decimated the ranks of the advancing militia units.

The Russians Are Coming (and the Cubans too)

The Soviet Union usually kept its client states in black Africa on a short leash. Weapons were provided, but ammunition, spare parts, and technical assistance were tightly controlled. This meant that if the country wanted to go to war it needed Moscow's blessing. Something went wrong in the case of Somalia, however. For years there was intense intelligence interest in reports of underground storage facilities in Somalia, fear that they could conceal Soviet weapons of mass destruction or perhaps missiles. I would not be surprised if those facilities housed stockpiles of ammunition, because for the first few months of the war there was no sign of shortages by the SNA.

Moscow did come through for its new darlings on the Horn. Shortly after their expulsion from Somalia, Soviet military advisors appeared in Ethiopia in great numbers. In fact, Moscow set up a complete Soviet general staff to run the war for Mengistu, a first for the Russians. Once more, they were joined by thousands of Cuban combat troops. Some Cubans were flown in from Angola, where they had recently secured a military victory for Marxist forces there; others came by sea and air from Cuba. Castro's troops married up with Soviet equipment and supplies delivered to Ethiopia.

The Soviets pushed supplies to the front, and the Cubans launched an attack in early 1978 that turned the Somali's right flank in the northern Ogaden, where the opposing forces were concentrated. Facing a growing threat in their front and with Cubans threatening their rear, the SNA began a general withdrawal and were out of the Ogaden by early March. Siad Barre ordered the retreat to save his army from being destroyed, but it would cost him dearly in the end. In April, the "Afgoye coup" attempt led by disgruntled SNA veterans of the Ogaden nearly succeeded.

The Ogaden war was followed with great interest at EUCOM. It played into the thinking of the CINC and DCINC who believed that NATO could be outflanked to the south. Soviet and Cuban boldness reached new heights, and two African states proved that they could fight a conventional war. Analytically the most amazing thing about the war was the reluctance to accept the fact that the Somalis could and did invade Ethiopia. Making the mental leap that what was happening was not a guerrilla campaign but a conventional war was excruciatingly difficult for many, but at least EUCOM had been out in front with the right call.

TANZANIA-UGANDA WAR, 1978-1979

In the fall of 1978, I was a veteran analyst of almost two years at EUCOM. I thought I had seen everything.

Ugandan dictator Idi Amin Dada, who came to power in a 1971 military coup, was still one of the most reviled despots in the world. Lately he had been siding with the Libyans and Palestinians, having been "victimized" by the July 1976 Israeli raid on Entebbe to free hostages being held by Arab terrorists.

Amin was a product of the British colonial system having served as a sergeant in the King's African Rifles. A six-foot-five-inch 300-pound brute of a man, Amin was an embarrassment to Africa. He terrorized the Ugandan people, even his own soldiers. When he played basketball, he scored all the points; when he donned the boxing gloves he always won by a knockout. His army was ruled and motivated by fear. Rumors abounded, with some basis, that Amin practiced cannibalism. Nevertheless, the Organization of African Unity (OAU) did nothing about Amin. In fact, he became president of the OAU for one year during his rule! The OAU did not intervene in the internal affairs of member states, a policy that has only changed in recent years.

The Teacher versus the Thug

In October 1978, there had been several violations along the Ugandan-Tanzanian border by out-of-control Ugandan soldiers. On 30 October, Amin's troops crossed the border in force into Tanzania's Kagera Salient, a piece of land wedged between the western shore of Lake Victoria and the Rwandan border. For two weeks, his troops plundered the Salient, which was defended only by rural police and militia. Hundreds of Tanzanian civilians were murdered. Amin proclaimed that he had "annexed" the Kagera Salient.

Tanzania was one of those African countries that asserted its nonalignment during the Cold War, though it adopted socialism. The country was led by a soft-spoken intellectual, Julius Nyerere, known to his adoring people as the *Mwalimu*, or teacher. His army was the Tanzanian People's Defense Force (TPDF), Chinese trained and equipped, but untested. Tanzania's security orientation had been to the south, as it was a charter member of the Front Line States of southern Africa in the protracted conflict to free that region from white minority rule. Now it faced a threat from the north.

After a couple weeks of rampaging through the Kagera Salient and conducting other high jinx, including Amin's challenge to Nyerere to settle this matter with a boxing match between the two leaders, the Ugandans pulled out. At this point the popular U.S. perception was that Amin had done it again, just another bizarre episode in his seamy career. Besides, Nyerere had neither the means nor the will to strike back. It was not his style.

However, mind the old adage: look at what they do, not what they say. There were reports of the TPDF mobilizing. Interesting enough, there were two streams of reporting, diametrically opposed to each other. In the majority were reports of all the reasons it did not make sense for Nyerere to militarily retaliate against Amin, to stoop to his level. The TPDF might not even have the capability to get its forces up to the Salient. Meanwhile another series of reports detailed TPDF military preparations: troop movements, reorganization, mobilization of the militia, and the commandeering of trucks and buses off the streets of Dar es Salaam. This last cinched the case: Tanzania was going to war.

Nyerere wanted a balanced mobilization to reflect all the regions and ethnic groups of Tanzania, but in some areas there were few volunteers while in others the response was overwhelming. Nyerere was not deterred. The hot pockets of volunteerism were among the very same ethnic groups that had been recruited into the German colonial forces. In its conquest of what became German East Africa before World War I, Berlin had incorporated warriors of the tribes that fought well against it into its own colonial army. The Schutztruppe, as the force was known in East Africa, went on to enjoy remarkable success against the British during the Great War.

Much doubt persisted at EUCOM and elsewhere in intelligence circles that the TPDF was up to the task of securing the Salient, no less invading Uganda. It was a daily battle to defend assessments that the Tanzanians were about to launch a major campaign, even as thousands of TPDF troops were arriving on the border. The doubters said the TPDF vehicles would be bogged down; but when some of them were, the Tanzanians just walked. Ultimately, the TPDF walked over four hundred miles all the way to the Uganda-Sudan border. Tanzanian resolve had not been factored in strongly enough.

The Counter-invasion Begins

It was plain to some that this was not going to be tit-for-tat retaliation. Julius Nyerere was taking it upon himself to rid Africa of its deadly buffoon. In January 1979, the TPDF began a military campaign that would deploy seven brigades containing roughly 30,000 troops into Uganda. The TPDF's prewar strength of 20,000 would peak at 60,000. A 10,000-man occupation force would stay behind for a year after the war.

The Ugandan Army was an unprofessional mob compared to the TPDF. A force of about 20,000, it melted away steadily as the war progressed. Several hundred fighters from the Palestine Liberation Organization (PLO), which maintained a training base in Uganda, and perhaps 1,000 to 2,000 Libyan troops supported the Ugandans. Libya's Colonel Gadhafi, forever trying to win influence in sub-Saharan Africa, had befriended Amin, a fellow Muslim.

The Ugandan Army was composed essentially of Amin's henchmen. If nothing else, they had colorful names like the Simba (lion) Regiment, the Tiger Regiment, and the Eagle–Colonel Gadhafi Battalion. The analysts' favorite was Amin's own: the Airborne, Seaborne, Suicide Commando Battalion. We often wondered if suicide was their mission.

The Tanzania-Uganda conflict had much in common with other African wars in that there were few pitched battles, casualties were mainly civilian, and progress was slow and road-bound. What was different was the ability of the TPDF to maneuver by brigade and tactically employ forces by battalion, and, perhaps of greatest importance, their will to fight. This showed a well-developed command-and-control capability. Armor and especially artillery were used effectively; air power was not.

The Air War Such as It Was

Air forces provided tragic and comic results. Early in the war, Tanzania sought to deploy a squadron of Chinese-built MiG-19 jet fighter-bombers to Mwanza on the southern shore of Lake Victoria. Following their squadron commander, they got lost overflying Mwanza, ran out of fuel, and crashed. In just a few hours, the Sunday punch of the TPDF's air wing had been lost.

The Ugandans managed to get one or two of their MiG-21s airborne, but they were not a factor in the conflict. The MiGs' short range prevented them from striking Tanzania, but the Libyans had an answer. They had Russian-built Tu-22 long-range bombers. The first attempt to deploy them failed, however, when the Libyan pilot couldn't find Uganda (no less the airbase), ran out of fuel, and bailed out over eastern Congo (then Zaire). Miraculously, the same pilot made his way back to Libya, was given another Tu-22, and successfully flew it to Nakasongola Airbase north of Kampala.

His next mission was not as successful. Taking off, fully armed, and intending to hit Mwanza in Tanzania, he dropped his bombs prematurely, hitting instead a game preserve on an island in Lake Victoria. The only casualties were a number of animals. The Tu-22 and its crew were recalled to Libya. It made no difference whether he had hit the target or not. One air raid by one plane on any target would not have affected the outcome of the war. In SSA, combat aircraft, namely, fighters and bombers, are rarely militarily significant. More often than not, their impact is psychological.

Marching to Kampala (to the Tune of "Marching to Pretoria")

The TPDF campaign in Uganda was thorough and methodical. The main thrust was along the road parallel to the western shore of Lake Victoria, from the border to Kampala, but every major town was liberated. Tanzanian forces worked west of the lake to insure that no major pockets of resistance that Amin might choose as a hiding place would remain. At first, progress was slow, but as the TPDF gained confidence they advanced at a measured pace. Amin's troops had to make a stand on the road to Kampala, and they eventually did. Using the Palestinians and Libyans to anchor their defense, the Ugandan Army tried to turn the tide at Lukaya and then at Mpigi. After brief but relatively sharp fighting, Lukaya fell on 10 March and Mpigi a couple of weeks later.

From Mpigi the Tanzanians were in striking distance of both the airport at Entebbe and the capital itself. A two-brigade attack won control of Kampala on 10 April. Although Amin was still at large in Uganda, after the fall of Kampala and the death and capture of hundreds of Libyans and PLO fighters, the game was up. The next two months saw the complete occupation of Uganda without any serious resistance. Amin had fled the country shortly after the fall of Kampala, leaving his remaining forces leaderless.

The United States was not involved in this war at all. Diplomatically we called for caution. There were rumors that the British secretly stage-managed the conflict, but that has never been proven. This war was a wakeup call that African armies were beginning to acquire enough capability to invade their neighbors and beginning to change the rules of the game in SSA. Tanzania would go on over the next few years to deploy small forces to the Seychelles, where they thwarted a white mercenary coup attempt, and to its ally Mozambique, provoking Professor William Foltz to coin the term "Tanzanian rent-a-troops."

(For a detailed account of this war, see Avirgan and Honey, *War In Uganda: The Legacy of Idi Amin* [Westport, Conn.: Lawrence Hill, 1982].)

Two Antagonistic Regimes Collapse

SOMALIA'S CIVIL WAR, 1980s–1991

By the time I made my second visit to Somalia in the 1980s, Mogadishu was in the Western camp. The United States had use of the Soviet-built air and naval facilities at Berbera in northern Somalia on the Gulf of Aden, there was a U.S. military assistance group in Mogadishu, and – best of all – a friend from my EUCOM days was the defense attaché. Much had changed since my 1977 visit, but I could not have fathomed how much more change was to come.

After the Ogaden War (chapter 9) ended with Ethiopian victory in 1978, the border with Somalia remained hot. Troops from both countries faced each other from dug-in positions. There were harassing attacks, Ethiopian air raids, and Somali guerrillas supported by Addis Ababa. When I returned to DIA from EU-COM in 1980, I went to an interagency meeting on the Ethiopia–Somalia situation. Before the meeting, I had read a couple of raw field reports that indicated Ethiopia might carry the fight deep into Somalia, perhaps cutting the country in two. This was not being discussed at the meeting.

When I brought up this information, another DIA analyst verbally attacked me, saying that this had all been hashed out at a previous meeting. The Ethiopians did not invade; the analyst was correct. The other analyst's violent reaction to my comments, though, was symptomatic of the power game and clash of personalities that often goes on at interagency meetings. The analyst would not brook a challenge to his established position, and the huddled masses followed sheeplike in his analytical wake.

After the Ogaden War: Things Fall Apart

Aside from two armies facing each other across a contested border, both Ethiopia and Somalia were backing insurgents fighting against each other. Somali president Mohamed Siad Barre was having problems at home managing clan politics, and Ethiopia's Chairman Mengistu faced growing armed opposition in the north in Eritrea and Tigre. On his way back from an overseas trip, President Siad Barre was stoned when he stopped in Hargeisa, Somalia's northern capital, an indicator of growing discontent. In April 1988, Siad and Mengistu signed an agreement pledging not to interfere in each other's affairs and to normalize diplomatic relations.

Members of the dissident Somali National Movement (SNM) and Somali Democratic Salvation Front (SDSF) were given three choices by Mengistu: become Ethiopian citizens and settle in the Ogaden, keep their weapons and join the Ethiopian Army, or disarm and return to Somalia. The SNM elected to return to Somalia but neglected to turn in their arms. Instead, in May they launched a desperate campaign in northern Somalia, capturing Hargeisa, Burao, and threatening Berbera.

Forces loyal to President Siad Barre continued to hold the airport and collocated military base several miles outside Hargeisa. Over the next few months, loyal elements of Siad's Somali National Army (SNA) bombed and shelled Hargeisa into oblivion. Tens of thousands of civilians were killed, earning General Mohamed Siad Hersi Morgan the moniker "butcher of Hargeisa." Siad Barre may have recaptured the north temporarily, but he lost his army in the process. The SNA was disintegrating along clan lines. SNA commanders found they could only trust troops from their own clan.

The "Mayor of Mogadishu"

The SNM and SDSF were the forerunners of a dozen or more armed groups in opposition to Siad Barre's regime. In the late 1980s, the rebellion spread south and gathered momentum. The SNA melted away until its only reliable troops were Marehan, and soon even some of them came to oppose Siad. Soon the president's authority extended only to the Mogadishu city limits. After his son-in-law General Morgan, leading the Marehan remnants of the SNA, was defeated just outside the city in late 1990, Siad's fate was sealed. Soon he was just another warlord. And in January 1991 he fled the capital.

Power soon fractured into a dizzying array of warlords dependent on shifting clan and subclan loyalties. The United Somali Congress (USC) was the most prominent militia in Mogadishu, but it broke into the Aideed and Mahdi factions that fought each other in the streets. The Somali state ceased to exist. Somalia became the late twentieth-century symbol of the collapsed state. Gun battles between rival clans raged unchecked in the capital and in the countryside, especially in southern Somalia. Faction fighting exacerbated the drought and famine already afflicting the land. In the summer of 1992, an unprecedented humanitarian crisis appeared in the offing.

Operation Eastern Exit

When U.S.-Somali relations improved after the Ogaden War, Washington built a large embassy in Mogadishu. Witnessing the disintegration of the state in the late 1980s–early 1990s, the ambassador bravely kept the American flag flying despite the apparent hopelessness of his diplomatic efforts. Non-essential embassy personnel had been drawn down, but, as the 1991 New Year arrived, a sizable number (36) remained. Once more, diplomats from other countries also remained virtually trapped in Mogadishu.

At this time, the United States had its focus up the road in the Persian Gulf, where Operation Desert Shield was about to become Desert Storm. Africa was getting a reputation for creating rescue missions as the United States was gearing up for military operations elsewhere. When our ambassador in Mogadishu,

Jim Bishop, requested evacuation, it resulted in one of the most daring rescue missions Africa had ever seen.

Helicopters from two U.S. Navy ships flew hundreds of miles with Seals and Marines on board. The harrowing mission required two mid-air refuelings over water at night by fixed-wing tanker aircraft, something that had never been done before. The helicopters were launched from nearly five hundred miles off-shore, flying just above the waves.

Two platoons of Marines and the Seal team landed at dawn on 5 January 1991 and secured the Embassy compound. In what must have looked like a scene from a modern day Alamo, they manned the walls and gates. A heavy machine-gun on a rooftop across from the Embassy belonging to some unknown faction was aimed at the helicopters. At one point, a Somali officer threatened to shoot down the helicopters if they tried to take off.

As the U.S. ambassador prepared to board the last helicopter, a Somali captain rushed up with a hand grenade. He threatened to blow up the helicopter if the ambassador did not let him on. Ambassador Bishop was a cool-headed veteran of several African emergencies. He deftly convinced the Somali officer that he could have all the vehicles in the compound if he gave up the grenade. Sure enough, the Somali bought into the deal and another disaster was averted. Amid all the chaos and confusion, Eastern Exit managed to safely evacuate 260 people from thirty countries, including the Russian ambassador and his staff.

Somalia Prostrate

Africa had seen just about every kind of political violence, warfare, and armed criminal activity in the era of independence, but what happened in Somalia between 1988 and 1992 was unprecedented. Every facet of life was broken down to its crudest, most base level: the power of the gun. Guns were essential whether you were a militiaman, a businessman, a farmer, or someone who just wanted to protect his family and survive.

The ruthlessness displayed by the 1988 leveling of Hargeisa went a long way toward hardening Somali attitudes against President Siad Barre. The use of such indiscriminate mass violence against Somali civilians by their president – the man defeated in the Ogaden – was too much for many Somalis to accept. With

Siad Barre's flight from the capital in January 1991, Somalia entered a phase of perpetual clan warfare and warlordism, a situation from which it has yet to emerge.

THE ETHIOPIAN CIVIL WAR: COLLAPSE OF THE MENGISTU REGIME, 1988–1991

Throughout the late 1980s, we already had seen some dramatic developments in sub-Saharan Africa. Wars were raging in Angola, Mozambique, Chad, and Somalia. Moreover, cooking on a slow burner until 1988 was Ethiopia. The Marxist regime of Chairman Mengistu Haile Mariam was one of two poles of Soviet Cold War influence in SSA. Unfortunately, for Moscow, both Angola and Ethiopia were coming under increasing pressures, and the clock was running out on the USSR itself. Moscow's enthusiasm for backing African clients at war was diminishing.

Mengistu came out of the Ogaden war in 1978 with a battle-tested 200,000-man army, an air force refurbished with modern Soviet aircraft, Cuban troops, and Soviet and East German advisors. He launched a series of large-scale offensives, often involving 100,000 troops, to retake all of the Province of Eritrea. The scale of the fighting in the 1980s and early 1990s was by far the largest yet experienced in SSA. Eventually, the Ethiopian Army grew to nearly half a million men.

Mengistu's "Red Star" offensives (military campaigns designed to crush Eritrean resistance) were effective in rolling back the tide of Eritrean nationalism with one important exception: the largely subterranean fortress of Nakfa, held by the Eritrean People's Liberation Front – EPLF. Situated in mountainous northern Eritrea, it withstood everything Mengistu's minions could throw at it. Aerial bombs, artillery shells, armored assaults, all failed to dislodge the EPLF from Nakfa. The name became synonymous with Eritrean resistance. While Texans might remember the Alamo that heroically fell, Eritreans would remember Nakfa that never fell.

The Tide Begins to Turn

Two events did the most to shape the opinions of intelligence analysts: the battle for Barentu, and Mengistu's dramatic survival of a coup attempt. In 1985 EPLF forces seized Barentu, a significant Ethiopian garrison town at a crossroads over the mountains west of Asmara. For the first time since the 1978–79 Ethiopian reconquest of Eritrea, the EPLF forced the Ethiopian Army to withdraw from a major base, abandoning much of its heavy equipment. This proved important, because the EPLF (and later the allied Tigrean People's Liberation Front – TPLF) relied on capturing most of its armaments from the Ethiopian Army. No external power provided the rebels with significant numbers of tanks, armored personnel carriers (APCs), artillery, or other heavy equipment.

What impressed the analysts, however, was the speed with which the Ethiopians launched a major counter-attack. Within weeks, an overwhelming force of 60,000 troops was assembled and launched; the EPLF had to abandon Barentu once again. The swiftness and size of the Ethiopian response left a great impression.

In May 1989, after the tide had already turned against the Ethiopian Army on the battlefields of the north, Mengistu was in Eastern Europe searching for additional military assistance. In his absence, a faction in the military leadership attempted to seize power. Instead of accepting his fate, Mengistu flew back to Addis Ababa, confronted his opponents, and re-established his authority. This display of courage and tenacity convinced many analysts that Mengistu's staying power was formidable, even in the face of battlefield reverses. This judgment by DIA analysts would soon prove to be problematic. His ability to rally the troops was apparently intact, or so it seemed.

The Slide Begins at Afabet

On the road to Nakfa was Afabet, the marshalling yard for Ethiopian attacks on the fabled Eritrean stronghold. In March 1988, the EPLF launched an attack against Afabet that was surprisingly effective. The Ethiopian garrison of more than a division was routed, abandoning a cornucopia of weapons and supplies. The fall of Afabet sent shock waves throughout Ethiopia and the region, but not to some analysts, who continued to see it as just another temporary reverse for Mengistu. After all, what is losing a division here or there when he has two dozen more? The Ethiopian Army – formidable on paper – was still fighting back, launching offensive operations.

Afabet was to be the first of four devastating February–March winter offensives by the rebels from 1988 to 1991. To the south of Eritrea lies the Ethiopian province of Tigre (pronounced 'TEE-gray'), also in revolt. The Tigre Peoples Liberation Front was allied with the EPLF, a relationship it benefited from immensely. Although there were periods of tension between the Eritreans and Tigreans, they had an effective marriage of convenience. Further, in 1989 the TPLF organized an umbrella group of several other factions fighting against the Mengistu regime. This new group – the Ethiopian People's Revolutionary Democratic Front (EPRDF) – was dominated by the TPLF. The EPLF,.the TPLF, and the EPRDF made common cause in an anti-Mengistu crusade.

In a February–March 1989 offensive, the TPLF captured Inda Selassie, the "Tigrean Afabet." A pattern emerged that became common to this war. The Ethiopian Third Army that had been formed to check the rebellion in Tigre launched a two-division offensive against the TPLF. As the offensive crumbled, the TPLF counter-attacked, and demoralized Ethiopian troops fled back toward Inda Selassie, where they caused a panic. The subsequent fall of Inda Selassie led to the collapse of the Third Army as the TPLF declared Tigre "liberated."

The major government defeats at Afabet and Inda Selassie led to many other garrisons falling to the rebels in Eritrea, Tigre, and elsewhere. With the loss of Tigre, the Ethiopian Second Army in Eritrea was becoming isolated. It now had to rely on air and sea resupply. In February 1990, however, a Second Army offensive faltered, leading to the EPLF's capture of the major seaport at Massawa. Ethiopian control of Eritrea was shrinking, as was the Second Army.

The EPLF and TPLF realized, however, that their political goals could not be achieved as long as Mengistu was in power. They needed a compliant government in Addis Ababa to assure Eritrea's independence and the EPRDF's own desires of peaceful self-determination. This reality led to ever-closer military collaboration. The EPLF fought along side the EPRDF all the way to Addis Ababa. Two brigades of EPLF-manned tanks played an important role and led to the Eritrean perception that the EPRDF could not have defeated Mengistu without their help.

The End Game Plays Out

Throughout 1990, government reverses continued. The Second Army in Eritrea launched several offensives to break out of its isolation as if in its death throes. Nevertheless, increasingly its area of control around Asmara diminished. Now dependent on an air bridge, the EPLF would on occasion get close enough to shell Asmara's airbase lifeline. To the south, EPDRF forces entered Welo and Shewa Provinces, threatening Addis Ababa from the north. The remnants of the Third Army held the northern front against the invaders.

In early 1991, the Ethiopian Army's position deteriorated further. The EPRDF took the provinces of Gondar and Gojam, opening a western front on Addis Ababa. This first phase of what became the final offensive ended with the seizure of the bridges over the Blue Nile gorge. This was accomplished by mid-March. The second phase in late March–April saw further EPRDF penetration west of Addis Ababa into Welega Province, setting up the strategic envelopment of the Ethiopian capital. The third phase in May saw heavy attacks by rebel forces now surrounding Addis Ababa on three sides (north, west and south) and in Eritrea. The EPLF armored assault on the Second Army's bastion at Dekemkare, south of Asmara, led to what was arguably the largest tank battle in Africa since World War II. With the road to Asmara now open to the EPLF, the Second Army surrendered five days later.

The Ethiopian Army: Quantity not Quality

Toward the end, Mengistu shuttled his reliable troops (an ever-diminishing commodity) from front to front in a desperate attempt to stiffen resistance to rebel attacks. His most reliable commanders were, ironically, the few remaining holdovers from the pre-Marxist army. However, purges, expulsions, and casualties took their toll on a once-proud professional army. Basic training went from months to weeks to days as Mengistu's Marxist mass army worsened. A revolving door army, it relied on massive recruiting and, increasingly, conscription.

Hundreds of thousands of men were conscripted and armed, only to desert, often with their weapons, which were later sold on the open market. Mengistu's army was a major contributor to Africa's future small arms proliferation problem.

Diminishing resources also played a role in the army's defeat. Having raised a huge army with Soviet support, it could not be sustained without Soviet aid. The Soviets actually armed three armies: those of Mengistu, the EPLF, and the EPRDF – the first intentionally, the latter two unintentionally. Although the Russians and their communist allies did supply the Marxist-leaning Eritreans with light weaponry in the pre-Mengistu days, the rebels feasted on captured military hardware to fuel their offensives in the last years of the war. Soviet military advisors that once numbered 1,500 or more, also evaporated. As for the Cubans, they never fought in the north, and were all out of Ethiopia by 1989.

The end came quickly. On May 21, 1991, with the enemy at the gates, Mengistu boarded a plane, ostensibly to inspect his troops at the front. Instead, he flew into exile in Zimbabwe, where an uncle he'd appointed was the Ethiopian ambassador. On May 27, the main air base at Debre Zeit south of the capital was captured, and the rump government left behind ordered Ethiopian troops in the capital to surrender. The next day EPRDF troops entered the capital from the south and west.

Lessons Learned

With all this evidence of impending doom for Mengistu, one would logically surmise that making the analytical calls would be easy – for example, Mengistu's days are numbered as his army collapses. Not so. Some analysts continued to see Mengistu as the Ethiopian "Rock of Gibraltar." Now, as the DIO for Africa, I spent a lot of time trying to make them see the forest as well as the trees. As late as April 1991, a senior analyst bet me that Mengistu would be in power a year from then. A month later Mengistu was out; it was the easiest five bucks I ever made.

One obvious lesson is not to confuse quality with quantity. The Ethiopian mass army was awesome on paper but rotten at its core – poor training and dismal morale. After the defeats at Afabet and Inda Selassie, it was never able to regain the strategic initiative vital for success. Its defenses, where strong, were often bypassed by the EPRDF moving ever closer to Addis Ababa.

Another lesson is to heed the tides of history. Marxist Ethiopia could not survive the fall of the Soviet Union. Soviet military largess was a thing of the past, and no one else would play that role. One of the most impressive yet sad sights I have seen in Africa was a field in Asmara brimming with the wreckage of war; hundreds of destroyed tanks, APCs, and other wrecked military vehicles. There were so many you could not get anything approaching an accurate count from the ground. What I was looking at was once the Ethiopian Second Army.

Somalia, Ethiopia, Eritrea, and Sudan in the 1990s

UN AND U.S. INTERVENTION IN SOMALIA, 1992–1995

By 1992, I was already a veteran DIO (Defense Intelligence Officer) with five years on the job and a half dozen major African crises under my belt. Continued factional fighting was exacerbating drought and famine in Somalia. With no central government, it was difficult to mount the kind of massive humanitarian rescue operation required. In April the UN formed UNOSOM, the United Nations Operation in Somalia (later referenced as UNOSOM I), a humanitarian operation without a mandate for peace enforcement. UN soldiers were to seize the airport and seaport in Mogadishu and supervise the distribution of food in the city.

At first, all went well. UNOSOM troops – 500 Pakistanis – landed at the airport, and then moved on to secure the seaport with its food shipments. When the UN troops attempted to escort trucks carrying food out of the port compound, however, the effort broke down. As the trucks emerged from the gate, hundreds of hands began removing the bags of grain as the trucks became mired in a sea of desperate humanity. Short of deadly force, nothing could prevent the looters from stealing the food.

Worse, once the mob besieging the port realized the UN soldiers would not fire on them, after all this was a *humanitarian* operation (with no peace to keep), they overran the port. UN troops quickly retreated to the airport, where they holed up in a small, fortified corner of the facility.

The Wheels Begin Turning in Washington

Aside from UN efforts in Mogadishu, cargo planes were delivering food to airstrips inland, with similar difficulty. Not only were the planes mobbed upon landing, but on occasion they were shot at as well. Food was becoming a weapon. Armed factions were competing for control of the food to enhance their power and prestige and gain adherents.

The summer of 1992 was typically hot and humid in Washington. The interagency players did not look forward to long meetings at the Old Executive Office Building adjacent to the White House's West Wing, with its fickle air-conditioning, or the stuffy State Department Building on 23rd Street. The White House had decided that the United States would respond positively to a July UN request to assist with humanitarian relief operations. At one meeting, a U.S. Air Force colonel was asked by the chair about providing American transport planes to deliver food to the interior. He responded that none were available, owing to training requirements to keep the fleet ready for military contingencies. The chair asked the colonel if the Air Force was still subordinate to the president as commander-in-chief. If the president decided to help, this was a military contingency!

Soon USAF transport aircraft were flying into Somali airfields, some returning with AK-47 slugs as souvenirs. This was Operation Provide Relief. However, things did not improve in Somalia; they got worse. By late 1992 the United States was moving to support a heftier UN mission in Somalia to be known as UNITAF. Southern Somalia had to be secured for the UN to perform its humanitarian mission.

Four options were on the agenda of the NSC Deputies Committee (DC) in late November. Option one was to do nothing more. Option four, the most robust, was to authorize the deployment of up to 5,000 U.S. troops to an enhanced UNITAF under UN command. To the surprise of virtually all in the room, the JCS representative pre-empted discussion of the four options, declaring that the Defense Department was prepared to deploy up to 28,000 troops as part of UNITAF but under U.S. command.

President George H. W. Bush quickly approved the major U.S. engagement, as did a surprised and pleased UN Secretary-General Boutros Boutros-Ghali. Operation Restore Hope was launched. U.S. Marines landed at Mogadishu on December 9, 1992. Insiders believed that the Thanksgiving holiday season and the news coverage of the human suffering and tragedy unfolding in Somalia influenced the decision. Prior to Operation Restore Hope, the U.S. policy maxim was that large numbers of American forces would never deploy to sub-Saharan Africa. Notwithstanding occasional training missions there, sending tens of thousands of U.S. combat troops to Africa had never been envisioned. Somalia stunned the policy community and changed this thinking.

Intelligence Responds to the Crisis

Before 9 December, DIA analysts were overly pessimistic about the Somali reaction to U.S. troops on the ground. Their warnings of immediate disaster failed to materialize. Rather, the Somali warlords and their followers were at first over-awed by the large show of force. And these were U.S. troops under U.S. command, not some patchwork of military ne'er-do-wells. Back at the Pentagon a Somalia Intelligence Task Force was established under the J2 in the DIA Alert Center. Suddenly there was a shortage of Somali experts. The flood of questions was overwhelming. A professor who was expert on the Somali clan and subclan structure was a godsend in sorting out shifting clan alliances.

I found my niche coaching the analysts on the Task Force. A colonel was assigned to run the Task Force, but he was out of his element. The five or six analysts who manned each shift looked forward to my early morning and afternoon visits. We established a dialogue on what was going on in Somalia and what it meant, what new intelligence reports were important and what were not, and why. Soon, I was influencing the content and judgments of the DIA's morning flagship briefing.

This briefing was presented to the SECDEF and the Chairman of the Joint Chiefs of Staff by the J2, not by J2 analysts or DIA's most senior Africa analyst, the DIO. Therefore, DIA's most knowledgeable people were not in the room when this briefing was given, and their expertise was not available to our most senior consumers. That was because the J2 was the senior substantive intelligence analyst in the DIA for crisis intelligence. This meant that in normal times the DIO was perceived as the most senior expert, but once a crisis was declared by the J2, he became the senior substantive authority no matter what countries or issues were involved. I did have the pleasure of sitting in on the morning dry run briefing for the J2 in his office. As the only non-J2 employee in the room, I had a unique position, able to critique the briefing as almost the J2's coequal. (My appearance in the J2's office was the result of the incident previously described.)

When crisis blossoms, intelligence gets swamped with requests for information, especially in the first month or so. Everybody wants to know everything right away. Offices you didn't know existed are clamoring for information. Sometimes they want a library, not an intelligence office; they don't like being told that. Working in parallel with the J2, DIA set up a crisis desk at Bolling Air Force Base in its Defense Intelligence Analysis Center, the site of most DIA's analytic assets.

Requests for more basic types of information or lower-priority requirements went across the river to Bolling. Still, DIA developed the database that sorted out the order of battle (organization and strength) for some fifty Somali armed factions. This database went directly to the president, according to a senior analyst who worked on the project.

The Somali Enemy

As they became more acquainted with UNITAF and U.S. forces, Somali gunmen grew more daring. Somalis are good fighters. Lightly armed, but clever and fearless, they make excellent desert or urban guerrilla fighters. A colleague of mine who had served a tour as the U.S. defense attaché in Somalia during the 1980s told the following story that illustrates the ruggedness of the Somali soldier. Early in his assignment to Mogadishu, he was given a tour of frontline positions on the border with Ethiopia. He met a soldier living in a fortified trench, essentially a hole in the ground. Two years later, on a farewell tour, he visited the same area and met the same soldier living in that trench. The soldier hadn't received any leave and wasn't expecting any. That was just the way it was. The Somalis, like many African troops, are low maintenance, often inured to physical hardships.

When UNITAF arrived on the scene, the Somali factions hid their heavy weapons, namely, armor and artillery, in favor of the "technical." As in Chad, these 4x4 light pickup trucks mounted with machine guns, rocket launchers, and the like provided mobile firepower and transport for Somali fighters. Individual fighters armed themselves with the ubiquitous AK-47 rifles and RPG (rocket-propelled grenade) launchers.

The "technical" received its name from the arrangement used to pay freelance Somali gunmen employed by NGOs and others for protection. These forces were technically attached to the organizations that hired them. The term "technical" soon migrated to the armed little trucks they rode.

Confounding the intelligence picture was the constant reconfiguration of clan and faction loyalties. This was a maddening pursuit. In late 1992, there were an estimated 70,000 to 100,000 armed Somalis organized into at least sixteen major factions. Many were gunmen for hire or simply organized locally for their own protection. When there is no government to rely on, you must defend yourself.

Major Events in the UN and U.S. Intervention in Somalia

April 1992:	UNOSOM I formed to get food to starving Somalis.
July 1992:	UN requests U.S. assistance with relief airlift.
August 15, 1992:	U.S. Operation Provide Relief set up to support airlift.
November 1992:	United States agrees to lead UNITAF to restore order in southern Somalia.
December 9, 1992:	U.S. Operation Restore Hope lands 20,000-plus troops in Somalia.
March 26, 1993:	UNOSOM II with a mandate to use force replaces UNITAF.
March 26, 1993:	U.S. Operation Continued Hope provides less support to the UN.
June 5, 1993:	24 UN Pakistani troops are killed in Aideed ambush.
August 1993:	United States deploys Task Force Ranger in the "hunt for Aideed."
October 3, 1993:	18 U.S. Rangers are killed in "Black Hawk Down" incident.
March 1994:	Operation Quick Draw; United States pulls remaining forces out of Somalia.
February/March 1995:	Operation United Shield; United States leads multinational force to cover UN withdrawal.
March 31, 1995:	UNOSOM II terminated; all foreign forces out of Somalia.

The Mission Goes Wrong

As an intervention for humanitarian purposes, UNITAF was successful in saving tens of thousands of innocent lives, sustaining only minor casualties. UNITAF was succeeded by UNOSOM II, a UN-led mission with a Chapter VII peacemaking charter that allowed it more latitude to use force. The United States left behind a Quick Reaction Force to bolster UN forces and some logistic support assets to move troops and supplies. Before June 5, 1993, General Mohamed Farrah Aideed was one of the more successful warlords in Somalia. After that date, he would be held in infamy by the UN.

Aideed lured a Pakistani detachment of UN troops into an ambush that resulted in twenty-four killed. This action was perceived as an affront to the UN, a clear provocation; there had to be some face-saving response. And so began the hunt for General Aideed and the corruption of the UN/U.S. mission. The peacekeepers had lost their impartiality by taking sides in Somalia's unending civil strife. A reward posted for Aideed made this appear to be a personal crusade by New York and Washington.

The U.S. Answers the Bell

Washington once again responded to assist the UN. In the summer of 1993, the United States sent highly trained Special Forces to back up the Quick Reaction Force and join in the hunt for Aideed. Intelligence analysts were concerned about this mission creep, but not alarmed. After all, U.S. forces had acquitted themselves well, making an impression on the Somalis. Now, however, the heavy-handed approach included the shelling of suspected Aideed houses, garages, and other buildings in Mogadishu. Devastating attacks by helicopters and AC-130 gunships were carried out on targets that may or may not have been Aideed property.

Tactical decisions were being driven by tactical intelligence in the field, not by assessments coming out of Washington. The daily intelligence briefings from DIA reported on the results of actions against Aideed and were less analytical and forward-looking. It seemed that intelligence assessments from Washington were taking a back seat to infatuation with what was happening on the ground in Somalia.

Black Hawk Down, SECDEF Out

Much has been written and portrayed on film about the raid by U.S. Rangers on October 3, 1993. Despite a healthy respect for Somali fighters, things went wrong in rapid succession. SECDEF Les Aspin's denial of the military's request for heavy armor contributed to his later resignation. Imagine that – a SECDEF impacted by a bad decision concerning a military contingency in a far-off African country! The impact of the Somali operation extended to the highest office in the Pentagon.

When two Black Hawks went down and the 3 October mission began to fall apart, the Rangers found themselves facing more than just Aideed's militia. Gunmen affiliated with Aideed or otherwise joined in the fray. General Aideed's stand against the United States and the UN made him a popular figure among the urban dwellers of Mogadishu.

The swarming attack by various militias could not have been predicted. It was the product of the moment. The word got around quickly that American soldiers were in the dusty streets firing at Somalis. The firefights drew Somali gunmen like a magnet. Ultimately, eighteen U.S. Rangers were killed along with untold hundreds of Somalis. It was the most serious urban firefight experienced by U.S. forces since Vietnam.

What We Learned from Somalia

In the aftermath of the Black Hawk Down debacle, the United States pulled out of Somalia in March 1994. American forces returned a year later at the head of an international force to cover the UN's withdrawal from Somalia in Operation United Shield. General Aideed was killed a few years later in a firefight with a rival faction. The Somalis were left to their own devices. The world seemed to be saying to the Somalis "Give us a call when you get a country." The Somali intervention was the largest U.S. military deployment to the African continent since World War II. It was also arguably the largest deployment to sub-Saharan Africa period.

Somalia, above all else, proved that Africa was not immune to military entanglements. Despite our lack of self-defined national interest and planning documents that gave it short shrift, the United States could and would become more involved in sub-Saharan Africa. We also learned that humanitarian crises in dangerous environments pitted the need to alleviate suffering against the risk of becoming involved in local conflicts. Further, former countries that had become failed states complicated this situation.

Somalia was a clear case where "mission creep" led to disaster. The mission was a success as long as it stayed above local rivalries and was not perceived as favoring one group over another. But, Aideed successfully baited the UN and the United States with dead peacekeepers. The hunt for Aideed led directly to mission failure. The impact of the Somali disaster on future U.S. policy was enormous. It came to represent all that was wrong with military involvement in Africa. It was a corollary to the post-Vietnam syndrome, where Washington feared becoming entrapped in other unwinnable counter-guerrilla wars.

The October 1993 debacle in Somalia heavily influenced the U.S. decision not to intervene in Rwanda six months later, specifically the Defense Department's reluctance to provide any military support until well after the damage was done. On the more positive side, the Somali experience convinced some military leaders of the need for more emphasis on urban guerrilla warfare as well as peacekeeping operations. One untruth engendered by our experience in Somalia was endowing all African guerrilla fighters with the capabilities of the Somalis. This is a dragon that military intelligence has had to slay in places like Liberia, Congo-Kinshasa, and Sierra Leone.

Was the Somalia intervention a success or a failure? Certainly from the humanitarian perspective it was a success. Many thousands of lives were saved. From the political-military vantage point, success appears more illusive. For the most part, U.S. and UN forces brought limited security and stability to southern Somalia – some would argue only to Mogadishu. On the downside, UN forces could not avoid becoming involved in military operations. Aideed made certain of that, forcing the issue by taking the initiative. Certainly, there was no real progress on a political solution, as has been borne out by subsequent events over the past ten years.

THE ETHIOPIA-ERITREA BORDER WAR, 1998–2000: ALL IN THE FAMILY

When the alliance of Ethiopian and Eritrean rebel forces defeated the Mengistu regime in 1991, there was every reason to believe that at long last peace prevailed in those two embattled countries. Yet, seven years later the unimaginable happened. The troubles began the previous year when Eritrea introduced its new currency, the Nakfa, also the name of the town in the north. Eritrea had long used the Ethiopian monetary unit, the Birr. Eritrea was after all economically integrated into the Ethiopian state. Addis Ababa rejected the Nakfa and demanded payment in Birr or in hard currencies such as the U.S. dollar or French franc. But in rejecting the Nakfa, Ethiopia deeply insulted Eritrea.

Remember the Nakfa!

Nakfa is the Eritrean Alamo, only Eritrea didn't lose it. They held on to that largely subterranean northern town in the face of the Ethiopian onslaught following the Ogaden War. Nakfa came to symbolize the struggle of the Eritrean people against great odds. The rejection of the Nakfa sparked a growing sense of mutual betrayal magnified by Eritrean president Isaias Afwerki and Ethiopian prime minister Meles Zenawi – former comrades in arms. Some would say, however, that they had really been allies of convenience.

In the war against Mengistu, Eritrea – independent since 1993 – had shed its blood to free Ethiopia, while Ethiopia after the war had made itself landlocked to ensure that a free Eritrea remained territorially intact. But after the Nakfa insult, relations between Asmara and Addis Ababa deteriorated sharply. Seemingly minor border disputes became major issues. Isaias and Meles each believed his brother had stabbed him in the back.

Still, it was not that easy to connect the dots. Reports from the field characterized the disputes more as ruffled feathers than reasons to mobilize half a million men. The outbreak of hostilities near the remote border village of Badme in May 1998 set off analytical alarm bells. Eritrea had seized Badme by force and Ethiopia would retaliate.

Before May 1998 it just did not seem logical for Eritrea, with a population of three million, to attack Ethiopia, with a population of 55 million. It seemed an improbable war over a desolate land of no strategic or economic value, by people who until recently regarded themselves as brothers.

Shuttle diplomacy by the United States failed to halt the military buildup. While the issues seemed trivial and negotiable to Westerners, they were monumental to the combatants. And once again, as we have seen in other theatres of African conflict, the dispute was being driven by interests important to the

Africans, not necessarily to outsiders. Africans once again claimed the right to define their own interests and create their own destinies.

Sub-Saharan Africa's Biggest and Bloodiest War

The Horn of Africa is not called "the cauldron of conflict" without reason. Between the spring of 1998 and the summer of 2000, four major rounds of fighting took place on three main fronts, involving over half a million men and resulting in at least 30,000 fatalities, almost all of them military. After Eritrea's May–June 1998 success at capturing Badme, analysts could clearly see the Ethiopian counter-punch coming. Mobilization on such a scale on either side could not be disguised. And, when countries go to those lengths to prepare for war, they almost always follow through with hostilities.

This was a conventional war on a very large scale employing infantry tactics similar to those used in World War I, except for the lack of massed artillery as had been seen in Europe. It was a war between sovereign states that actually declared war – a rarity in today's world. It was fueled by pure nationalism, a product of state growth, not state collapse. Ethiopia had some 300,000 troops deployed, more than double the size of the force used by the United States in the 2003 invasion of Iraq.

The three major fronts from west to east along the border were Badme in a very rural area, Zela Ambessa near the main roads leading north into Eritrea, and Bure ('BYOO-ray') opposite the seaport of Assab. There were territorial claims in all of these areas, but it was the Bure front that made the most sense, because the capture of Assab would give Ethiopia a corridor to the sea. A quick study of the geography revealed that Assab's only real reason for existence was to serve Ethiopia as a seaport.

But Western logic would prove faulty again. The Ethiopian army probably could have taken back Assab but didn't make a serious attempt. A thrust north from Zela Ambessa toward the Eritrean capital Asmara to end the war might have proved inviting, but it was never in the cards. And Badme, in splendid isolation, remained a major focal point of the conflict. The strategic objective for Addis Ababa was more to teach impudent Eritrea a lesson and to prove that Ethiopia was still the dominant power on the Horn of Africa.

May–June 1998: Eritrean attacks at Badme; war begins

February–March 1999: Ethiopian counter-offensive on all fronts

June 1999: Eritrean counter-offensive

May 2000: Ethiopian offensive

December 2000: Algiers Peace Agreement

A Bad Day at Badme

In June 1999 Eritrea launched a large-scale offensive to regain territory lost to Ethiopia earlier that year. The Eritrean army employed a total of fourteen infantry divisions totaling some 100,000 men. They were opposed by the Ethiopian army's ten divisions, another 100,000 men. The results were inconclusive, the casualties staggering.

The degree of effort should not come as a surprise. People on the Horn of Africa have been raising large armies for centuries, especially Ethiopia, where rival warlords fought to claim the crown when an emperor died. We saw militia mobilized on a large scale during the Ogaden War and then during Mengistu's war with the rebels. Chairman Mengistu was, in effect, just another emperor, but in Marxist garb. Commenting on the conflict as a whole, the late Jim Woods – former deputy assistant secretary of defense for Africa in the Pentagon – said there had been nothing like it in Africa since the North Africa Campaign during World War II. The Ethiopia-Eritrea War was in a class of its own.

How Are You Going to Pay for This?

One of the biggest inhibitors to waging large-scale warfare in Africa, at least in the minds of the analysts, is the seeming inability of poor countries to finance military adventures. Ethiopia and Eritrea are consistently ranked among the world's poorest. Yet they have found a way to outfit hundreds of thousands of soldiers, provide them with massive amounts of consumables, such as ammunition, food, and fuel, and purchase some high-tech weapon systems, notably Su-27 and MiG-29 jet fighters and modern self-propelled artillery.

Though how they do it remains largely a mystery, arms merchants flood a region once they get scent of a conflict brewing. Terms and conditions for the purchase, delivery, and training (even operation in some cases) of weapons can usually be worked out. "They are not going to war because they can't afford it" is not a defensible analytic position. Futures can be mortgaged, long-term loans arranged, and diaspora contributions collected. It is also possible that donor funds provided for development or humanitarian relief can be diverted.

Eritreans Invade the Pentagon

Two vignettes may shed some light here. The Eritreans are remarkable. While working at the Pentagon some years ago, I began noticing people who looked to be from the Horn of Africa working in the cafeteria; they spoke to each other in their native Tigrinya. One day I asked a cashier when she was last in Asmara. That started a long-running lunchtime commentary lasting several years. The Eritreans overseas – and there are many – send a part of their earnings back to the homeland, much like Mormons tithing a percentage of their earnings to their church.

After attending a meeting with President Isaias at the State Department, I returned for lunch at the Pentagon. I said to the cashier: "You will not guess who I was just speaking with."

Without hesitation, she replied, "My president; I danced with him last night." Her president, Isaias, is quite a charmer. The last time I saw the cashier she was heading out of the Pentagon for the last time – "to work on my master's degree," she said. Another time I met with a groundwater expert – a typical white American – who was on his way out to Eritrea for a year to do a survey for the government. The owner of his California-based company was an Eritrean making good on his debt to his country; he was absorbing all costs.

A Policy Dilemma for Washington and the UN

In the 1990s President Isaias Afwerki and Prime Minister Meles Zenawi were among a group proclaimed the "new leaders of Africa." These were post–Cold War winners, people the United States embraced as allies in a new era. They spoke plainly and meant what they said. Their embrace of democracy was seemingly just around the corner. Going to war with each other was not what was expected, especially when they appeared to be doing it for spurious reasons.

Eventually, peace talks in Algiers led to a cease-fire agreement and the acceptance of a UN mission. In 2001 UNMEE (the UN Mission for Ethiopia and Eritrea) deployed 4,200 military observers and peacekeepers. It established a Temporary Security Zone to separate the opposing forces. Both parties initially hailed the 2002 ruling by an independent border commission, but ironically the status of Badme, where the dispute began, remained ambiguous. Delays in demarcating the border have not helped. Both Ethiopia and Eritrea through their harassing actions have made things difficult for UNMEE, which has been looking more like a vestigial organization as the months go by.

The Ethiopia–Eritrea conflict was an episodic war that remained on the margins of international consciousness. Between spasmodic combat lasting a few weeks, nothing much went on; the media vacated the region when the fighting stopped. Their focus was on the Balkans, although along a one-mile stretch of one front in Ethiopia more people died in three days than in the seventy-eight days of fighting in Kosovo. J. Brian Atwood, the former director of the U.S. Agency for International Development, sadly commented that we accept a level of violence in Africa we would not accept in Europe.

Ethiopia is, and will remain, at the crux of the Horn of Africa problem, what I have called Africa's crucible of conflict. U.S. policymakers have labeled it an anchor country, a focus of American efforts to engage regional problems with diplomacy. As the dominant power on the Horn, Ethiopia remains central to these efforts. John Prendergast correctly sees two interlocking clusters of conflicts on the Horn. One evolves around confrontations in Sudan, both the situation in the south and the war in Darfur. The second cluster joins the heated-up conflict in Somalia with the Ethiopia–Eritrea struggle.

What is significant about these conflicts is that they encompass an area from the African Horn (Somalia, Djibouti, and Ethiopia) westward to include parts of Kenya, Uganda, the Central African Republic, Chad, and western Sudan. Further, a dozen or more non-state actors are in the field backing the various players or acting as proxy forces. Therefore, the lines of communication are already in place to grow these conflicts into a major regional conflagration. The potentially most damaging conflict pits Ethiopia against Eritrea, the continuation of the 1998–2000 fratricidal conflict. Addis Ababa backs the weak, fledgling secular government of Somalia that would surely not survive without Ethiopian muscle, hence the late 2006 Ethiopian invasion of Somalia.

Ironically, Ethiopia seems to be playing a role in Somalia similar to the U.S. role in Iraq. Even roadside bombs, up until now not a major cause for concern in SSA, are being used against Ethiopian troops in Somalia. The Ethiopia–Eritrea conflict is playing out in Somalia through proxies, and some of them are reportedly linked to those hostile to U.S. interests (notably, terrorist cells). From my perspective, Ethiopia is once again fulfilling the role of respected U.S. ally who can function in concert with American policy and, if necessary, American forces.

The Ethiopian–Eritrean war did not make any sense from the U.S. perspective; therefore, it would not happen. That kind of reasoning is too dangerous, especially in today's Africa, and in particular, on the tumultuous Horn.

(See John Prendergast and Colin Thomas-Jensen, "Blowing the Horn," *Foreign Affairs* 86, no. 2, March–April 2007.)

WAR IN SUDAN: THE ENIGMA ON THE NILE

Sudan is one of those places that have been at war with itself longer than I have been an intelligence analyst, and for that matter longer than I have been a student of Africa. Territorially it is the largest country in Africa, nosing out the Democratic Republic of the Congo (a.k.a. "Congo big"), and as large as the United States east of the Mississippi River. Independent since 1956, Sudan has experienced two crippling civil wars encompassing thirty-one of its first fifty years.

Unlike Angola, where war engulfed virtually the whole country, Sudan's civil wars were mostly confined to the far south. Khartoum's residents remained 800 miles north of the fighting. For the United States, Sudan has been both an ally and an enemy at different times during the Cold War, and at times both a secular state and a Moslem fundamentalist state. It has harbored terrorist organizations and expelled them, its most infamous guest in the 1990s being Osama bin Laden.

It lies along the east-west fault line that separates the heavily Islamic and Arabic-influenced north from the more pluralistic south. In Sudan the people that reside in the north and dominate the political scene in Khartoum call themselves Arabs. They have a lighter complexion than their southern countrymen, although to the uninitiated they would appear black. The vast northern two-thirds of Sudan is mostly desert, while the extreme south enjoys relatively lush vegetation.

Sudan's second civil war began with an army mutiny in 1983. The late Colonel John Garang de Mabior, a southerner serving with the Sudanese army, became leader of the dominant rebel group, the Sudanese Peoples Liberation Army or SPLA. Colonel Garang was a Dinka, a people noted for their dark skin and height. Getting on an elevator with Garang and his bodyguards was a humbling experience even for me at six foot four.

In the 1990s Garang was an occasional visitor to Washington. At a Pentagon meeting, Garang and Defense Department officials poured over battle maps of the Sudan. The SPLA commander was clearly in his element pointing out the deployment of his troops and the enemy, the Sudanese army. After a while it almost seemed that he was playing a board game when he pointed out his 167th independent infantry brigade. There was an air of unreality about his comments. The SPLA was a lackluster guerrilla army, not the well-oiled military machine Garang seemed to be portraying.

The Bush Team Embraces Sudan

When President George W. Bush's foreign policy team arrived on the scene in 2001, their top interest in Africa was Sudan. Why Sudan? The religious right helped Bush win the presidency and was concerned about the persecution of Christians in southern Sudan. Most people in the south were either Christians or animists; very few were Muslims. Arab raiders employed by Khartoum to fight in the south engaged in slavery, an age-old practice now supported by the government. Worse, the government used its air force to bomb the south. While attempting to hit the SPLA, Khartoum's pallet-bombing campaign more often than not landed near civilians lining up to receive humanitarian aid at feeding centers. Pallet bombing is a crude method of dropping explosives from the air. Aerial bombs are lashed to a cargo pallet, then slid out the rear ramp of a transport aircraft from relatively high altitude. Highly inaccurate, pallet bombing is mainly a terror weapon.

The fundamentalist regime in Khartoum was easy to vilify. With allies such as Iraq, Libya, Iran, and Cuba, it was a charter member of a select club: those countries the United States accused of state-sponsored terrorism. Sudan also earned the distinction of the only sub-Saharan country ever directly attacked by the United States, which launched Tomahawk missiles in 1998 to take out a suspected chemical weapons facility.

When Brigadier General Omar al Bashir came to power in 1989, his fundamentalist regime established an open arms policy for all Muslims visiting Sudan, including those of known terrorist groups. My take on this behavior was that it had more to do with the responsibility to show hospitality to fellow Muslims than it did with support for terrorist groups. Nevertheless, Bashir was duped by his guests and eventually came around to expelling them, but not without dissension in his government.

Hassan al Turabi, a fundamentalist zealot, led the extremist wing of Bashir's government. Eventually, Bashir survived the Turabi challenge and placed his rival under wraps. Before that, however, I had the opportunity to see Turabi in action on his visit to the United States and Canada. A man clearly possessed by his beliefs, Turabi would levitate out of his chair when speaking and chuckle at his next remark not yet out of his mouth. On his ensuing visit to Canada, a political opponent, a 300-pound karate expert, attacked Turabi, a small wiry man. The life-threatening beating put a serious kink in Turabi's political career, and also his neck.

A Slow-Motion War in the South

The conflict that began in 1983 in the south pitted Garang's SPLA against the Khartoum government's standing army of about 60,000. Offensives and counter-offensives over the years led to inconclusive results. Juba, the southern capital, was threatened at times by the SPLA, and other southern towns changed hands several times. Khartoum employed local militias that frequently changed sides, supporting Garang one day and the government the next. The SPLA rebels, with the help of Isaias's Eritrea, attempted to open a front in eastern Sudan closer to Khartoum. This effort, characterized by shallow penetrations of Sudanese territory, failed to threaten the government.

For me and other analysts, the image that most accurately depicted this war was lethargy. Government forces operating at the end of a long logistic pipeline from Khartoum were dependent on supply by barge, rail, and air over a distance of nearly a thousand miles. Government offensives were slow and cautious. One such attack was stalled for two weeks when a convoy pulling out of Juba hit a land mine twenty miles down the road. Tanks were a clear signature of government forces on imagery. A T-55 tank or two would remain in the same exact position for weeks, sometimes months, while reportedly being "on the offensive."

The SPLA, too, was constrained by logistics. Southern Sudan is an isolated place to fight a war. A short-lived alliance in the 1990s by Uganda, Ethiopia, and Eritrea to support the SPLA showed some promise but dissolved when the latter two countries went to war with each other.

Darfur and the Oil

In 2003, just as the government was inching closer to a pact with Garang to end the war in the south, a rebellion broke out in the west. The peace deal in the south stopped most of the fighting and improved the lot of suffering masses there. But intelligence analysts were justifiably concerned about last-minute details that kept cropping up and the six-year course of the southern peace plan. Analysts will be jaded by long-term plans that allow so many opportunities for unraveling.

The discovery of oil in south-central Sudan, and the rapid development of the country as an oil exporter, was a major factor in the north-south peace negotiations. Garang and the SPLA knew that oil revenue would allow Khartoum to re-arm and expand its military. The government saw an opportunity to buy off Garang with oil money and end the long-running conflict with the south. Unfortunately, the non-Arab peoples of the Darfur region in western Sudan feared exclusion from any settlement with oil wealth entitlements. They had little stake in the political negotiations and would get no oil benefits. The rebels were a poor, threadbare lot, even by SPLA standards. (Garang was killed in 2005 in a helicopter crash, but his untimely death has not negatively affected the peace process.)

Aping the SPLA, which gained Khartoum's attention and concessions through rebellion, the rebels in the west rose up and attacked government positions in Darfur. Khartoum reacted swiftly, employing many of the same tactics it had used in the south against the SPLA. Pallet bombing, attacks by armed helicopters, deployment of regular army units, and worst of all the use of Arab militias employing a scorched-earth policy all contributed to the growing crisis. Labeled the world's worst humanitarian crisis, Darfur threatens three things: a spillover of the war into Chad, the future of the peace pact with the SPLA, and political turmoil in Khartoum itself. Many of the inhabitants (or former inhabitants) of the Darfur region are ethnically linked to Chad. The president of Chad is of the same ethnic group as the bulk of the refugees and internally displaced persons from Darfur. Chad is thus linked to the crisis, with the possibility of more regional violence.

Once again Arab militias are running wild, raising the question of who actually controls them. Can we assume that Khartoum can turn them on and off like a faucet? These militias operate in remote areas and once unleashed are difficult to control. What we are seeing in Sudan is another case of a large state fighting off centrifugal forces since independence. The political power of the

Muslim, Arabized north is fighting against these forces, exacerbated by the oil factor, to keep from breaking apart.

MODERN SUDAN

1956: Independence from the UK

1962: First civil war in the south

1972: Peace of Addis Ababa ends first war

1983: Mutiny leads to second war in south

1989: General Bashir takes power in Khartoum

1994: Largest government offensive against SPLA

2003: Peace talks with SPLA; Darfur rebellion erupts

Two Improbable Conflicts: Zaire (Congo) and Chad

THE SHABA I AND SHABA II INCURSIONS INTO ZAIRE, 1977–1978

In March 1977 I had only been working as the Africa analyst at the U.S. European Command for two months. It was a time of concern because the communist powers were still on a roll. Marxist regimes had emerged in Angola and Ethiopia with Soviet and Cuban backing following the fall of South Vietnam. The pro-West regime of President Mobutu Sese Seku in Zaire (since 1997, once again the Democratic Republic of the Congo-DRC) seemed a probable next target for communist expansion in Africa. As corrupt as it was, Mobutu's Zaire was widely perceived in the U.S. government as a bulwark against communism and a de facto base for contingency operations in the area.

When Mobutu changed the name of the DRC to Zaire in 1972, he also changed the name of mineral-rich Katanga Province to Shaba, as if to metaphorically close the door on the rebellions that had swept through the eastern regions of his country in the 1960s. Among those groups that fled Zaire in the mid-1960s were the former Katangan Gendarmes, paramilitary police forces that had bitterly opposed Mobutu and fought for Katanga's secession. These relatively well-trained troops entered neighboring eastern Angola, then still an overseas province of Portugal, and gained employment with Lisbon as counter-insurgents. They fought for Portugal against Angolan nationalist guerrillas, and later fought for the MPLA (Popular Movement for the Liberation of Angola) when that group emerged victorious in the 1975–76 civil war and established its government in Luanda, the Angolan capital.

The Katangans formed the National Front for the Liberation of the Congo, known by the French acronym FLNC, and variously referred to by intelligence analysts as "flink" or "flunk." The FLNC fought with distinction in the early days of Angola's civil war, helping the MPLA into power, but never lost sight of its objective: the overthrow of Mobutu and Katanga's secession. In love and war there is no substitute for experience, and the Katangans had it. Their encampment in eastern Angola was an armed village, with family members; communications were maintained with Shaba through ethnic ties. The older gendarmes trained the youth in the profession of arms. Receiving ample support from the Marxist Angolan government, the Katangans were essentially a mercenary tribe.

What stood between the FLNC and its objective was the Zairian Armed Forces (FAZ). Zaire had one of Africa's worst armies. Sizable but feckless, the FAZ had been trained at one time or another by countries as diverse as the United States, France, North Korea, Israel, Belgium, and China. The pattern was always the same: a satisfactory period of training, initially good results, but once foreign advisors withdrew, a quick reversion to type, that is, an undisciplined mob. A pillar of Mobutu's kleptocracy, the FAZ was an army never seriously expected to fight, except perhaps against its own people.

African dictators were fearful of competent armies, and Mobutu was no exception. They would rather keep their armies anemic, without ammunition and without serious training. Frequently, armies were balanced against paramilitary forces such as a gendarmerie, presidential guard, or militia.

Shaba I

On March 8, 1977, the FLNC, about 1,500 strong under the command of "General" Nathaniel Mbumba, launched a three-pronged attack into Shaba Province, southern Zaire.

At EUCOM headquarters the response was swift. I was the J2 (intelligence) representative on my second command battle staff since arriving less than two months before. At headquarters we were receiving raw intelligence on an almost daily basis claiming the FLNC were about to attack. A steady diet of this over the months led to a certain intellectual numbness, resulting in surprise when the attack actually materialized. Several towns in Zaire fell quickly, fanning U.S. fears of another communist victory in Africa.

Someone, perhaps the Angolans or the Cubans, apparently gave the Katangans new camouflaged uniforms that quickly became known as "tiger suits." "Who are those men in tiger suits?" became the intelligence question of the day for many days. With so many EUCOM eyes focused on the iron curtain, developments in sub-Saharan Africa – when they became important enough for senior-level attention – always required a quick history lesson. In fact, one of the most useful things I ever did when covering an emerging African crisis was to put together an unclassified one- or two-page paper explaining the background to the problem at hand.

The U.S. Commander in Chief Europe (CINCEUR), who was based in Brussels, rarely visited his staff in Stuttgart, where his deputy ran the show. But CINCEUR General Alexander M. Haig did visit at the time of the Shaba crisis, and I had the job of briefing him. Haig's lack of familiarity with the situation was evident. I can only remember him fixating on the fact that the Katangans had communist weapons and came from a Marxist country (Angola). President Mobutu claimed that the attack was the behind-the-scenes work of the Soviets, Cubans, and Marxist Angolans, a charge sure to register in the minds of our Cold Warriors.

Mobutu's appeal to the West was successful. France, Belgium, and the United States came to his aid. The French set up an inter-African force whose teeth were provided by 1,500 Moroccan troops. A Moroccan-led counter-attack, with the FAZ in tow, forced the FLNC back into Angola and the rebel invasion ended in May. When things cooled down at EUCOM J2, I was haunted by the feeling that the Katangan incursion was like a bad movie I had seen before. During the war we dumped all of our classified trash into burn bags as usual but did not have time to cart them out for destruction. Before this could happen I went through the trash and eventually found a report of a FLNC battle plan issued just days before the attack. It was an exact blueprint for the operation, giving times and locations of the invasion.

That piece of intelligence could have made me look like a hero predicting the Shaba I invasion; but we received scores of reports of impending Katangan attacks, and a prediction of a FLNC incursion based on any one such raw report would not have been credible. In a reverse of the normal situation, sometimes too much raw reporting on a given problem can obfuscate when and where an attack will occur.

Shaba II

The Katangans had not been destroyed, however. A year later, the FLNC attacked again. While the 1977 attack aimed at provoking an uprising to oust Mobutu, the 1978 attack had a more limited objective. It was the mining center at Kolwezi, a target the FLNC failed to reach the previous year. Cobalt, copper, and other minerals were vital to the Congo's economy and the West's strategic interests. Uranium from the Congo was used to make the first atomic bomb. This time the Katangans took a short cut, attacking from the south through sparsely populated northwestern Zambia. The Zambians did not collaborate in this invasion; they were simply unaware or powerless to stop it.

The FLNC had infiltrated Kolwezi months before the attack. Kolwezi was a sensitive target because the mining industry employed hundreds of Europeans (mainly Belgian and French) who would be in great danger. Since the atrocities of the early 1960s in the Congo, visions of nuns being raped and other murderous acts propelled the West into immediate action when Europeans were in danger. This was not always the case when Africans were in danger, as in the 1994 Rwandan genocide as well as the horrific violence in Liberia and Sierra Leone in the 1990s. The FLNC attacked Kolwezi on 13 May, routing the FAZ garrison and capturing the airport outside of town. The result was immediate chaos and mayhem. At EUCOM headquarters there was quick action to coordinate military operations with the French and Belgians. Liaison officers arrived at Patch Barracks from Paris and Brussels. This would be a well-coordinated response to rescue the Europeans in Kolwezi, crush the FLNC, and save Mobutu yet another time.

When it came to Africa and especially Zaire, there was a certain amount of tension between Belgium and France. Paris saw an inherent responsibility for the world's second largest francophone country and derided Brussels' poor record in the former Belgian Congo. A few days after the attack, my office received information about unusual activity at bases in the south of France and at the Foreign Legion base on Corsica. It looked as though the French were preparing to jump the gun on a joint U.S.-Belgian-French response.

I warned of independent French action in the next morning's J2 briefing. It was challenged at the pre-brief for the J2. He and the J2 staff could not believe such French deception, and that part of the briefing was dropped. The next day, the Foreign Legion landed in Zaire in French airliners, changed to shorter-range military transport planes, and went on to parachute into Kolwezi. Paris obviously felt compelled to act and may have saved lives by acting independently. The French action, however, did nothing to improve the confidence level between Paris, Brussels, and Washington.

Actually, a French-trained FAZ rapid reaction unit had parachuted into Kolwezi the day before and retaken the airport, while up to 2,000 Katangans still held the town. The first French jump by the Foreign Legion was nearly a disaster, as it occurred in near darkness and had no reinforcements until the next day. The FLNC force largely withdrew toward the Zambian border without any serious resistance to the French Foreign Legionnaires. Aerial photography later showed the FLNC column heading south with captured vehicles and other booty – a forlorn sight in the African bush.

At EUCOM it was another African brush fire extinguished, another communist thrust at NATO's soft underbelly parried. The Shaba wars added to the growing perception that Africa south of the Sahara was a troublesome area that had to be watched, and who better to watch it than the U.S. European Command? (At the time, EUCOM did not have geographic responsibility for sub-Saharan Africa, only for North Africa. In fact, all of Africa south of the Sahara was technically unassigned in the United States Unified and Specified Command Plan, the only major landmass to have such an "honor.")

(For a fuller understanding of the Shaba Wars, see Roger Glickson, "The Shaba Crises: Stumbling toward Victory," in *Small Wars and Insurgencies,* vol. 5, No. 2, Autumn 1994, 180–200.)

CHAD'S "TOYOTA WARS," 1986–1987

One of the most remarkable military conflicts in modern Africa took place in the mid-1980s in Chad. A former French colony about three times the size of California, Chad's northern two-thirds comprise a desert wasteland. The French called the less-arid agricultural southern third *le Tchad utile* (useful Chad). Libya to the north was forever meddling in Chadian affairs and in 1973 annexed the Aouzou Strip along its southern border with Chad. In the mid-1980s, Libya was backing Chadian rebels, led by Goukouni Oueddei, who were fighting against the regime of Hissene Habre. The Libyan-Goukouni forces occupied all of northern Chad above the sixteenth parallel. Attempts to advance farther south toward the capital at N'djamena failed. Meanwhile, the Libyan Army of Colonel Mouammar Gadhafi, 16,000 strong in country, built heavily fortified bases in the Aouzou Strip and elsewhere in northern and central Chad.

The Chad-Libyan war also marked my transition from Africa military capabilities branch chief in DIA at Bolling Air Force Base to the DIO for Africa position at the Pentagon. For me this was a move from line management to senior substantive expert for Africa. As branch chief I recognized that military developments in Chad were potentially significant to U.S. military operators and policymakers. A brilliant young analyst who was covering Chad at the time and I put together the "Toyota Wars" intelligence assessment that became an intelligence community bestseller.

There were plenty of lessons to learn from Chad, and our leaders had to be made aware of them. But, as the cliché goes, intelligence like life insurance must be sold. When I became the DIO-AF in the summer of 1987, my predecessor said that he spent 90 per cent of his time on Chad. I vowed not to succumb to that fate. There were just too many other pots boiling in SSA. A particularly avid consumer of intelligence was the late James L. Woods, the first deputy assistant secretary of defense (DASD) for Africa. The DASD for Africa was, and is, DIA's most important customer for information on SSA, and our most influential client. As the most senior official for Africa in the Defense Department, the DASD uses DIA as his other main source of intelligence. A DASD is the equivalent of a three-star general, placing him on par with the director of DIA.

Early on in this relationship between the DASD and the DIO for Africa, the demanding Mr. Woods requested detailed imagery analysis of Libyan defenses in Chad. DIA balked at this because it was "too tactical." What need would a DASD have for such analysis? Jim Woods set me straight, I set DIA straight, and it was the beginning of a rewarding professional relationship. You see, the DASD for Africa would participate in policy-operator conclaves that would decide on whether the United States would engage in this conflict and, if so, exactly how. The point here is that DIA does not decide what a DASD gets or does not get.

Why "Toyota Wars"?

In the 1980s, at least a half-dozen warlords fought for control of Chad. Most all of them were based on northern and eastern tribes with desert warrior traditions. They went by a bevy of French acronyms that analysts strung together into the "Chadian cheer" – FAN, FAP, FAT ... FROLINAT! – a tension-breaker in the office when the going got tough.

When Colonel Gadhafi's alliance with Goukouni broke down in 1986, Libya was left alone in control of northern Chad. In December, Habre began a military campaign to drive the Libyans back; this led to an episode in Chad's military history that became known as the "Toyota Wars."

With logistical help from France and later the United States, Habre developed a highly mobile desert cavalry force that relied on light 4x4 Toyota trucks – mostly pickups. The trucks were platforms for weaponry that included French Milan anti-tank missiles, heavy machine-guns, multiple rocket launchers, and mortars. Others carried soldiers armed with rocket-propelled grenades (RPGs), other light anti-tank weapons, and the ubiquitous AK-47 assault rifle.

The Toyota replaced the horse and camel in executing the age-old raiding tactics of Chad's modern-day desert fighters. Westerners may have helped with logistic and other support. The daring of the Chadian soldiers, however, corsairs on the Sahara's sea of sand, was unsurpassed, almost to the point of lunacy. The Chadians believed, for example, that if you drove your truck fast enough through a minefield you could safely outrun the explosions.

Their ability to maneuver on the desert and close quickly with their heavily armed enemy raised havoc with the Libyan forces, whose tanks and artillery were ineffective against so many small moving targets at close ranges. Chadian troops dismounted and engaged Libyan armor with light anti-tank (AT) weapons at ranges as close as twenty yards (about the distance from the pitcher's mound to home plate). These tactics were extremely effective, but often resulted in injury or death to the shooter!

Chad's 4x4 Toyotas were an inspiration if not the model for the so-called "technical" in Somalia in the early 1990s. This also fit the trend toward using light, easily maintained civilian platforms for lethal military purposes. Around Africa these ranged from small motorboats to light aircraft as well as a variety of truck and weapon combinations. For example, the Ethiopians mounted anti-aircraft guns on flatbeds and used them in a direct ground-fire role.

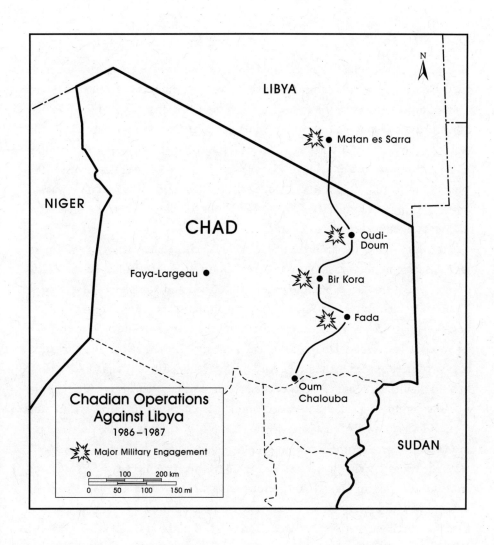

Chadian Operations
Against Libya

1986–1987

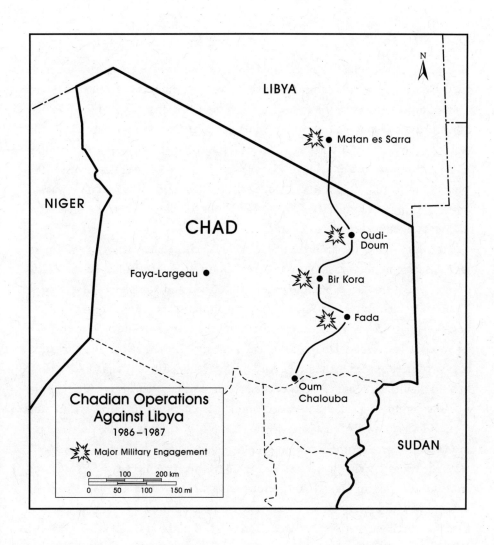 Major Military Engagement

0   100   200 km
0   50   100   150 mi

Libya Bites the Dust

Habre's counter-offensive against the Libyans began unspectacularly enough in late 1986 with a guerrilla campaign in the Tibesti Mountains in far northwestern Chad. But in January of the following year, the Chadians attacked the fortified Libyan base at Fada and overwhelmed its defenses. The garrison panicked. The rest is history. Of the 1,000-man Libyan force at Fada, 700 were killed and 80 taken prisoner, and 100 vehicles and pieces of equipment were destroyed. The Chadians suffered 20 killed and three trucks destroyed. This outcome was an omen of things to come. The Libyans could not handle a fleet and agile enemy willing to fight at such close quarters.

In March Gadhafi ordered a relief column dispatched from Libya's main logistics base in northeast Chad at Ouadi Doum to retake Fada. Caught in the desert, two of the three battalions were ambushed and completely destroyed at Bir Kora in a running two-day battle, with similar catastrophic results. About half the 1,600 Libyan troops were killed. As the remnants of the Libyan force fled back toward Ouadi Doum, the Chadian army followed. When the retreating survivors were guided through the base's defenses, the Chadians charged in right behind them! The result was one of the greatest military defeats on African soil.

The mounted Chadians moved quickly from point to point within the sprawling base, which encompassed a 12,500-foot runway that could accommodate large transport planes, and neutralized Libyan resistance. The base's outer defenses became a barrier entombing Libyan soldiers trying to escape from Ouadi Doum. Over 1,200 Libyan troops were killed and an enormous amount of military equipment was destroyed or captured. N'djamena claimed that the Chadians had destroyed or captured 100 tanks and 120 other armored vehicles, along with eighteen aircraft. The loss of Ouadi Doum forced the Libyans to withdraw its 2,500 troops from Faya Largeau, the administrative center for northern Chad, to the Aouzou Strip. After Ouadi Doum, all but the Aouzou Strip had been retaken from Gadhafi's army.

After a five-month hiatus from major fighting, Habre sent his forces sixty miles across the border in a dramatic raid on the Matan es Sarra airbase in southeastern Libya. Surprise was complete and the result predictable: another staggering loss of men and equipment for Tripoli. The toll according to Habre's government was 1,700 Libyans killed, seventy armored vehicles and twenty-five aircraft destroyed. Chad admitted to taking just under 200 casualties. According to one story, Libya made a futile effort to use chemical weapons against the Matan es Sarra raiders, reportedly rolling barrels of a chemical agent out of the back of a transport plane at high altitude. The barrels landed harmlessly in the Saharan sands.

The events described here were one-sided clashes in which the Libyans were unprepared for what they encountered. In combat a small tactical advantage can lead to a complete unraveling of a force superior on paper. Man-for-man the Libyans were not good soldiers; the Toyota Wars merely confirmed that. Gadhafi's military did learn from their ineptitude and won some clashes with Chadian forces. After all, they did retain control of the Aouzou Strip.

TOYOTA WARS: KEY ENGAGEMENTS

January 5, 1987	Battle of Fada
March 19–20	Battle of Bir Kora
March 23	Battle of Ouadi Doum
August 8	Chadian forces take Aouzou village
August 28	Libyan troops retake Aouzou village
September 5	Chadian Raid on Matan es Sarra (Libya)

LIBYAN LOSSES (JANUARY THROUGH SEPTEMBER 1987)

4,400 killed

1,000 wounded

1,300 captured

Over 400 pieces of equipment captured

About 40 aircraft destroyed (on the ground)

The Foreign Factor

Libyan retaliation came mainly in the form of a few bomb attacks into southern Chad by Tu-22 BLINDERS; these were the same long-range, supersonic bombers that Gadhafi used in the Tanzania-Uganda war. The attacks in Chad were ineffective; the French shot down one plane with a U.S. Hawk missile. That was about as far as U.S.-French cooperation would go in Chad.

The French military never really left Chad. They usually maintained a garrison in N'djamena of 2,000–3,000 men. French troops in Chad were reinforced during the Toyota Wars (Operation Epervier), and there has been speculation that they did more for Habre's army than help with logistics, ranging from planning the attacks to actually participating in them. With the French reinforcing the capital and controlling the airspace, Libyan forces had no realistic chance of moving against the Habre regime in the south. Not much can happen in a former French colony without Paris knowing about it or being involved in it. And the French were not about to roll over and play dead for the Libyans.

The Americans were involved, too, especially in encouraging the raid on Matan es Sarra in Libya. September 1987 was only sixteen months after the U.S. air strike against Libya known as the "El Dorado Canyon operation." Could Washington resist the urge to take the opportunity to smack Gadhafi once again, this time on the cheap and from the south, using non-U.S. forces? I think not!

Toyota Wars in Retrospect

The conflict in Chad revealed several lessons. It demonstrated that U.S. collaboration with an African army against a pariah like Libya was not only feasible but also workable. It also showed that light anti-tank weapons as employed by Habre's army could be used to great effect in a desert environment. Libyan ineptitude on the battlefield was once again exposed. Libya's formidable base defenses on imagery were not impregnable, and decentralized combat by Chad's Toyota warriors could be very effective.

Chadian victory could be attributed to their light maneuverable vehicles, their decentralized scheme of combat, their exercise of a great amount of initiative, and the sheer tenacity of the Chadian soldiers. The twirling combat, an adaptation of age-old desert tactics and the traditional way of fighting of desert warriors, suits the Chadians well. At DIA I tried to use the Toyota Wars story to catch the policymakers' attention and create favorable interest in Africa. Having seemingly unsophisticated desert warriors running rings around the Libyan invaders in little Japanese trucks was good stuff, well-illustrated and entertaining. During one of the Toyota Wars briefings, an admiral remarked, "Those tactics will work; you just need to have testicles the size of basketballs."

The locus of interest, however, was on Libya, not Chad. Without the Libyan bad boy poking his nose into Chad (Gadhafi liked to play powerbroker in SSA), there would have been little or no interest in Habre's accomplishments. On one occasion, my Pentagon policy customers scolded me because DIA did not inform them about a U.S.-provided Chadian C-130 transport plane that blew some tires during a hard landing. They informed me that they had been fighting a bureaucratic battle over the military aid package for Chad and that just such an event (the plane had to be grounded because Chad had no spare tires for its two C-130s) would have helped make their case for a larger assistance program. This was an early part of my education as a DIO.

I once had the pleasure of sitting across from one of the heroes of the Toyota Wars at a Pentagon conference. Idress Deby led Chadian forces in the field and later went on to unseat Habre and become president of Chad. Deby had all the warmth of a calculating killer. Today, some two decades after Toyota Wars, Chad is once again a battleground. The threat is internal insurrection exacerbated by the spillover of the violence in Darfur. It certainly figures in the war against terrorism, still has unsecured borders, and has just become a significant oil producer.

(See Captain Mank-Koefoed, French Army, "Routing the Libyans," *U.S. Marine Corps Gazette*, August 1987, p. 26; and Dr. William J. Foltz, *Chad's Third Republic*, CSIS Africa Notes #77 [Washington, D.C.: Center for Strategic and International Studies, October 30, 1987]).

The Great Lakes Crises:
Rwanda, Burundi, and the Congo

RWANDA'S CIVIL WAR AND GENOCIDE CRISIS, 1990–1994

Africa is beset with many dormant, inactive conflicts. Like sleeping volcanoes, they wait patiently for their day of reckoning. One such tempest in waiting was Rwanda, a small country in the heart of central Africa in an area known as the Great Lakes Region. About the size of Maryland and with 8 million people, it is one of the most densely populated countries in the world. Rwanda is one of the two countries where the Hutu-Tutsi rivalry has led to large-scale violence; the other is neighboring Burundi. In both countries, the Hutu majority (85 per cent of the population) are mainly agriculturalists, the Tutsi (14 per cent) mainly herders. Strictly speaking, they are not ethnic groups because people can move between them; it is more like a caste system. I listened to a diplomat from Rwanda spend the better part of an hour trying to explain the differences and similarities between Hutu and Tutsi and came away still somewhat confused.

Background to Crisis

Over the years there has been occasional fighting. Prior to 1959 the Tutsi minority was in control. The Tutsi were the pre-colonial rulers of Rwanda and the Belgians, who took over the colonial role from the Germans during World War I, favored them. In 1959, however, on the eve of independence, the Hutu majority rose up and seized power. Tutsi fled to neighboring countries, including Uganda to the north. The Tutsi refugees became known as the "59ers," those who fled in 1959. They vowed to return one day to their homeland, and on October 1, 1990, thirty-one years later, they did.

In the interim, the Tutsi in Uganda became a significant militarily force. Many joined Yoweri Museveni's National Resistance Army in post-Amin Uganda, and 2,500 Rwandan Tutsi soldiers helped him fight his way into power in 1986. Subsequently, the Tutsi exiles formed the Rwandan Patriotic Front (later Army); some held critical posts in the Ugandan Army such as deputy commander and director of intelligence.

On the first day of the 1990 Tutsi invasion, Rwandan Patriotic Army (RPA) commander Fred Rwigyema was killed under mysterious circumstances. The RPA recalled Ugandan Army major (soon RPA general) Paul Kagame from his studies at the U.S. Army Command and General Staff College in Fort Leavenworth, Kansas. Kagame proved to be the right man for the job.

In the early days of the war, the RPA enjoyed great success, penetrating deep into Rwanda. Swift reaction by France, Belgium, and Zaire helped blunt the offensive, and for practical purposes their military presence in Kigali precluded the possibility of an RPA victory. The war became a stalemate, with the RPA occupying northern portions of Rwanda along the Ugandan border. Diplomacy led to cease-fires and long-running peace talks at Arusha in Tanzania.

Begun as a conventional military campaign, the war reverted to guerrilla warfare. By 1992 it had bogged down into trench warfare. A DIA analyst who visited the area was surprised to see government and RPA troops holding dug-in positions within shouting distance.

The talks in Arusha produced several cease-fires. One allowed the RPA to station a battalion in Kigali as a good faith measure. The UN also deployed a

2,500-man monitoring force known as UNAMIR to Kigali, replacing the foreign troops supporting the government.

The Fuse Is Lit

On the night of April 6, 1994, Rwandan president Juvenal Habyarimana, a Hutu, was returning from Arusha in his executive jet along with the president of Burundi. On its final approach to Kigali airport, the plane exploded and crashed, killing all aboard. Mystery surrounds the event. The RPA and even the French were accused. The best explanation is that Hutu hardliners used a shoulder-fired surface-to-air missile to down the aircraft and kill Habyarimana, fearing that the president had given away too much to the Tutsi at the peace talks.

Subsequent events show that this was a carefully planned attack. Within hours, soldiers of the Hutu-dominated Rwandan Armed Forces (FAR) and paramilitary Hutu militia called the "Interahamwe" began vicious attacks on Hutu moderates – those who cooperated with the Tutsi and disavowed violence – and on Tutsi still resident in Rwanda. In succeeding days these attacks in Kigali, led by Hutu militants and encouraged by government-controlled hate radio, mushroomed into the 1994 Rwandan genocide in which some 800,000 people were slaughtered.

The fact that Hutu and Tutsi lived side by side in villages around the country facilitated the massacre. Neighbor slew neighbor in an indescribably horrific mass murder. Over the next weeks, the killing of Tutsi and moderate Hutu by Hutu extremists wielding machetes would outpace Hitler's gas chambers in speed and efficiency, killing so many so quickly.

Another Intelligence Failure?

U.S. intelligence did not predict the genocide but would argue it was not predictable. As always, reports of impending Hutu-Tutsi mass violence were extant, but who could have made a judgment along the lines of what actually happened? Intelligence and the U.S. Embassy Kigali actually got lucky on April 6. DIA had no resident military attaché in country but the attaché in Cameroon was accredited to Rwanda. Fortuitously, he had arrived in Kigali for a scheduled visit that very morning. When hell broke loose, we had a military officer on the scene to help coordinate the embassy's evacuation and report on the situation.

Close Calls amid Chaos

Hutu militants went from door to door looking for Tutsi and others on their hate list like Hutu moderates and Belgians. An African American woman visiting the embassy at the time and who fit the general appearance of a Tutsi – tall and thin – was held for hours at a diplomatic residence by a gang of marauding Hutu killers. Finally, a resident diplomat convinced the *genocidaires* that she was indeed a visiting American.

The evacuation of U.S. Embassy Kigali a few days later was probably the most dangerous operation of its kind in my experience. We came very close to losing many people. Analysts believed an airlift staging out of Burundi was the best choice, but it required evacuees to leave Rwanda via road convoy to Burundi. Ambassador David Rawson led the last convoy out, with American flags flying on his car. A few kilometers outside Kigali, FAR troops looking for Belgians stopped the convoy at gunpoint. Hutu militants had already tortured and killed ten Belgian members of UNAMIR. The convoy was held up for some twenty minutes that must have seemed like days. Any discharge of a firearm would have likely led to indiscriminate firing at the convoy.

With a Little Help from Our Friends

Back at the Pentagon, a Rwanda Working Group had been set up. It was struggling to establish a database by pulling together material on Rwanda to answer the many questions coming in. On my first walk through, I saw a veteran Africa analyst and asked him what we knew about the FAR Presidential Guard that was reportedly directing the violence. After a sigh and a crimped smile, he replied, "That it exists." This may have been a bit of an exaggeration, but it captured the sense of frustration. African databases were not important until something happened; then it was too late.

In this case we benefited from a NATO ally. I saw the Belgian military attaché walking around the Pentagon. He had a pouch full of papers, and as he passed me, he asked, "Which way to the joint staff?"

In the inter-agency arena, a battle was brewing over the "G" word: "genocide." As the weeks and months went by, the enormous scope of the Rwandan tragedy came into focus. Yet resistance to using the word "genocide" persisted. The reason for this is simple. By recognizing a situation as genocide, you commit the United States to doing something about it. Washington is on record with the UN in Geneva to never again stand by and allow a holocaust.

Fearing another disaster like the October 1993 fiasco in Somalia, however, policymakers were reluctant to take any bold actions that could lead to military entanglement. U.S. action was slow in coming; and when it did come, it treated the survivors after the worst was over. When President Clinton made his 1996 "contrition tour" of Africa, he stopped ever so briefly in Kigali. Never leaving the Kigali airport, the U.S. president promised never again – again.

Back on the Battlefield

The Tutsi RPA launched a general offensive two days after the genocide began. Enraged by the mass murder of their kinsman, the smaller (10,000–20,000) RPA began to slowly push back the FAR, twice its size, in what was once more a conventional contest. On July 4, Kigali fell to the RPA, ending the chaos in the city.

With the tide turning against the FAR, Hutu began to flee the country. In June the French established a safe haven for displaced persons in the south, known as Operation Turquoise. The operation, however, attracted only Hutu fleeing the advancing RPA. Turquoise was quickly labeled proof of continued French support of the Hutu over the Tutsi. U.S. Operation Restore Hope, a humanitarian rescue mission, got underway in July and was to last two months. Restore Hope was based at Uganda's Entebbe airport and deployed to Goma, a teeming border town in eastern Zaire. The American effort was limited to assisting those fleeing the victorious RPA in Rwanda. Only a handful of U.S. troops ever went into Rwanda to establish liaison in support of this mission.

SECDEF William Perry visited Operation Restore Hope and met RPA commander Paul Kagame, with whom he developed a personal friendship. Long after Restore Hope expired, Secretary Perry would ask about Rwanda, Kagame, and how things were going. This helped the Africa corps in DIA to fend off resource management's efforts to dump Rwanda quickly back into the ash heap of insignificant African countries.

Kagame was a charmer, no doubt. Tall and thin, with razor-sharp features, he fit the stereotypical image of the Tutsi warrior perfectly. Possessed of a sharp mind and wit, he does not fail to impress. American officials who are not Africa specialists sometimes seem surprised at the polish and intellect of African leaders when they meet them.

KEY DATES IN THE RWANDA CRISIS

October 1990: Rwandan Patriotic Army (RPA) invades Rwanda.

August 1993: Arusha Accord signed; paves way to peace.

October 1993: UNAMIR deploys to monitor cease-fire.

April 1994: President Habyarimana's plane shot down; genocide begins.

April 1994: RPA begins desperate offensive.

April 1994: United States evacuates American Embassy Kigali.

June 1994: French Operation Turquoise begins.

July 1994: RPA captures Kigali; massive Hutu refugee flow underway.

July 1994: U.S. Operation Restore Hope begins.

September 1994: Operation Restore Hope ends.

The War Spreads beyond Rwanda

Through the remainder of 1994, the RPA gradually consolidated its control of Rwanda, setting up a government with a moderate Hutu president and General Kagame as vice president. The Hutu enemy fled Rwanda to neighboring countries, chiefly Zaire and Tanzania, but was not defeated. An estimated 40,000 ex-FAR soldiers and untold thousands of Interahamwe – collectively referred to as Hutu militants – took up residence in eastern Zaire, where they could camouflage themselves in a sea of refugees. Fearing retribution, by mid-1994 some 2.2 million Rwandan Hutu had crossed the border into Zaire, Tanzania, and Burundi.

Of these, 1.3 million went into Zaire along with the overwhelming majority of the Hutu militants. The ex-FAR in particular maintained command of its forces and took control of the refugee camps that UNHCR had established and used them as rear bases for attacks into Rwanda. From the RPA's perspective, militant Hutu power in the camps had to be broken.

The Zairian government of President Mobutu Sese Seko never did have firm control of its eastern provinces and now was unable to deal with 40,000-plus foreign armed forces on Zaire's territory. The weak Zairian Armed Forces (FAZ) were unable to secure the camps and soon embraced the Hutu militants as allies. This evolving situation led to the next phase in the central African conflict.

The Rwandan civil war and the genocide it spawned created a militant Tutsi state psychologically akin to Israel. The "Israelis of Central Africa" were not about to allow a neighboring country to support Rwandan Hutu militants responsible for genocide. This pursuit of Hutu militants led directly to the war against Mobutu and what later became known as Africa's First World War. For the Africa-watchers in the intelligence community, Rwanda was proof that the U.S. involvement in Somalia was not just a freak occurrence. Perhaps a new day was dawning, one where African conflicts were important enough to impinge on strategic planning as never before.

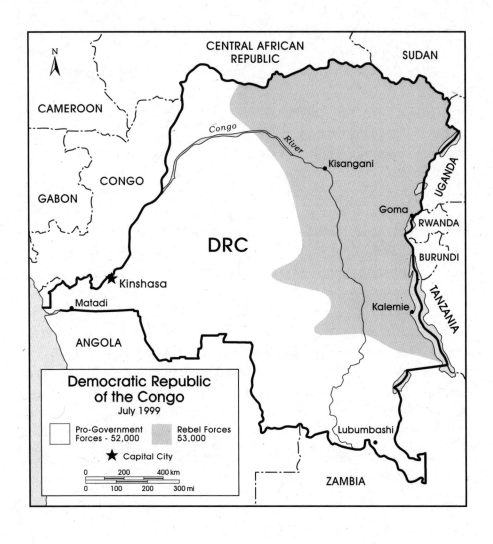

N

CENTRAL AFRICAN
REPUBLIC

SUDAN

CAMEROON

Congo

River

• Kisangani

CONGO

GABON

UGANDA

Goma

RWANDA

DRC

BURUNDI

★ Kinshasa

Matadi

Kalemie

TANZANIA

ANGOLA

**Democratic Republic
of the Congo**
July 1999

Pro-Government
Forces - 52,000

Rebel Forces
53,000

★ Capital City

| 0 | 200 | 400 km |
| 0 | 100 | 200 | 300 mi |

Lubumbashi

ZAMBIA

THE DEMOCRATIC REPUBLIC OF THE CONGO (DRC) IMPLODES, 1996–2002

The military situation in eastern Congo in the mid-1990s was unacceptable to the new Tutsi rulers in Rwanda. They were not about to stand by and allow the Hutu militants to reconstitute themselves and launch a guerrilla campaign from the Congo into Rwanda. They would take things into their own hands, if necessary, and they did.

This situation led to three wars in the Congo: the 1996–97 war that resulted in the ouster of President Mobutu Sese Seko; the 1998–2002 unprecedented coalition war that led to a de facto partition of the country; and the post-2002 conflict among sub-state actors – insurgents and tribal militias, sometimes acting as proxies.

At the start, the Rwandan objective was to break the militants' hold on the Hutu refugees and destroy their capacity to wage war. This was to be accomplished with the help of ethnic Tutsi living in eastern Congo and Congolese rebels recruited for that purpose.

Laurent Kabila, the Man of the Hour

Laurent Desiré Kabila was an old-school Marxist left over from Africa's liberation struggle. Kabila never came close to becoming a threat to his nemesis, President Mobutu, the West's anti-communist stalwart in Central Africa. Rather, Kabila remained holed up in the remote mountains of extreme southeastern Congo, where he assaulted Mobutu with rhetoric, not bullets. In the mid-1990s he had one thing going for him: he had never been bought off or compromised by Mobutu.

In 1996 Kabila was just what Kagame and the RPA needed, a recognizable name they could co-opt as a front man to nominally lead a rebellion in the eastern Congo. Kabila became the leader of the Alliance for Democracy and Liberation of Congo-Zaire. Trained, armed, and led by the RPA, the Alliance was the tool Kagame and company required to expunge the Hutu militants from the refugee camps and drive the remnants deeper into the Congo. As Kagame later admitted, the Alliance was entirely a creature of the RPA. In October 1996 a local official gave the ethnic Tutsi living in eastern Congo an ultimatum to leave the country or suffer the consequences. This anti-Tutsi action became the spark to begin the RPA offensive in the eastern Congo.

In November 1996 the Alliance rebels took Mugunga camp just west of the Congolese border town of Goma. Mugunga was the largest refugee complex, with some 700,000 residents. Upon liberation from the Hutu militants, most refugees chose to return to Rwanda; others either chose not to return or were still under militant control. In any event, one result of the Alliance-RPA campaign was to drive the militants deeper into the Congo.

Back at the Pentagon

Throughout the rebel campaign, the United States was interested in the plight of the refugees in the event Washington would once again become involved in humanitarian operations. The alliance rebel attacks, especially the one on Mugunga, had the effect of shattering the camps like a row of ten pins. Not that there were numerous casualties (there weren't), but the refugees were scattered. Intelligence was asked to find them.

Traditional imagery from satellites and reconnaissance planes was not very effective because of the heavy foliage. One platform did work, however – DIA's little C-12 attaché aircraft that could fly low in the valleys and spot the refugees. The twin-engine military version of the Beech King Air was very handy until word came that Hutu militants, presumably, had fired at it. C-12 operations were immediately terminated.

From Buffer Zone to War against Mobutu

The RPA and its allies soon discovered that advancing in the Congo (still called Zaire by the Mobutu regime) was like pushing on an unlatched door. Everywhere the rebels advanced, Mobutu's army – the FAZ – melted away. Ironically, Mobutu's best soldiers were the Hutu militants, who were fighting for their lives. With Mobutu's forces fading away, the RPA and their friends shifted gears and upgraded their objectives. Why settle for a buffer zone in eastern Congo when you can install a puppet regime in Kinshasa?

In January 1997, the FAZ launched a countrywide counter-offensive, its only serious attempt to turn the tide. Air strikes on rebel-held towns, hiring of French, Belgian, and Serbian mercenaries, and employing guerrilla fighters from Angola all failed to halt the Alliance-RPA advance. Regular forces from Uganda and Angola joined the Alliance and RPA in what was rapidly becoming an anti-Mobutu crusade. This was a typical African bush war. Moving along roads and dirt paths, there was very little actual fighting. Long marches were punctuated with brief skirmishes. The invaders succeeded against minimal opposition.

The advance on Kinshasa accelerated after Kisangani, Congo's third largest city, fell on 15 March 1997. By early May, the allied forces were but a hundred miles from Kinshasa. Concern mounted in the United States and elsewhere that a Mobutu last stand would result in a bloodbath. Thousands of FAZ troops, including Mobutu's Special Presidential Division, had retreated hundreds of miles to the capital. Estimates had some 45,000 Congolese troops in Kinshasa. How would they react to a rebel take-over?

Congo's All–but–Forgotten Hero

Mobutu, suffering an advanced case of prostate cancer, was delusional. Like Hitler in the bunker looking for those phantom divisions that could yet turn the tide, Mobutu was giving orders to fight to the last. His army commander was not buying it. General Marc Mahele, who had led an airborne assault against rebels during the 1978 Shaba invasion, was one of a rare breed, a Congolese military hero. Mahele defied Mobutu and ordered the FAZ and other troops in the capital not to resist the rebel take-over. For his courage, Mahele was executed by a Mobutu loyalist the day before Kinshasa fell, the day Mobutu flew out of his capital and into history.

On May 18, 1997, soon after allied forces secured the city without any real resistance, Laurent Kabila was installed as president of the Democratic Republic of the Congo. Foreign advisors, mostly from Rwanda and Angola, were everywhere. Colonel James Kabarebe, a.k.a. "Commandant James," was the commander of the new Congolese army, composed mainly of the Alliance rebels and ex-FAZ. Kabarebe, a Rwandan Tutsi, had been a key RPA commander during the recently concluded war.

ANALYST HUMOR

Despite the seriousness of the craft of the military intelligence analyst, humor would occasionally come into play to relieve the tension. Andy Roberts, one very fine analyst, and an even better person, came up with this spoof when Mobutu's fortunes were sinking:

Radio reports have picked up Kabila's rebels singing a spin-off from an old Hank Williams tune:

Goodbye Moe, you gotta go, meo myo

Son of a gun, you had too much fun on the Congo

Mobutu fly or you be crocodile pie and Ngbandi gumbo

'Cause tonight there will be no Sese Seko

Pack your car, head for C.A.R. some time todayo

Son of a gun you had too much fun on the Congo

All Not Quiet on the Eastern Front

From June 1997 to August 1998, Congo (now no longer Zaire) had a brief interlude without major fighting. Kabila found he had a fragmented army under the command of Commandant James, one of Kagame's right-hand men. Kabila's new army, the Congolese Armed Forces, proved no better at policing the eastern hinterland than Mobutu's FAZ. Worse, from the Rwandan viewpoint, Kabila appeared to be following the same path as Mobutu in the east: his army couldn't control the Hutu militants, so his soldiers began collaborating with them. There were even reports (later confirmed) that Kabila was providing them with arms.

At least 10,000 well-armed Hutu militants were operating in the east; some had even infiltrated Rwanda. Relations between Kinshasa and Kigali deteriorated sharply. Anti-Tutsi feeling was again growing in Kinshasa and in the countryside. In July 1998 relations reached the crisis point. Kabila fired James Kabarebe as his army commander and replaced him with a crony. A new rebellion broke out in the east, this time against Kabila's government. The RPA's Congolese rebel foil this time was the Congolese Rally for Democracy.

Kagame's Gambit to Shorten the War

In August 1998 Rwandan and Ugandan forces invaded eastern Congo. Much of Kabila's army quickly deserted or defected, and the RPA-backed rebels soon controlled the central portion of Rwanda's border with the Congo; the Ugandan army took control of the northern section of the border; and the Tutsi-dominated Burundi Army was active in the south. Kagame, however, was not about to start another thousand-mile trek across the Congo to Kinshasa; he had a better idea.

In one of the most daring military exploits ever attempted by an African army in the era of independence, Kagame flew some of his best troops to Kitona Base, a large military facility near Congo's Atlantic coast some two hundred miles west of Kinshasa. When the RPA troops landed, they were able to convince the Congolese garrison to join the rebellion and march on Kinshasa. At first, the plan worked. RPA troops and the mutineers took all the main towns between Kinshasa and the sea, including a naval base, the country's main seaport, and the dam that supplies electric power to Kinshasa.

Only one flaw appeared in Kagame's plan: he had not cleared it with the Angolan government. Luanda saw the western end of the Congo, close to its oil fields, as belonging in its sphere of influence. It also backed Kabila because of his strong stance against the Angolan UNITA rebels. The Angolan army –a battle-tested force like the RPA – intervened and blocked the RPA move on Kinshasa from the west. Angola sent additional troops to Kinshasa to back up the Kabila government. Zimbabwe and Namibia also sent troops. The Western Front collapsed as the RPA force was trapped between the capital ahead of them and the Angolan Army advancing from behind them. The Rwandans scattered or cut deals with their pursuers to escape.

Africa's "First World War"

For the first time, sub-Saharan states took sides in a developing civil war. Yes, it is true that in the past the French had stage-managed coalitions of African forces led by Paris or a surrogate. This time it was a strictly African affair. Angola and Zimbabwe in particular eventually sent division-sized forces (some 10,000–12,000 troops) into the Democratic Republic of the Congo (DRC) in support of the Kabila government.

The alliance that brought Kabila to power broke into two groups and attracted some additional players. The forces involved can be divided into pro- and anti-DRC forces and into state and non-state actors. Rwanda was again the big player with 40,000 troops (80 per cent of its army) deployed in the Congo.

MAJOR PARTICIPANTS IN THE 1998–2002 CONGOLESE CIVIL WAR

Pro-Government Forces	Anti-Government Forces
Congolese Armed Forces (FAC)	Rwandan Army (RPA)
Angolan Army (FAA)	Ugandan Army (UPDF)
Zimbabwe Defense Force (ZDF)	Burundi Army (FAB)
Namibian Army	RCD Rebels and factions**
Chadian Army*	MLC Rebels**
Sudanese Army*	Tutsi Militia**
Rwandan Hutu Militants**	
Burundi Hutu Militants**	
Mai Mai and other militias**	

* Participated briefly at the start of the war then withdrew

** Sub-state actors

In August 1999, a year after the war began, the rebels and their allies controlled about half the country. You could draw a line diagonally from the extreme northwest corner of the DRC southeastward to the southern shores of Lake Tanganyika to delineate government-held and rebel-held territory. Everything to the east of that line would be rebel-controlled, everything to the west government-held. The 1998–2002 conflict was a semi-conventional war, displaying both conventional and non-conventional aspects. The fighting was more serious than in the 1996–97 war. This time it was an infantry war, typified by the RPA, a light infantry force operating at times in conventional and guerrilla modes. The DRC is a territory the size of the United States east of the Mississippi River with a largely non-existent road system. The main forces – especially those of the national armies involved – nevertheless moved along the roads and tracks, such as they were.

Airlift was critical to all the operations. Regular forces at the fronts, often hundreds of miles from their supply depots, relied on contract airlift to provide them with consumables, mainly ammunition, fuel, food, and repair parts. Angola and Zimbabwe in particular made good use of private contract airlift, as did Rwanda. The deployments in this conflict could not have been sustained without airlift support. Prominent among the purveyors of contract airlift was one Victor Butt, a former colonel in the Soviet air force. Butt had amassed a fleet of some sixty aging transport planes that would fly anything anywhere for a price.

Aside from airlift, the combat air arms of the national forces, although deployed for combat, played only a minor role. The government did try to use the Congo's natural highway: the river system. The army assembled a small armada of riverboats and barges in an attempt to move north on the Congo River and penetrate rebel-held Equateur Province. But the force was ambushed. Fire from the shore ignited ammunition and fuel on barges that had been set up as platforms for crew-served weapons such as machine-guns, rocket launchers, and mortars, and secondary explosions set the whole fleet alight.

After the War, Still No Peace

The conflict evolved into a strategic stalemate in which the foreign forces played a diminishing role. When these foreign armies withdrew in 2002 in accordance with various peace negotiations, the war continued by other means. First, the guerrilla forces of the sub-state armies continued as proxies still representing the interests of their now-discreet backers. Second, seven years of war had torn the eastern Congo asunder. No reliable administration existed. In the northeast Ituri Region, Uganda was asked by the Congolese government to delay its pull-out and leave a thousand soldiers behind to help police the area.

The terrorized population was at the mercy of local warlords, many of whom were little more than economic insurgents or bandits taking what they will from the helpless. There were too many armed factions and no one to disarm them. Those who might have the means to disarm them would not take on such an arduous task for practical reasons, wishing to avoid sustaining casualties and risking entanglement.

The Significance of the Congo Wars

The Congo wars of the 1990s and 2000s were symptomatic of the changes in international relations in the post–Cold War era. In the end, Mobutu, a Cold War edifice, had been left on his own. Further, African states in the region actively conspired against him, and no extra continental power came to his rescue. Genocide proved to be a powerful motivator and justifier. It propelled the Rwandan Tutsi to pursue their sworn enemy across the continent not once but twice. Today it is still the force that drives regional politics.

The coalition war showed that African states could and would band together militarily to achieve common goals based on a confluence of national interests. Sizable conventional forces, amassed and transported a thousand miles or more, deployed and then continued in combat. Africans were calling the shots, not former colonial powers, Cold War icons, or superpowers. As they say in Africa, when bull elephants fight, the grass suffers. Here the grass consists of the internally displaced, legitimate refugees, and traumatized villagers of eastern Congo. In the wake of these conflicts stand well-armed tribal militias, spiritually oriented insurgents, warlords, and private armies claiming to be forces for positive change.

The UN was again slow to learn from other recent experiences in Africa. UN involvement was too little too late, waiting for someone else to bring the peace that it could then keep. UN peacekeepers were not initially authorized to protect civilians, just as in 1994 Rwanda. And the force was ridiculously undersized. The UN authorized 17,000 troops for Sierra Leone and only 10,800 for DRC. The Congo is thirty-two times larger than Sierra Leone. But nobody wanted to talk about a 50,000- or 60,000-man peace enforcement mission in the Congo.

Another kind of mass looting took place: that of Congo's natural resources. The main countries that fought in the coalition war gained economic rewards, or simply took what they could grab. The sub-state actors took their share too.

BURUNDI'S CIVIL WAR, 1993–2006

No discussion of the Great Lakes conflicts in Central Africa would be complete without Burundi. On the surface Burundi appears to be a twin of Rwanda to the north. It has similar demographics, geography, and to some extent history; and it shares the legacy of bloody Hutu-Tutsi rivalry.

In 1972 an aborted Hutu uprising against their Tutsi overlords resulted in 100,000 to 200,000 deaths in a frenzy of bloodshed that lasted for months. Media coverage of the massacres was paltry. In most major U.S. newspapers, coverage of the carnage in Burundi was far from the front page. With today's depth of media coverage worldwide, it is difficult to imagine such a tragedy being given such short shrift.

The more recent troubles in Burundi began in 1993 when the elected president, a member of the Hutu majority, was assassinated. In a 1997 coup, the Tutsi-dominated Burundi Army took over the government in Bujumbura, the capital, and installed Colonel Pierre Buyoya as president. Soon several Hutu armed factions were in open rebellion against the ruling Tutsi minority. Insurgency by armed Burundi Hutu militants swept the country as civil war developed.

Burundi: Part of a Tutsi Conspiracy or the Weakest Link?

Following the 1994 genocide in Rwanda and the bellicose Tutsi response, people throughout the region became alarmed over rumors of a Tutsi plan to dominate all of Central Africa. This preposterous theory had Tutsi-dominated Rwanda, Burundi, and Uganda (yes, Ugandan president Yoweri Museveni was a "secret Tutsi") scheming to secure all the wealth of the Great Lakes Region by force. Ugandan-Rwandan clashes in Kisangani later knocked some wind out of this theory.

Refugees from the fighting in Burundi fled into Tanzania, the Congo, and even Rwanda at times. The Burundi Army pursued Hutu rebels into the Congo, marking Bujumbura as a player in the regional struggle. The region's anti-Tutsi forces involved in the Congo's coalition war began to see Burundi as the weak link in the Tutsi alliance but were unable to do much to exploit it. Instead, Burundi became a sideshow to the fighting in the Congo.

Intelligence Requires a Complete Picture

From the mid-1990s through the early 2000s, Burundi became an oscillating target for U.S. policymakers. Driven by concern about another possible genocide, they wanted weekly, if not daily, updates (reassurance) on the region. They felt the need to be prepared in the event of a worst-case scenario, with Burundi becoming another Rwanda. Intelligence analysts from around the community spent many a meeting explaining why Burundi was not a cookie-cutter Rwanda.

Policymakers dealing with Africa would drop Burundi as soon as another new crisis emerged, a frequent occurrence. When the interest and fascination with the crisis of the day ended, the policymakers would return to Burundi. Every few months, it seemed, Burundi was rediscovered. Throughout the critical 1990s, DIA had no military attaché assigned to Burundi. State Department pressured DIA to open an office in the tiny U.S. embassy, but the best DIA would do was to assign a series of temporary attachés. These were trained military officers from another embassy, or from Washington, who would be assigned to Burundi for a number of weeks or months on TDY (temporary duty) status. Being the DIO for Africa with one foot each in the policy and intelligence worlds, I balanced in the middle.

The bureaucratic battle over establishing USDAO Bujumbura had a silver lining. It resulted in a complete change in DIA's approach to attaché staffing in Africa south of the Sahara. DIA sought and received funding to open many new attaché offices in the region, a move that was not only prudent, but one that probably saved lives.

A Difficult Transition to Peace

The civil war in Burundi was characterized by armed factions using guerrilla tactics against a Tutsi-led army supported by extremist Tutsi militias. It was a strange conflict in that the rebels were capable of infiltrating the capital and other large towns, threatening security but not the government. Bujumbura was the scene of occasional fighting, and for a time one rebel group established a strong point just north of the city. Harassing mortar and small arms fire into the city, as well as raids into Bujumbura's suburbs, were not unusual. While the civil war has ebbed and flowed over the years, there have been no military turning points of note.

The peace process, though, has borne fruit, thanks to the perseverance of the UN and the African Union (AU) – formerly the Organization of African Unity. The UN and South Africa have collaborated to move the process along, despite great difficulty in getting all the rebel factions to the table, and have denounced the armed struggle – a situation we have seen in many other conflict-prone countries around Africa.

The Burundi conflict is also significant because it was post-Apartheid South Africa's first venture into peacekeeping, despite its inward focus. In January 2003, to improve security in Bujumbura, South Africa sent in a small, battalion-sized force, which later became part of an expanded AU peacekeeping force known as the African Force. In 2004 the force was folded into a 5,650-man UN peacekeeping operation known as ONUB (United Nations Operation in Burundi) that carried on through 2006.

Whither Burundi?

The main points of the peace agreement signed in 2001 for a transitional government called for eighteen months of Tutsi rule, followed by eighteen months of Hutu rule, culminating in national elections, with some provisos for proportional ethnic representation. Stalking the peace process was the ever-present fear of a return to mass violence. A 2004 attack on a Tutsi refugee camp near the border with Congo massacred nearly two hundred and once again exposed the fragility of Burundi and African peace agreements.

In August 2005, successful elections were held, bringing to power Pierre Nkurunziza, a Hutu and member of the former rebel Front for Defense of Democracy. Scattered fighting continued throughout the peace process, however, until the last rebel group, the Forces for National Liberation, laid down its arms in the summer of 2006.

A 30,000-man force, half Hutu and half Tutsi, is replacing the former Tutsi-dominated army. ONUB is reverting to an AU Special Task Force, once again led by South Africa. Everything seems to be coming full circle in Burundi. The country does not have a strong government like those of its erstwhile allies, Rwanda and Uganda. If the peace process holds up, Tutsi power in Burundi will be further diluted. Nevertheless, accommodating the Tutsi minority will be a challenge that no one will take lightly.

Vicious Civil Conflicts in West Africa

LIBERIA'S CIVIL WAR, 1989–1997

For most of my early career the small countries of West Africa were considered a quiet backwater, an excellent place to assign new inexperienced analysts who could learn from their mistakes without jeopardizing anything important. But one West African country had a special relationship with the United States.

Founded by freed American slaves in 1847, Liberia was, and is, widely viewed as "America's colony." The colonizers – known as Americo-Liberians – were 2 per cent of the population, yet dominated the leadership of the country. They succeeded in recreating a piece of the nineteenth-century American south on the western hump of Africa. This time, however, it was the black Americo-Liberians, not white plantation owners, who were the masters. America's "special relationship" with Liberia was such that when the Firestone rubber plantation's trees were bent by the prevailing winds, it was said they bowed to Akron (Ohio). Liberia was also a safe place for Washington to build global communications and other facilities because of the absence of threats. In Monrovia, the Cold War seemed light years away.

The Armed Forces of Liberia (AFL) were little more than a vaudeville troop of a few thousand men. They rarely had live ammunition; their biggest weekly event was donning the uniform for church on Sunday. The AFL was so incompetent that a home movie of a training exercise made by one of our military attachés was the comic hit of a 1974 attaché conference in Germany. Later when Liberia began to fall apart, a senior U.S. official acknowledged that Liberia was a pile of ****, but it was *our* pile of ****.

Paradise Lost

Relative serenity was shattered in 1980 when, after a night of drinking, a dozen or more AFL soldiers from indigenous ethnic groups stormed the Executive Mansion and murdered President William R. Tolbert, breaking 133 years of Americo-Liberian rule. The soldiers had deposed Tolbert's regime, but who was to rule? One story has it that the gang's leaders could not agree on who was to become president, so instead chose a compromise candidate acceptable to all: twenty-seven-year-old Sergeant Samuel K. Doe (who had once flunked an English language proficiency test required for military training in the United States).

Sergeant Doe was a member of the Krahn ethnic group, only 4 per cent of the population. Tribalism was reborn as Doe began staffing his government with Krahns. Despite the bloody coup and executions that followed, Washington soon recognized Doe's regime. Doe ruled for ten years, and the United States supported him despite his bloody ascent to power. As elsewhere in Africa, Doe seemed to be the only game in town. The Liberian dictator even made an official state visit to Washington to cement his regime's relationship with the United States.

Enter Charles Taylor, an Americo-Liberian and minor official in Doe's government. Taylor had been charged with embezzling funds, fled the country, and was apprehended in Massachusetts, where he later escaped and made his way back to Africa, stopping in Libya for military training. On Christmas Eve 1989, Taylor led a small group (a few dozen) across the border from Ivory Coast into Nimba County in northeast Liberia.

War Comes to Liberia

The Taylor incursion was to complement an uprising against Doe in Monrovia. The uprising failed, however, forcing Taylor to Plan B: starting an armed insurgency in Nimba County. Taylor rallied the Gio and Mano people of northeast Liberia, who had grievances against Doe; his ranks quickly filled.

Taylor unveiled the banner of his political movement, the National Patriotic Front of Liberia (NPFL). Militarily, he consolidated his position in Nimba and organized his newly trained guerrilla army, now several thousand strong, for a drive on Monrovia. He was allowed this respite due to the AFL's continuing incompetence. Slow to recognize the seriousness of the NPFL invasion, Doe sent his forces piecemeal into the northeast. Much like the early stages of the American Civil War in northern Virginia, each force sent to check Taylor was defeated, resulting in the appointment of a new commander of dubious competence.

The AFL's employment of its few heavy weapons was comical, as there seemed no one in the AFL capable of sighting an artillery piece. On occasion, the AFL would fire a field gun in the direction of the enemy as simply determined by sound. When suspected sounds of the enemy were heard to the front, they fired in that direction; when the noise came from the rear, they fired in that direction, and so on. Soon they would be out of ammunition and flee the area, leaving the gun behind.

This was not a war where armor and artillery were of any real significance. It was an African bush war fought by often drugged and lightly armed soldiers. The rebels rarely had uniforms, and they frequently wore women's garments and other charms to protect them in combat. Their leaders took outrageous names, such as "General Butt Naked," who led his men into battle wearing only combat boots. It was difficult for many U.S. officials to take seriously a war fought by men with women's underwear on their heads. However, not taking the war seriously would lead to further complications for U.S. policy formulation.

By late March 1990, Taylor had begun his offensive. Moving along the road and rail lines toward the capital on the coast, NPFL forces used the facilities of commercial enterprises and NGOs, such as timber camps, plantations, and relief agencies, for logistic support. Each captured site yielded vehicles, fuel, food, communications gear, and recruits to join the NPFL bandwagon. To the intelligence analysts, this tactic was so obvious that it became easy to predict Taylor's next move by simply looking at a map showing the facilities between the rebel advance and Monrovia.

Methodically, the NPFL closed in on Monrovia. By June the rebels had captured the Firestone Plantation near Monrovia and Roberts International Airport outside the capital. By August Taylor's men controlled most of Liberia, including parts of the capital, but not the mythical Executive Mansion or the Barclay Training Center – the downtown headquarters of the AFL.

With NPFL forces infiltrating the capital, President Doe and his followers felt surprisingly secure as long as they held the Executive Mansion, as if physical possession of the building was their refuge against all harm. Some wanted insurance, however. One of Doe's lieutenants was not taking any chances. He purchased a charm he believed would make bullets pass safely through him. When tested, he literally shot himself in the foot. Furious, he deduced that he had been sold an ineffective charm! Magic ,or "Juju," played a major role in Liberia's civil war, something it was difficult for policymakers and operators to understand.

The spiritual component of most African conflicts is difficult for the uninitiated to accept. Yet, it is a key motivational factor in many African wars. The belief in magic is strong and real. Young men who believe they can be protected in battle by charms are often willing recruits for warlords and other troublemakers. Another spiritual factor is belief in a religious zealot who sanctifies the combatants by proclaiming a holy war.

The encroachment of the NPLF, and a breakaway group, the Independent NPFL, threatened the U.S. Embassy in the Mamba Point section of the city, a small peninsula jutting out into the Atlantic.

In June 1990, the first of four U.S. military deployments to Monrovia took place (the others came in 1992, 1996, and 2002). Their mission: protect the U.S. Embassy and rescue Americans that may have been trapped by the fighting in the capital. The situation was growing desperate, as people fled into the city, while others were now caught "behind the lines" in territory controlled by Taylor. Ethnic reprisals were taking place. A Doe government official pleaded with the United States for "forty Marines," all that would be needed to end the crisis. Such was the respect and prestige the American military enjoyed in Liberia.

There's No MOG like an ECOMOG

Foreign citizens from Nigeria and Ghana were also trapped in Monrovia, and they were the initial motivation for the formation of a West African peacekeeping force. The Economic Community of West African States (ECOWAS), an economic grouping of sixteen countries dominated by Nigeria, authorized the formation of a peacekeeping force for Liberia. That force became known as the ECOWAS Monitoring Group, or ECOMOG.

In August 1990, ECOMOG landed about 3,000 troops – mostly Nigerian and Ghanaian – in the port area of Monrovia. At first there was confusion as to what ECOMOG's mission was and what its rules of engagement were. Soon, someone fired mortar shells at its headquarters in the port area. A Nigerian general was appointed field commander, replacing an over-the-hill Ghanaian, and was assigned the job of clearing the NPFL out of Monrovia. As armor arrived with the Guinean contingent, ECOMOG proceeded to evict the rebels, house by house and block by block. Taylor was stopped just a couple hundred yards short of the Executive Mansion by a force, namely ECOMOG, he could not have imagined when he began his campaign less than a year earlier.

Defense Intelligence to the Fore

All through the first half of 1990, the Liberian crisis grew and policymaker concern intensified. By spring inter-agency meetings occurred almost daily, and DIA was the key player for intelligence. At the outset I carried the analytic ball for DIA but soon realized that I needed to delegate responsibility to other DIA analysts, because the daily intelligence traffic required too much detailed attention and I was still responsible for the forty-seven other sub-Saharan countries. This new responsibility provided opportunity for our analysts, one of whom, Margaret Culbert, went on to become the intelligence community's leading authority on Liberia and Sierra Leone.

DIA's success was the result of being able to provide a daily military analysis for inter-agency meetings at which policymakers discussed the situation and mulled over policy options. Inter-agency leaders became hooked on DIA briefings and would not start a meeting without one. The popularity of these briefings with senior U.S. officials won accolades for the analysts involved.

When ECOMOG prepared to land in Monrovia, one big question was whether the United States should assist the West African force and, if so, how. I attended a Pentagon policy conclave on the subject. The mood around the room was universally hesitant. The group (not one of them a true expert on African militaries) felt that the West Africans not only would be ineffective but would actually add to the problem. They were viewed as no better than Charles Taylor's rebels or the AFL. The United States could be tarred if it supported a force that would rape, pillage, and add to the horror.

I reminded the group that ECOMOG would place the West Africans in a highly visible role on the world stage. They would send their very best and conduct themselves in a fairly professional manner. No one really listened. Within six months of the U.S. decision to steer clear of ECOMOG, the following unfolded: ECOMOG cleared the NPFL out of Monrovia and established order; two U.S. military attachés who observed the operation first-hand told me that it was conducted professionally (one of the attachés actually said he wouldn't mind serving a tour of duty with the Nigerians or Ghanaians); and the Pentagon was looking for ways it could assist ECOMOG, now convinced of their effectiveness.

The Rest of the Story

Unfortunately for all concerned, with the exception of Taylor, ECOMOG failed to maintain that high level of professionalism for the next seven years. While the bottom line is still positive – ECOMOG did save tens of thousands of lives – its performance was inconsistent. A pattern developed where ECOMOG would atrophy into a lackluster outfit, partaking in theft, drug peddling, and business deals and shaking down the locals. Each down cycle would result in ECOMOG's getting burned by the rebels, the assignment of a new Nigerian Field Commander, and an instantaneous force revival.

Things did not go smoothly for Charles Taylor and the NPFL either. The INPFL was only the first of several splinter groups to emerge. By the mid-1990s, there were six significant rebel factions. Although the NPFL remained the largest and most capable group, it had serious competition. When President Doe was murdered by the INPFL in November 1990, the AFL became just another armed faction. Ethnic Krahns who had been loyal to Doe established other factions. ECOMOG mismanagement, if not treachery, was implicated in Doe's capture, torture, and death.

Throughout the early and mid-1990s, warlords and their armed factions controlled parts of Liberia. Occasional fighting was the rule of the day on most days. The political map of Liberia resembled a patchwork quilt. Monrovia and the Executive Mansion remained the prize; it was not only the seat of government but ECOMOG headquarters as well.

LIBERIAN ARMED FACTIONS, 1990–96

(Figures show the highest strength obtained during this period; not all groups existed throughout the period.)

Armed Forces of Liberia (AFL, 1990, Samuel Doe)	3,500
National Patriotic Front of Liberia (NPFL, 1990, Charles Taylor)	8,000
United Liberation Movement for Democracy (ULIMO, 1991)	7,000
Liberian Peace Council (LPC, 1993, George Boley)	2,000
Lofa Defense Force (LDF, 1993)	2,000

SPLINTER GROUPS:

Independent NPFL, Prince Johnson	1,500
NPFL Dokie/Woewiyu	4,000
ULIMO Kromah	4,000
ULIMO Roosevelt Johnson	3,000

Source: *Africa Confidential*, 4 November 1994, and other press accounts.

Intermittent fighting continued through the mid-1990s. The NPFL made two other major attempts to seize Monrovia. The first occurred in October 1992 when Taylor attacked ECOMOG forces in and around Monrovia. The NPFL's "Operation Octopus" involved infiltrating the capital from its eastern suburbs, crossing the swamp that separated this area from Monrovia proper, a north-south coastal strip. Before ECOMOG realized the threat, it was too late; NPFL marauders were everywhere and the peacekeepers had to rally, deputizing AFL and ULIMO troops to help resecure Monrovia. It took about a month to drive Taylor's men out of the capital once again.

ECOMOG STRENGTH IN LIBERIA:

1990	3,000
1991	8,000
1993	11,000
1994	12,000+
1996	12,600

COUNTRIES PROVIDING A SIGNIFICANT NUMBER OF TROOPS TO ECOMOG (1990–97). Forces from Sierra Leone, Senegal, Uganda, and Tanzania did not participate throughout the period; Uganda and Tanzania are not ECOWAS members:

Nigeria	Division Equivalent 10,000+
Ghana	Battalion+ 1,000
Guinea	Battalion+ 1,000
Sierra Leone	Battalion 700
Senegal	Battalion 1,000
Tanzania (Expanded ECOMOG)	Battalion 1,000
Uganda (Expanded ECOMOG)	Battalion 1,000

Source: *Africa Confidential*, 4 November 1994, and various press accounts.

During Operation Octopus, the NPFL killed five American missionary nuns. That incident refocused world attention, however briefly, on Liberia. The media interest and political concern in Washington over the loss of the five nuns weighed more heavily than the hundreds, even thousands, of hapless civilians massacred in Liberia simply because they were of the wrong tribe or in the wrong place at the wrong time.

The third battle for Monrovia took place in April 1996 when, once again, ECOMOG was caught unprepared. This episode ended in a military stalemate and a recommitment by ECOMOG to see the peace enforcement mission through. As it became clear that the rebel factions had no prospect of winning militarily, the fourteenth peace accord finally took hold and the way was opened for July 1997 elections.

The Warlord President

Charles Taylor won the election fair and square. The man who was a three-time loser militarily in attempts to take the capital by force won it in peaceful elections. And to what did Taylor owe his success? The most accepted story is that the bulk of Liberians simply believed electing Taylor was the surest bet for peace. If Taylor lost, he would almost certainly return to the warpath, prolonging Liberia's misery.

Taylor did bring a period of relative peace. The price for that peace, however, was Taylor's becoming a kingpin in the regional arms trade, the illicit diamond trade, the systematic plunder of what was left of Liberia's resources, and the brutal suppression of dissent. Taylor simply continued to act as a warlord, and his regime was unstable to boot. He relied on several different paramilitary forces that he played off against each other. His old enemies, the Krahns and others, were biding their time to move once again against Taylor when ECOMOG left the scene.

In 2000, a new armed faction took the field against the NPFL: Liberians United for Reconciliation and Democracy (LURD), later joined by the Movement for Democracy in Liberia (MODEL). At first the LURD insurgency was localized along the border with its sponsor Guinea. By 2002, however, they were threatening the capital and infiltrating internally displaced persons (IDP) camps on Monrovia's outskirts. Taylor's vow to crush the insurgency, and later to fight to the last man, gave way to his August 2003 negotiated exile in Nigeria. Taylor's regime had lasted a little more than five years.

Lessons from Liberia

The reluctance to put U.S. military personnel on the ground, even in a place where they are widely respected and feared and where we have historic familial ties, shows the depth of Washington's revulsion to African entanglements. Certainly, perhaps four thousand, not forty thousand, Marines could have done wonders to stabilize the situation early on. U.S. policymakers also have difficulty differentiating among African forces: the good, the bad, and the ugly. The difference between Liberian and Somali guerrilla fighters is not like apples and oranges; it is like apples and bricks!

ECOMOG's ups and downs should not distort its achievements. It was the first purely African peacekeeping operation and the first major security commitment by an African sub-regional economic organization. It also illustrated the folly of committing to "peacekeeping" when peace enforcement is required. No country should sign up for classic peacekeeping operations in SSA. No one can guarantee that the former combatants will remain exactly that: former combatants. Always assume combat can become part of the deal.

The more common operation is UN Chapter VI peacekeeping deployment. This relies on having a peace to keep. If the diplomats succeed, both parties to the conflict (and this assumes that there are only two) agree to a cease-fire and the insertion of UN forces between them. UN forces are not empowered to use military force, except for self-protection. Under a UN Chapter VII operation, in contrast, the need for peace enforcement is recognized. Peace enforcers have limited authority to use force. But, even here UN troops are constrained to engage in fighting depending on the particulars of the mission.

Another lesson from Liberia is the difficulty in dealing with rebel factions that divide, subdivide, and change allegiance based on ethnicity, religion, or some other local consideration. Getting them to the table and getting them to commit to what they signed on a piece of paper are formidable obstacles. We also learned that sometimes democratic elections can result in unpalatable outcomes such as a president Charles Taylor.

A final lesson is not preparing for the peace. Once a peace accord was signed, policymakers tended to lose interest in Liberia. There were few provisions for effective disarmament and adequate economic inducements to support the peace plan.

DDR: DISARMAMENT, DEMOBILIZATION, AND REINTEGRATION

DDR is a term widely used in the peacekeeping/conflict resolution world to address imperatives – the follow-on steps – once a cease-fire and a peace agreement have been obtained. This usually includes incentives, monetary or otherwise, for ex-combatants to hand in their weapons and begin demilitarization training. Taking the guns away from the former fighters is usually the key sticking point in the whole process. Reintegration can refer to reincorporation of ex-rebels into the national army or preparing them for a return to civilian life. Sometimes the process is called DDRR, or DDDR, or another combination of letters, as each negotiation leader seeks to give greater visibility to his mission.

SIERRA LEONE'S CIVIL WAR, 1991–2001

In March 1991, unidentified insurgents began attacking soft targets in eastern Sierra Leone, a West African coastal state about the size of South Carolina bordering Liberia's northwest. At first, Charles Taylor's NPFL was blamed for the attacks; the violence that had gripped Liberia was spilling over into Sierra Leone. Taylor was merely paying back a favor to Foday Sankoh, a former corporal in the Sierra Leone Army, who earlier had helped the NPFL organize its guerrilla campaign in neighboring Liberia.

Liberian rebels were involved in these early attacks, but Sankoh went on to form his own insurgent organization, the Revolutionary United Front (RUF).

This group of killers became synonymous with African brutality and mayhem. In March 1992, however, Sierra Leone was still considered safe enough for a high-profile U.S. visitor, General Colin Powell, chairman of the Joint Chiefs of Staff. Powell was on a swing through West Africa to thank four countries – Senegal, Sierra Leone, Nigeria, and Niger – that had contributed to Operation Desert Storm in the Persian Gulf.

Ironically, the chairman's visit to Niamey, Niger, was cancelled because of a recent military coup. The war in Sierra Leone was still restricted to the frontier with Liberia and seemingly posed little threat to a VIP in the capital, Freetown.

The Accidental Coup

In April 1992, barely a month later, Captain Valentine Strasser of the Sierra Leone Army (SLA) led a group of officers and soldiers from the "front lines" in the east back to Freetown to protest the lack of logistic support. President J. S. Momoh was not at State House, the seat of government, located about a block away from the U.S. Embassy. An argument ensued between Strasser's group and the staff at State House. Shots were fired and the confrontation escalated.

Back at DIA, we received a message from our embassy in Freetown. The ambassador described the events and concluded that the situation was now under control; the shooting had stopped and cooler heads had apparently prevailed. About twenty minutes later, we received a rare Flash precedence message (the highest priority communication) from American Embassy Freetown, stating that stray bullets had struck the Embassy, at least one of which lodged in the ambassador's desk. The embassy staff was taking shelter in the safe haven within the building.

Up the street at State House, it was learned that President Momoh – who had heard all the commotion – had fled the country. Captain Strasser was now in control in what became known as the "accidental coup." The British-trained SLA was historically not a bad army by African standards, but, ironically, Momoh, a former force commander, had weakened it years before the war broke out, fearing it posed a threat to his presidency. Once confronted with a serious military challenge (and any challenge to the SLA would be a serious matter), he expanded the ranks by recruiting riff-raff and under-aged youths.

The Pentagon Discovers Sierra Leone

Early one morning in the Pentagon's mezzanine basement, I was making my rounds conferring with the Africa analysts of the J2 joint staff intelligence directorate. The J2's main customers – the Joint Chiefs Chairman and the SECDEF – had become accustomed to receiving an update briefing on Liberia once or twice a week. This particular morning, however, the RUF was infiltrating Freetown, and the J2 called for a briefing on Sierra Leone that had to be put together in about an hour!

Luckily, our J2 Liberia analyst also handled Sierra Leone and was on top of the situation. Using a Shell Oil map of the country (oil and tire company road maps were often the most reliable ones), we plotted information on our hands and knees and put together a quick assessment. From that time on, we had two West African crisis countries. In the inter-agency arena, this meant that the DIA Liberia update briefing would include a Sierra Leone update as well.

During his tenure as leader of Sierra Leone, the twenty-something Captain Strasser paid a visit to the Pentagon. There was not exactly a groundswell of interest in seeing him. Often in cases like this, the Office of the Secretary of Defense (OSD) would request DIA (and me as the DIO) to brief our respected but not always welcome guests from SSA. On his OSD rounds, Strasser was a pathetic sight with his runny nose and zombie-like demeanor. Discussions were never more vacuous. This is what the State and Defense departments call a self-invited visit – low profile, with no visit to the White House or calls on cabinet-level officials. Strasser's highest courtesy call in the Pentagon was with an assistant secretary, small potatoes for a head of state.

The RUF Defines Economic Insurgency

Up through the mid-1990s, the RUF insurgency covered most of the country. Like Taylor's NPFL, Sankoh's RUF was essentially an economic insurgency, i.e., glorified banditry. There were no higher political or social motivations for the RUF. They were out for plunder and profit. And like most African economic insurgencies, they eventually would produce a piece of paper stating their supposed goals and objectives.

Economic insurgency can occur when the following are present: crushing poverty, a youth bulge of males between 12 and 24 years old, and ineffective, corrupt and weak national government, especially where it fails to control its own territory. Once more, bombarded by images of First World wealth, thanks to the global communications revolution, many of these alienated youths see no peaceful path to a better life. They become easy prey for warlords seeking recruits, offering instant rewards through the barrel of a gun.

And Sierra Leone possessed diamonds, mostly alluvial, in the north and east of the country. Under RUF control, and with a Liberian conduit to market them, they became known as "blood diamonds" or "conflict diamonds," because their sale financed the RUF, the NPFL, and others, possibly including terrorist groups laundering their funds.

Despite security problems, elections were held in 1995 and Ahmad Tejan Kabbah, a mild-mannered professor and longtime UN official, won the presidency. Kabbah hired Executive Outcomes (EO), the South African private military company (a.k.a. mercenaries) to suppress the RUF insurgency. EO enjoyed short-term success, driving RUF back into the interior, adding to the accolades it had won in Angola. Meanwhile, West Africa was growing mercenaries of its own. Freebooters, roving bands of thugs, sought new frontiers of violence or revisited old ones. Liberian and Sierra Leonean professional rebels moved about, usually away from where they were hunted down to areas more hospitable. Later, they would show up in Ivory Coast, Guinea, and perhaps elsewhere. These regional renegades make peace settlements difficult because they rarely participate or simply renege on any peace agreements.

Things Fall Apart ... Again

On May 25, 1997, Major Johnny Paul Koroma (ex-SLA) was liberated from prison by a gang of his followers. Koroma immediately marched on State House with a few hundred followers and deposed President Kabbah. He formed the Armed Forces Revolutionary Council (AFRC). The RUF rallied to support the AFRC and streamed into Freetown, creating instant chaos. The wolves were in control of the sheep. Freetown was sacked in biblical fashion. Murder, mutilation, rape, and plunder continued around the clock. A Nigerian battalion in

Freetown under a bilateral agreement with the Kabbah government was isolated on a peninsula, under attack by the RUF, and powerless to stop the carnage.

The crisis in Freetown called for evacuation of U.S. citizens and other foreigners. It just so happened that the U.S. Navy had the Amphibious Warfare Ship, the USS *Kearsarge*, in West African waters to support a possible evacuation of U.S. personnel from Kinshasa in the Congo. Fortuitous indeed. Helicopters and Marines from the *Kearsarge* evacuated 1,200 people from Freetown. Within a matter of days, Nigerian reinforcements and troops arriving from Ghana and Guinea drove the RUF and AFRC forces from Freetown, restored Kabbah to power, and formed the ECOMOG Task Force Sierra Leone (ETFSL).

MAJOR ARMED FORCES IN THE SIERRA LEONE CIVIL WAR

Sierra Leone Army: Unreliable; called "sobels" (soldiers by day; rebels by night). 10,000–14,000 strong; eventually retrained by a British team in country.

RUF: The major rebel group; given to extreme violence and savagery. Owed allegiance to Charles Taylor and other warlords in addition to Foday Sankoh. Strength 10,000 plus.

AFRC: Anti-President Kabbah; about 1,000 men, most ex-SLA.

Kamajors: Pro-government militia based on rural hunter societies. Later, some became unlawful. Strength about 10,000.

Executive Outcomes: South African mercenaries employed by the government, 1995–96. Several hundred soldiers and aviation and other specialists.

ECOMOG Task Force Sierra Leone: Nigerian-led West African force to oppose RUF. Strength 6,500 early, 10,000 plus later. Backed by heavy weapons (armor, artillery, light-strike aircraft, and naval gunfire).

UNAMSIL: UN peacekeeping/peacemaking force, ineffective at first. Later became largest UN peacekeeping operation at the time, with 17,500 troops.

Nigerian Operation Sandstorm

An uneasy truce lasted until December 1998, when the pro-government Kamajors opened a guerrilla campaign against the RUF in the interior. Meanwhile, the Nigerians were building ETFSL into a division-size combat force. In February 1998, ETFSL launched a ten-day campaign that evicted RUF from most major towns, re-establishing government control. The RUF had hired its own mercenaries (some of whom had actually worked for EO and the Kabbah government earlier) and reorganized its expanding guerrilla army into a more conventional force. This made RUF battalions and headquarters good targets for the conventionally organized Nigerian force that fielded four brigades of its own, including one transferred over land from Liberia.

Nigeria and America have a peculiar military relationship. For example, the similarity between Nigeria's Operation Sandstorm and the U.S. Operation Desert Shield/Storm is likely not a coincidence. The Nigerian military (like Nigeria itself) has very deep respect for the United States and tends to copy America, although any nationalist would cringe at the thought. For example, soon after I graduated from the U.S. Army War College, I was able to tour the Nigerian War College; the similarity was uncanny. The Nigerians once had an 82nd Airborne/Seaborne Division inspired by the U.S. Army's 82nd Airborne Division. They say imitation is the sincerest form of flattery.

RUF Operation No Living Thing

The RUF reacted to its tactical defeat at the hands of ETFSL and the Nigerians by turning on the rural population. Instead of winning the hearts and minds of the people according to Mao's dictum, the RUF attacked and terrorized them. In 1998 the RUF launched Operation No Living Thing, later followed by other terror campaigns such as Operation Burn House and Operation Pay Yourself. The purpose of these campaigns was to demonstrate to the people that neither the Kabbah government, ECOMOG, the Nigerians, nor anyone else could protect them.

Some similarity exists with the situation in Iraq in 2003–2005. The enemy's objective was to cause chaos and extreme instability that can deny progress toward reconstruction and a transition to normalcy. Any post-war settlement requires security; without it, you have nothing except many angry people frustrated at not being able to resume a peaceful existence or develop economic possibilities. The RUF tactics of hacking off limbs and other horrors are well known. I shall not detail them here again. Suffice it to say, they constituted another example of man's inhumanity to man.

The Lomé Peace Accord

"It is generally a bad idea to strike deals with men who chop the limbs off thousands of human beings," wrote Ralph Peters, a popular military strategist. As the atrocities continued through 1998 and into 1999, the search for peace intensified. Despite the humiliation of negotiating with butchers, it was the only way forward short of outright military intervention by the United States and the other Western powers. Finally, in July 1999, an all-parties accord to the conflict was reached in Lomé, the capital of nearby Togo. Peace came at the cost of blanket amnesty for the RUF and others suspected of crimes against humanity. Rebel leaders turned politicians were given posts in President Kabbah's government.

The ETFSL would transition to a peacekeeping force, the UN Mission in Sierra Leone (UNAMSIL). UN troops began arriving in Sierra Leone in late 1999. In May 2000, however, UNAMSIL received a rude awakening. RUF forces challenged troops moving to secure the interior; some were killed, others disarmed and held captive. The rebels took more than five hundred UN soldiers hostage. The credibility of UN peacekeeping was immediately at stake. After a few weeks, the disarmed UN peacekeeper hostages were released, but most of their equipment was never returned.

This was yet another case of peacekeepers not prepared for peacemaking. The former is more palatable when recruiting countries to volunteer their forces for UN operations. It also highlighted the lack of training and proper equipment among UN peacekeeping troops and their lack of preparation for combat operations. The UN did respond by authorizing 17,500 troops for UNAMSIL, making it the largest UN peacekeeping operation in the world.

The RUF Makes a Costly Error

Rebels still roamed the interior in 2001, as Disarmament Demobilization and Reintegration (DDR), as called for in the Lomé Accord, had not taken place. In fact, a tedious cease-fire settled over Sierra Leone, with the RUF forces still largely intact. A refugee camp across the border in Guinea proved too tempting a target (a source of plunder), and the RUF crossed the border in strength. The Guineans, enraged by this affront, drove the RUF fighters back into Sierra Leone but did not stop there. In coordination with the Kamajors, they chased the RUF from village to village using blunt- force heavy weapons. The rebels suffered staggering losses. With the Guineans at their front and the Kamajors at their back, the RUF was seriously reduced as a military force. It was time for the RUF to get out of the armed insurgent business, perhaps for good. Most rebels thus eschewed the armed struggle and became a political party. Others gravitated to remote locations, frequently across borders, to ply their murderous trade.

The Rise and Fall of the RUF: From Gangs to Brigades to Politicians

The RUF went through a cycle that resulted in its collapse as a military force. It began with banditry, and then became better organized as an insurgency. The difference here was moving from haphazard, random attacks against villages to the emergence of a command structure and central direction. With this, RUF became a semi-conventional force capable of holding ground. It targeted military and police forces and employed more conventional tactics. With the availability of diamond revenues, it began to acquire and employ better and heavier weapons and the mercenaries to train and resupply its forces. Arms were bought on the black market. Finally, with a good communications capability, the RUF became an even more conventional force, with its troops organized into brigades and battalions with fixed headquarters.

As we have seen elsewhere in sub-Saharan Africa, the move into the conventional arena led to the demise of the RUF as a potent military force. Large troop formations and their infrastructure made good targets for conventionally trained opponents, in this case, the Nigerian army, the Guinean army, and UNAMSIL. The UN's decision to beef up UNAMSIL, backed by growing world opinion that something had to be done about the repugnant human rights abuses in Sierra Leone, persuaded many RUF leaders to join the political process, this time for real.

Looking Back: The Tragedy of Sierra Leone

The war in Sierra Leone has been described as one of the most barbaric Africa has ever seen. For one reason, all sides were compromised at one time or another, except the UN. Members of the SLA and the Kamajors fought alongside the rebels at times, used indiscriminate violence against the civilian population, and employed child soldiers. For years a photo hung in my office of one of our military attachés accredited to Sierra Leone carrying a boy of about eight or nine years old wearing a red beret and clutching an automatic weapon that looked as big as he was.

Children saw their parents killed and were sometimes forced to participate in their murder. The RUF or local warlord became their father; the rebels became their family. Boy soldiers were given the power of life and death over adults, undermining the moral, psychological, and physical authority of the culture. RUF rebels in their campaigns against the population sought out community leaders such as teachers and police for punishment or elimination.

Drugs and magic were motivating factors as well. For many, this war was too bizarre to understand. A U.S. four-star general on a visit to Freetown found himself seated at dinner next to Hinga Norman, a Kamajor leader who became the deputy minister of defense in the Kabbah government. The general was impressed with the urbane and articulate British-educated Norman and asked him about the unusual clothing and charms worn by the rebels. Norman told him the clothing allowed bullets to pass through the body or in some cases turned them into water. The general was shocked; not so the old Africa hands in the intelligence community.

African Wars I Did Not Get to Know

Starting my career in 1967, I was not present for some of the early wars of independent Africa, or was too junior to cover conflicts outside of southern Africa. There are other wars that deserve a mention here to round out the deck of African conflicts and attempt to place them in an overall context. I did have responsibility for all of Africa south of the Sahara once I joined the U.S. European Command in January 1977. That made my career somewhat unique.

THE CONGO CRISIS

The early 1960s civil war in the former Belgian Congo placed Africa on the map, making an immense negative impression. The largest UN peacekeeping operation since Korea, the Congo crisis dashed hopes of a smooth African transition from colonial rule to independence. It also placed central Africa in the gun sights of the Cold War antagonists. Poor, fragile African countries were literally "up for grabs" between East and West.

The Congo crisis brought the horrors of African bush warfare to black and white TV screens around the world. Symbolized by the image of raped Belgian nuns, the Congo war left an imprint of black African savagery that seems to linger in the popular mind. The trite journalist's phrase "cannibal copy from Africa" was born. Even today, the 1960s Congo crisis evokes extreme negativity.

THE NIGERIAN CIVIL WAR

The big conflict in Africa when I began my career was the Nigerian civil war. In the late 1960s, Nigeria was already of some strategic importance to the United States, even though the extent of its oil wealth was not yet understood. As a result, only the more experienced Africa analysts at DIA got to work the Nigerian account. The three-year conflict – also known as the Nigerian-Biafran War or the War of the Biafran Secession – raged from 1967 to 1970.

The war pitted the Ibo people of southeastern Nigeria against the federal government and the rest of the country. The Ibo were seeking to establish their own country, an independent Biafra, but were violating one of the Organization of African Unity's most sacred strictures: the inviolability of the inherited colonial borders. African leaders feared altering borders would lead to chaotic instability; something one might argue is similar to what we have today. This was independent Africa's first big war. The federal government's army expanded quickly from 11,000 troops to 250,000. It took decades to demobilize this force when the war was over and unity prevailed. Nigeria emerged from it a budding regional power.

OTHER AFRICAN CONFLICTS

Mali and Niger have for years had to contend with nomadic Tuareg insurgency in the northern parts of their country. These mini-conflicts are mostly off rather than on; the Tuaregs have never threatened the governments but have resisted governmental authority.

Congo Brazzaville (the other Congo) has had its share of civil war in the late 1990s and early 2000s. It was like a protracted military coup in which no claimant was strong enough to prevail, at least until an outside power (Angola) intervened. The country's military and paramilitary forces dissolved into three militias (estimated at 25,000 strong) that contended for power.

For twenty years, a brutal guerrilla force known as the Lord's Resistance Army (LRA), led by Joseph Kony, has menaced northern Uganda. Despite the

Ugandan Army's successes in the Congo and Rwanda, it has been unable to cope with this vicious insurgency at home. Kony was a beneficiary of two contemporary security conditions. First, Kony and the LRA have survived by striking at defenseless civilians in rural areas, capturing children and making them slaves whose only way out of the LRA was by moving up and becoming gun-toting marauders. Second, the LRA has adopted a religious theme for its activities no matter how incongruous that might be.

Senegal, too, has successfully contained a low-level sporadic insurgency in its southern Casamance region. Concern for rebel support coming from Guinea-Bissau to the south resulted in Senegal's involvement in the 1998 civil war there.

OTHER WARS SINCE INDEPENDENCE

All of the wars described in this book kept Africa analysts around the intelligence community busy, even if high-profile interest was not always there. Of the forty-eight sub-Saharan states, only seventeen have not been involved in fighting a civil war, a cross-border war, or a major insurgency. If the criteria were expanded to include violent military coups or participation in peacekeeping operations, the number drops to seven. Moreover, some arguments could be made raising doubt about the remaining seven.

SOME FINAL OBSERVATIONS

Looking back, it has been a real privilege having access to classified raw intelligence traffic that allowed me to track political-military events in Africa over the course of my career. Information gathered, even on sub-Saharan Africa, a low-priority region, provided deep insights into the critical issues of the day and the motivations behind key decision-makers. Many an academic would give his or her right arm for access to the classified intelligence reporting that crossed my desk every day. It is too easy to complain about deficiencies in collection, staffing, and other resources. Generally speaking, we "Africa hands" at DIA had what we needed to keep going analytically through dedication to the job. I have always admired the professionalism of analysts – military and civilian – who made the system go despite those deficiencies.

Tracking developments in SSA can be stimulating but also depressing. In the early 1980s, I worked in a high-rise office building in Rosslyn, Virginia, across the Potomac from Georgetown in the District of Columbia. The two main building occupants were DIA and the State Department's Agency for International Development, AID. I soon discovered that when I got on the elevator in the lobby each morning I could easily tell which individuals worked for AID and which worked for DIA. The intelligence people had a serious demeanor, usually looked down at the floor, and rarely said anything. They wore suits and carried attaché cases. All business. The AID employees were quite different. They spoke freely and jovially to colleagues and dressed down. I remember one big fellow wearing a Hawaiian shirt and a straw hat. They were relaxed and looked happy to be going to work.

The AID people were in the business of giving away money and supplies to help people overseas, to make their lives better. This was a positive experience. The intelligence people, on the other hand, focused on the flaws in human character. Conflict, corruption, and political instability were the topics of the day, every day. National foreign intelligence dissects these problems, then makes judgments about them, and those assessments are almost always negative – especially when you are dealing with SSA.

Africa South of the Sahara Is Gradually Gaining Respect

Over the past forty years, slowly, ever slowly, both policymakers and intelligence professionals have taken Africa more seriously. Several converging factors are driving this evolution in perception. Analysts and policymakers for the most part are keeping an open mind and a straight face. A remarkable achievement was President George W. Bush's 2007 decision to create a U.S. Africa Command on the continent. Formerly a stepchild of the U.S. European Command in Stuttgart, Germany, AFRICOM, as it is called, turns the military spotlight on an area of the world long downplayed and studiously avoided by the Defense

Department. It is, as they say, a sign of the times. One of my DIA directors, LTG Pat Hughes, was an early advocate of an Africa Command.

There Is Too Much Levity in Intelligence

One repeated experience has always annoyed me, however. When presenting an assessment for a group of policymakers and/or intelligence officers, they too often drifted into a jocular state. How an African war can become a comedy by seemingly trivializing it has always depressed me. One reason is ignorance that breeds insecurity. As the intelligence analyst presenting the assessment catalogues all that is going wrong in country *X*, eyes begin to roll in the audience. Soon it's: "Oh no, not that too!" It begins to resemble a Bob Newhart skit. "You mean the rebels think bullets will turn to water, and army recruits are selling their weapons to teenage insurgents, and child soldiers are running amok terrorizing people in internally displaced persons camps?" The collective response frequently is, "What a mess!" The body language is clear: "Stay away from Africa!"

I want to differentiate here between the inside jokes and slogans that Africa analysts share with each other and the negativism described above. The difference is that the negativism is often the product of revulsion. Africanists, on the other hand, may make light of a situation to take the edge off, make it more tolerable. Facing difficult situations on a daily basis can wear a person down, lead to depression. In my mentoring capacity I advised young Africa analysts to maintain a balance between their personal and professional lives and stressed the advantages, such as they were, of working the region. I know that looking at all the ills of Africa over a long period of time influenced my retirement decision.

Africa's Growing Importance

On balance, it is becoming more difficult to disregard Africa. The global war on terrorism has extended into SSA. There is simply too much lawless territory to ignore (that is, ungoverned spaces), too many places for terrorists to hide, and too many corrupt officials willing to take bribes to look the other way. Americans there have already been attacked (the 1998 East Africa embassy bombings), and the threat to U.S. interests in Africa is likely to persist indefinitely. There are many soft American and allied targets. International terrorists also need a place to go, a safe haven for training and planning.

Another strategic factor that is slowly growing in American consciousness is the value of West African oil. According to various sources, 25 per cent of U.S. imports will come from this region by 2025. A disruption in oil flows out of the Middle East or elsewhere could make West African oil critical to the United States overnight.

A third factor is the moral imperative. As the world's only global super-power, and possessing a strong sense of empathy, the United States senses a responsibility to intervene to alleviate human suffering in worldwide disasters, whether natural or manmade. In Africa it is often a combination of both. Geno-cide, the violence in Sudan's Darfur region, the battle against HIV/AIDS and other deadly infectious diseases, recurring famine, and the plight of displaced persons fleeing conflict situations all draw the United States to Africa.

This isn't just about America doing the right thing. It is also in our long-term strategic interest. For a variety of reasons, including those mentioned here, the United States needs to maintain a capability to engage in sub-Saharan Africa. At times we will need access to Africa and the help of African allies to snuff out budding threats, whether they take the form of counter-terrorism, protection of oil supplies, or stopping the spread of a deadly disease. (See Klare and Volman, "Africa's Oil and American National Security," *Current History*, May 2004.)

Africa's Thirty Years' War?

People frequently ask me where Africa is going; will security get worse or im-prove? My answer is never a precise one. Certainly, insecurity and violence will persist in some regions around the continent. Africa seems to be reawakening from a long slumber as it shakes off the specter of colonialism and the distor-tions of the Cold War. Africa is in a desperate search for its own identity, a metamorphosis from which a new Africa will emerge. Some colonial borders may have to change. Yes, this has been a sacred commandment in post-colonial SSA: thou shall not tamper with the colonial borders for fear of creating wide-spread instability. Non-interference in the internal affairs of African states was another commandment that has since been disregarded by the African Union (AU). Refugee flows to neighboring states incur serious problems as a result and have fostered the realization within the AU that they cannot ignore "internal" problems that create "external" crises, such as hundreds of thousands of refugees in the receiving state.

What is really exciting is that African states are setting their own agendas, acting on their own sense of strategic importance. Countries are acting independently or in unison to meet security challenges, or they intervene in conflicts when their interests seem threatened. The AU in collaboration with the UN has established a peace operation mechanism to address every major security problem in SSA. South Africa and Nigeria, as expected, are in the front rank of these efforts, but countries such as Angola, Rwanda, Ethiopia, Ghana, Uganda, Senegal, and Zimbabwe have emerged as important players on the African scene. In addition, what will the "new Africa" look like? It may not be truly democratic, but it will be more stable.

Cold War Foibles

Throughout most of my career, Washington's obsession with the Cold War placed America on the wrong side of Africa's history. We just could not see the forest for the trees. We used the flimsiest "evidence" to condemn liberation movements as "communist." Therefore, the white minority regimes of southern Africa were viewed as the lesser of two evils. Most of the liberation movements were communist at least on paper, but Africa analysts for the most part knew that Marxism was hardly even skin-deep. It was, in fact, primarily a badge of convenience. Who else – other than the communist bloc – would supply these insurgents with arms to use against defiant white minority states who would scoff at holding serious peace talks with their black majorities?

Leave Your Logic and Biases at Home

As in many Third World environments, Western logic and unfavorable comparisons can lead an analyst astray. Many of the African conflicts and events outlined in preceding chapters occurred despite the prevailing thinking in the intelligence and policy communities, which held that these military forces were incapable of performing the task. In any case, the conflicts seemingly made no sense.

Military intelligence analysts can make the mistake of judging African militaries and insurgent forces incorrectly. They are not comparable to NATO forces, the U.S. military, or the armies of the former Warsaw Pact countries. But that doesn't mean they can't accomplish things in their own way. After all, they will be fighting other African armies, not modern First World forces. Presuming to know what is going on in a key leader's mind is a dangerous thing. The history of Africa, and the world at large, is replete with examples of the unexpected actions taken despite logical contradicting arguments. The late Tanzanian president Julius Nyerere's decision to invade Idi Amin's Uganda; Fidel Castro's decision to have his expeditionary force in Angola march on Namibia; and President Paul Kagame's decision to airlift his Rwandan soldiers to Kitona Base in order to attack Kinshasa from the West are but three examples of the unimaginable happening.

Finally ...

We have not seen the last of Africa's many conflicts. Africa analysts around the intelligence community will remain gainfully employed. I have cautioned policymakers and senior intelligence officials alike, telling them Africa will not go away, and that if you ignore it, you do so at your peril. That is still good advice.

Epilogue

It was a typically hot summer day in 1967 as I hit the Jersey Turnpike bound for Washington accompanied by a college friend of the liberal persuasion. My colleague assured me that choosing the upstart Defense Intelligence Agency (DIA) over graduate school and the Peace Corps was a smart idea, especially with the draft hanging over my head. He assured me that "anything in defense of intelligence can't be all bad." As the warm humid air rushed through the cabin of my bottom-of-the-line Plymouth Valiant, I pondered what fate lay ahead of me. Some forty years later, as I was tying up some loose ends in *African Wars*, it occurred to me that a few comments on one of the most far-reaching events of our day might be in order.

President George W. Bush established the U.S. Africa Command (AFRICOM) in 2007. It became fully operational by late 2008 and should become a watershed moment in U.S. relations with Africa. The coming of AFRICOM is important chiefly for two reasons. First, it is institutional recognition that Africa (particularly Africa south of the Sahara) is now a full-fledged member of the club and not that ne'er-do-well we could afford to dismiss. Commander/AFRICOM will have the same voice as other four-star commanders. This will elevate Africa to a new, previously unheard of position of influence within the U.S. defense establishment.

Second, "build it and they will come" might be a fitting motto. Once AFRICOM is up and running and fully staffed and becomes the moral equivalent of other U.S. commands, pressures will grow for its involvement in various African contingencies. Depending on how it is employed, the command could be a good, bad, or ugly thing for U.S. policy on the continent. On the positive side, AFRICOM is an idea whose time has come – and may be significantly overdue. It is a logical conclusion that reflects what has been going on in Africa south of the Sahara for the past decade or so. Set to be a key cog in the "Global War on Terrorism," the new command will have a unique humanitarian/nation-building bent that should make it beneficial to U.S. policy objectives.

Oil is the third strategic factor here. These days, it is not unusual for news broadcasts to cite "trouble in Nigeria" as affecting the price we pay at the pump.

As long as the United States remains dependent on foreign oil, sub-Saharan Africa will be of growing importance to Washington. According to recent prognostications, the region, and primarily the Gulf of Guinea in West Africa, will be supplying 25 per cent of U.S. imports. Despite the euphoria surrounding this prediction, it has yet to happen. Nevertheless, competition for African oil is growing. There is plenty of oil in sub-Saharan Africa, both in proven reserves and, more important, in unproven but anticipated reserves.

All beginnings are difficult, and AFRICOM's is no exception. Despite its dual personality (military and diplomatic), "boots on the ground in Africa" will leave many policymakers uneasy. Finding the right place to plant the commander's flag will be a major challenge. Then there is the "large footprint" (i.e., military presence) the command will leave on the continent if its headquarters is located there. The worst case, however, is that an AFRICOM based in Africa would provide terrorists with relatively easy targets. This could be exacerbated if the command were to become over-extended and drift into uncharted waters. Could AFRICOM become a "little Iraq" in some remote sub-Saharan country? The answer is, no one knows. It is possible but unlikely.

Nevertheless, force protection will be a major concern. Only one combatant command, EUCOM, is located outside U.S. territory, and that command is located in efficient, responsive, and security-conscious Germany. Further, the United States has a record of vulnerability in Africa, evidenced by embassy bombings and attacks on aircraft. Perhaps the ultimate disaster scenario is a short-notice evacuation operation that theoretically could result from a change of government in the host nation or from threats to Americans there.

On balance, the benefits clearly outweigh the risks. This is particularly true should AFRICOM be based on U.S. soil or in a strong European ally. No part of Africa can be allowed to become fertile ground for terrorist activities. Beyond the struggle against terrorism, the United States must act to protect its other growing equities in the sub-Saharan region, principally oil. The word is out – Africa is in.

Glossary of Acronyms

AID (Agency for International Development): The U.S. agency that administers foreign aid.

AFL (Armed Forces of Liberia): The feckless state army of Liberia that was reduced to just another warring faction during the 1990s Liberian civil war.

AFRICOM (Africa Command): The U.S. military command established by President Bush in 2007.

AFRC (Armed Forces Revolutionary Council): The transitory government established in Sierra Leone during the 1990s civil war.

AHS (Arlington Hall Station): The small army post about two miles west of the Pentagon in Arlington, Virginia, where most of the DIA's analysts were housed during the 1960s through the mid-1980s.

ANC (African National Congress of South Africa): South Africa's principal liberation movement, led by Nelson Mandela; later the dominant political party in South Africa.

ARMSCOR (Armaments Corporation of South Africa): The parastatal company that led Apartheid South Africa's arms production and procurement efforts.

AT (anti-tank): A weapon designed primarily to destroy armored vehicles and other hardened targets such as bunkers.

AU (African Union): The continent-wide cooperative organization of African States that replaced the Organization of African Unity.

CD (Civil Defense).

CF (Citizen Force): The ready reserve component of the South African Defense Force during the Apartheid era.

CIA (Central Intelligence Agency).

CINC (Commander in Chief): The most senior U.S. military commander in a theatre of operations, e.g., CINCEUR is the top commander in the U.S. European Command that, until recently, has been responsible for nearly all of Africa.

CIO (Central Intelligence Organization): The national intelligence apparatus of Southern Rhodesia, today's Zimbabwe.

CJCS (Chairman of the Joint Chiefs of Staff): The most senior U.S. military officer; his office resides in the Pentagon.

COIN (counter-insurgency): A set of tactics used to combat guerrilla warfare.

CT (Counter-terrorism).

CTs (Communist Terrorists): The name the white minority regime in Southern Rhodesia gave to the armed liberation movements fighting for their independence.

CTW (Cuban Troop Withdrawal): The negotiated process by which Cuba agreed to pull its forces out of Angola in exchange for South African withdrawal from Angola and Namibian independence.

COCOM (Combatant Command): A term used to refer to a U.S. unified command, such as the European Command or Central Command.

DARSP (Defense Academic Research Support Program): A DIA-sponsored program in the 1980s and early 1990s that funded academic research papers and annual conferences.

DAS (deputy assistant secretary): A State Department official, often of ambassadorial rank, who works under an assistant secretary of state, in this book the assistant secretary for Africa, the highest-ranking State official who deals only with African affairs.

DASD (deputy assistant secretary of defense): The DASD for Africa in the Pentagon is the highest-ranking defense official who deals only with African affairs and is DIA's most important customer for Africa.

DAO (Defense Attaché Office): The military office in a U.S. embassy that is responsible for liaison with the host nation's armed forces. Most embassies in Africa now have DAOs.

DCINC (deputy CINC): The four-star general or admiral who serves as second in command. In the European Command, the DCINCEUR is usually responsible for Africa, allowing the CINCEUR to concentrate on Europe and parts of the Middle East.

DDR: disarmament, demobilization, and reintegration.

DE (Directorate for Estimates): A senior analytical office within DIA that focused entirely on longer-range forecasts. It was eliminated in the early 1990s.

DIA (Defense Intelligence Agency): A defense agency headed by a three-star general (or admiral) designed to provide a homogeneous analytic defense position on strategic military intelligence. DIA was created to overcome the bickering among the army, navy, and air force intelligence chiefs.

DIAC (Defense Intelligence Analysis Center): A building on Bolling Air Force Base in Washington, D.C., designed to consolidate nearly all of DIA's personnel and functions at one location. Never able to achieve that goal, the DIAC was undergoing significant expansion in the mid-2000s.

DIO (Defense Intelligence Officer): The senior expert in DIA and the defense intelligence community for a given geographic or functional area. Located in the Pentagon down the hall from the director of DIA, the DIOs served as advisors to senior intelligence and policy officials. The DIOs were disbanded in 2003.

DIO-AF (DIO for Africa): The chief Africanist in defense intelligence; the position the author held from 1987 to 2002.

DRC (Democratic Republic of the Congo): Formerly known as the Belgian Congo and then as Zaire under President Mobutu, the DRC is sometimes referred to as Congo-Kinshasa to differentiate it from the much smaller former French colony of Congo-Brazzaville.

ECOMOG (Economic Community of West Africa Monitoring Group): The military arm of ECOWAS, whose forces, led by Nigeria, have been involved in extensive peacekeeping missions in West Africa.

ECOWAS (Economic Community of West Africa States): An economic grouping of fifteen West African states, dominated by Nigeria. During the 1990s, it developed a security component called ECOMOG.

E.O. (Executive Outcomes): A private military company composed mainly of former South African, and South African–trained, troops. Despite being labeled as mercenaries by some, in the 1990s E.O. worked successfully for the governments of Angola and Sierra Leone. The organization splintered and disintegrated.

EPLF (Eritrean People's Liberation Front): The dominant Eritrean liberation movement, it is now the government of an independent Eritrea.

EPRDF (Ethiopian People's Revolutionary Democratic Front): The rebel movement that in 1991 ousted the Mengistu regime in Ethiopia and now rules the country. It is dominated by the Tigrean People's Liberation Front.

ETFSL (ECOMOG Task Force Sierra Leone): The ECOMOG force originally sent into Sierra Leone to differentiate it from continuing operations in Liberia.

EUCOM (European Command): The U.S. command headquartered in Vaihingen, Germany, that has most of Africa in its geographic area of responsibility.

EUCOM J-2 (EUCOM Directorate for Intelligence): Headed by a two-star general (the J2), responsible for intelligence in the European theater of operations.

FAA (Angolan Armed Forces): Title of the Angolan military since the 1990s.

FALA (Armed Force for the Liberation of Angola): The armed wing of UNITA, the liberation movement led by the late Jonas Savimbi.

FAPLA (Armed Forces of the Popular Movement for the Liberation of Angola): The army of the Popular Movement for the Liberation of Angola prior to the 1990s.

FAR (Rwandan Armed Forces): The Hutu-dominated army of the government in power when civil war erupted in 1990. When that regime was ousted in 1994, government soldiers fled into neighboring countries, especially the DRC, and became known as the "ex-FAR."

FAZ (Zairian Armed Forces): The ineffective army of President Mobutu's government in what was then Zaire, now the DRC.

FDD (Force for Defense of Democracy): The former Hutu rebel group that became a highly successful political party in Burundi; its leader, Pierre Nkurunziza, was elected president.

FLNC (National Front for the Liberation of the Congo): Rooted in the former Katangan Gendarmes that fled their native Katanga Province in the Congo for Angola in the mid-1960s, this group has persisted in being a military factor in central Africa. Widely known as the "ex-Katanga Gendarmes."

FLS (Front Line States): Black-ruled countries in central and southern Africa that banded together to support liberation movements and confront the power of South Africa. Zambia and Tanzania were later joined by Mozambique, Zimbabwe, and Angola.

FNL (Force for National Liberation): The last Burundi insurgent group to surrender its arms and join the peace process in 2006.

FNLA (National Front for the Liberation of Angola): A Western-backed liberation movement that was a factor during the 1975–76 fighting in Angola. It has long since dissolved.

FRELIMO (Mozambique Liberation Front): The dominant liberation group in Mozambique, it continues to rule the country today, thirty-five years after independence.

GDIP (General Defense Intelligence Plan): A planning document that provides guidance on resource allocation for DIA and all the other defense intelligence components.

GS-12, GS-13, GS-14 (mid-level General Schedule pay grades): mid-level grades on the U.S. Civil Service payscale.

HUMINT (Human Intelligence): Information collected directly from human sources.

IDP (internally displaced persons): People uprooted by natural or manmade humanitarian crises but who do not cross international borders when they become refugees.

IGAD (Inter-Governmental Authority for Development): A cooperative union of states in the Horn of Africa; at first an economic and developmental organization, IGAD has become involved in peacemaking efforts.

I–NPFL (Independent–National Patriotic Front of Liberia): Led by Prince Y. Johnson, this rebel group was the first to break away from Charles Taylor's NPFL in Liberia.

ISA (International Security Affairs): Led by an assistant secretary, this part of the Office of the Secretary of Defense is responsible for security policy formulation. The deputy assistant secretary of defense for Africa works in ISA.

J2 (Intelligence): The part of a joint military staff that is responsible for intelligence. It could refer to the intelligence section of the Joint Chiefs of Staff (also a part of DIA), a large military command such as EUCOM, or a lower echelon military formation (e.g., a corps or division). J2 also refers to the person who heads a J2 section.

JCS (Joint Chiefs of Staff): The supreme U.S. military staff in the Pentagon.

JOCs (Joint Operations Center): A regional headquarters established by the white minority regime in Southern Rhodesia in the 1970s to stem the tide of the black nationalist insurgency.

LDF (Lofa Defense Force): One of a half dozen or more armed factions in the 1990–97 Liberian civil war. This group was based in Lofa County.

LPC (Liberian Peace Council): An armed faction in the 1990–97 Liberian civil war.

LRA (Lord's Resistance Army): A rebel/terrorist group that has ravaged northern Uganda since 1989. Led by Joseph Kony, the group purports to follow the Ten Commandments, but in reality is a vicious gang that victimizes the civilian population.

LURD (Liberians United for Return to Democracy): The primary rebel group that weakened and eventually destroyed the Charles Taylor regime in Liberia.

LTG Lieutenant General in U.S. Army usage.

MLC (Congolese Liberation Movement): A guerrilla army led by Pierre Bemba that operated in the northwest part of the Democratic Republic of the Congo during the 1998–early 2000s civil war (a.k.a. "Africa's First World war").

MNR (Mozambique National Resistance): A vicious insurgent group that devastated Mozambique for more than a decade. Also known as RENAMO.

MOD (Ministry of Defense): The senior cabinet department for the military in many nations.

MODEL (Movement for Democracy in Liberia): Another rebel group that fought against Charles Taylor's regime in Liberia.

MPLA (Popular Movement for the Liberation of Angola): The formerly Marxist-oriented liberation movement that fought the Portuguese, the South Africans, and rival Angolan groups to wrest control of the country.

MRL (Multiple Rocket Launcher): A popular area-fire artillery weapon used in many African wars; the Russian-made BM-21 carrying forty 122-mm rockets was prominent among these.

NATO (North Atlantic Treaty Organization).

NCEUR (National Security Agency office in EUCOM in the late 1970s.

NCOs (non-commissioned officers): military ranks such as coroporal, sergeant.

NGO (nongovernmental organization): Ranging from humanitarian relief organizations to large bureaucracies, these organizations act to pick up the burden where individual nations do not get sufficiently involved. Hundreds of NGOs operate in Africa.

NIC (National Intelligence Council): A group of senior officials in the U.S. intelligence community that previously served under the Director of Central Intelligence but now is under the new Director of National Intelligence.

NIO (National Intelligence Officer): A member of the National Intelligence Council and the senior substantive authority in the U.S. intelligence community for a given region or functional area.

NIO–AF (National Intelligence Officer for Africa): The senior authority for Africa in the U.S. intelligence community.

NPFL (National Patriotic Front of Liberia): The guerrilla movement led by Charles Taylor that took power in Liberia's 1997 elections after eight years of civil war.

NR (National Reconciliation): The process in Angola to bring together the country's warring factions following Cuban troop withdrawal.

NSA (National Security Agency): The U.S. Defense Department agency responsible for signals intelligence, notably intercepting foreign communications.

NSC (National Security Council): The White House national security advisors to the president.

NSSM (National Security Study Memorandum): A U.S. policy document focusing on a specific issue or crisis in foreign affairs, providing an assessment of the situation and a suggested course of action.

OAU (Organization of African Unity): A regional organization of African states established in the 1950s and replaced by the African Union in 2000.

OB (Order of Battle): The part of military intelligence that focuses on the strength, organization, deployment, equipment, and formation of foreign armed forces. Sometimes referred to by the derogatory term "bean counting."

OSD (Office of the Secretary of Defense): The staff and sub-staffs of the secretary of defense in the Pentagon; this staff numbers in the hundreds.

ONUB (United Nations Operation in Burundi): The UN PKO in Burundi from 2003 to 2006. It was brought in to assist an African Union force; it handed control back to the AU when it departed.

PAC (Pan-Africanist Congress): The South African liberation movement second in importance to Nelson Mandela's ANC – African National Congress.

PAIGC (African Party for the Independence of Guinea and Cape Verde): The successful liberation movement that achieved the independence of Guinea-Bissau (formerly Portuguese Guinea) from Portugal.

PF (Permanent Force): Fulltime professional soldiers of the South African armed forces during the Apartheid era.

PKO (Peacekeeping Operation): The negotiated deployment of troops to a country in order to prevent a resumption of hostilities.

PLO (Palestine Liberation Organization): A militant group that opposed Israeli control of Palestinian territory; it also became involved in at least one African conflict.

RAR (Rhodesian African Rifles): A Southern Rhodesian army unit comprised of black African troops, except for the officers, who were white.

RCD (Congolese Rally for Democracy): The rebel group opposed to the Kabila government in Kinshasa that fought alongside Rwandan forces in the coalition war, also called "Africa's First World War," that began in 1998; largely a product of the Rwandan Tutsi government.

RENAMO (Mozambique National Resistance): A rebel group that fought against the ruling Front for the Liberation of Mozambique (FRELIMO) government in the 1980s and early 1990s. Originally founded by white Southern Rhodesia and latter backed by Apartheid South Africa, RENAMO became a vicious countrywide insurgency in Mozambique; also known at the MRN.

RLI (Rhodesian Light Infantry): A major formation of all-white troops in the army of Southern Rhodesia.

RPA (Rwandan Patriotic Army): The Tutsi-dominated army that defeated the Hutu-dominated Rwandan Armed Forces in 1994, forcing them into exile in neighboring countries, especially the Congo.

RPG (rocket propelled grenade): The ubiquitous direct-fire hand-held weapon that launches a rocket-propelled projectile. Extremely popular in Africa, it is used against all types of targets, including aircraft.

RUF (Revolutionary United Front): The Sierra Leonean rebel group infamous for its use of terror tactics against the country's hapless civilian population.

SADF (South African Defense Force): The armed forces of Apartheid South Africa.

SAN (South African Navy): South Africa's naval forces.

SANDF (South African National Defense Force): The title of the South African armed forces after majority rule was established.

SAS (Special Air Services): An elite company-sized special operations force in the armed forces of Southern Rhodesia.

SDSF (Somalia Democratic Salvation Front): An armed faction that fought against Somali president Mohammed Siad Barre's regime.

SECDEF (Secretary of Defense): The head of the U.S. Department of Defense.

SIGINT (signals intelligence): The method of intelligence collection using listening devices to intercept all kinds of communications.

SLA (Sierra Leone Army): The government army of Sierra Leone.

SNA (Somali National Army): Somali president Siad Barre's national army led by his own Marehan clan. The disintegration of this force led to Somalia's collapse.

SNM (Somali National Movement): A rebel group that opposed the Siad Barre regime in Somalia.

SPLA/M (Sudanese People's Liberation Army/Movement): The major guerrilla army led by the late John Garang that fought against the Arab-oriented government in Khartoum for many years. The Movement traditionally controlled much of southern Sudan.

SSA (sub-Saharan Africa): All of Africa except for the northern tier of states (Morocco, Algeria, Tunisia, Libya, and Egypt). Island states around the continent (e.g., Madagascar, Cape Verde, and Sao Tome & Principe) are usually included as part of Africa south of the Sahara (another way of saying sub-Saharan Africa).

SWAPO (South-West Africa People's Organization): The major liberation movement in South-West Africa, now known as Namibia.

SWATF (South West Africa Territorial Force): The indigenous army raised by Apartheid South Africa to bolster its control of the territory of South-West Africa.

TAN-ZAM (Tanzania-Zambia): the railroad built by China in the 1970s that connects the rail systems of Tanzania and Zambia, creating an alternate rail corridor.

TPDF (Tanzanian People's Defense Force): The army of Tanzania.

TPLF (Tigre People's Liberation Front): The rebel movement that fought against the Mengistu regime in Ethiopia in the 1980s and early 1990s.

UDI (Unilateral Declaration of Independence): The illegal separation of Southern Rhodesia from Great Britain in 1965. White Rhodesians refused to go along with London's plans for independence that would in effect transfer power to the black majority.

ULIMO (United Liberation Movement): A rival Liberian warring faction that opposed Charles Taylor's group in the 1990s.

UN (United Nations).

UNAMIR (UN Mission in Rwanda): The UN force deployed to Rwanda prior to the 1994 genocide.

UNAMSIL (UN Mission in Sierra Leone): The UN peacekeeping operation in Sierra Leone that was initially ill prepared but later became the largest UN security mission in the world.

UNAVEM (UN Verification Mission in Angola): A UN military observer mission deployed to Angola.

UNHCR (United Nations High Commissioner for Refugees).

UNITA (National Union for the Total Independence of Angola): Led for decades by the late, charismatic Jonas Savimbi, it became the only real military challenge to the government during the country's long-running civil war.

UNITAF (Unified Task Force): The peacekeeping/enforcement operation set up in 1992 in cooperation with the UN but led by the United States. The Task Force was established to pacify the situation in southern Somalia to allow in humanitarian assistance after a UN mission failed.

UNMEE (UN Mission in Ethiopia and Eritrea): A UN verification and observation force deployed along the common border in 2000 to monitor the cease-fire between Ethiopia and Eritrea.

UNOMOZ (UN Observer Mission in Mozambique): The early 1990s UN peacekeeping operation in Mozambique to monitor the cease-fire between the government and the rebels.

UNOSOM (UN Operation in Somalia): Usually differentiated as UNOSOM I and UNOSOM II, these missions encompassed UN security operations in Somalia from 1992 to 1995.

UPDF (Ugandan People's Defense Force): The Ugandan Army.

USC (United Somali Congress): The warlord army that controlled most of Mogadishu Somalia during the UN intervention but was divided between the Aideed and Mahdi factions.

USDAO (U.S Defense Attaché Office).

USG (Government of the United States).

USSR (Union of Soviet Socialist Republics): The Soviet Union.

WMD (weapons of mass destruction): Nuclear, chemical, biological, or other catastrophic weapons.

WSLF (Western Somali Liberation Front): A Somali-sponsored guerrilla force that contested Ethiopian control of its Ogaden region for many years.

ZANLA (Zimbabwe African National Liberation Army): The military arm of the Zimbabwe African National Union.

ZANU (Zimbabwe African National Union): The Zimbabwean liberation movement backed by China, it was ultimately successful and is now the country's ruling party.

ZAPU (Zimbabwe African People's Union): The liberation movement supported by the Soviet Union.

ZIPRA (Zimbabwe People's Liberation Army): The military arm of the Zimbabwe African People's Union.

Bibliography

Adebajo, Adekeye, and Ismail Rashid, eds. *West Africa's Security Challenges*. Boulder, CO: Lynne Rienner Publishers, 2004.

South African Parliament. "Parliamentary Briefing Reveals SANDF Equipment Figures." Supplement to *African Armed Forces Journal* (July 1996).

Arlinghaus, Bruce, and Pauline Baker, eds. *African Armies: Evolution and Capabilities*. Boulder, CO: Westview Press, 1986.

———. *Military Development in Africa: The Political and Economic Risks of Arms Transfers*. Boulder, CO: Westview Press, 1984.

Avirgan, Tony, and Martha Honey, eds. *War in Uganda*. London: Zed Press, 1982.

Barnett, Michael. *Eyewitness to Genocide*. Ithaca, NY: Cornell University Press, 2002.

Bayham, Simon. *Military Power and Politics in Black Africa*. London: Croom-Helms, 1986.

Bienen, Henry. *Armed Forces, Conflict and Change in Africa*. Boulder CO: Westview Press, 1989.

Bowden, Mark. *Black Hawk Down: A Story of Modern War*. New York: Atlantic Monthly Press, 1983.

Breytenbach, Col. Jan. *Forged in Battle*. Cape Town: Saayman and Weber, 1986.

———. *They Live by the Sword: 32 Buffalo Battalion – South Africa's Foreign Legion*. Alberton, South Africa: Lemur Books, 1990.

Bureau of Intelligence and Research. *Arms and Conflict in Africa*. Washington: U.S. Department of State, 1999.

Butts, Kent Hughes, and Steven Metz. *Arms and Democracy in the New Africa: Lessons from Nigeria and South Africa.* Carlisle Barracks, PA: U.S. Army Strategic Studies Institute, 1996.

Butts, Kent Hughes, and Arthur Bradshaw, eds. *Central African Security: Conflict in the Congo.* Carlisle Barracks, PA: Center for Strategic Leadership, U.S. Army War College, 1996.

Cawthra, Gavin. *Brutal Force: The Apartheid War Machine.* London: International Defense and Aid Fund for Southern Africa, 1986.

Cawthra, Gavin, and B'jorn Moller. *Defensive Restructuring of the Armed Forces of Southern Africa.* Brookfield, VT: Ashgate, 1991.

Cilliers, Jakkie, and Peggy Mason, eds. *Peace, Profit or Plunder: The Privatization of Security in War Torn States.* Halfway House, South Africa: Institute for Security Studies, 1999.

Clapham, Christopher, ed. *African Guerrillas.* Bloomington: Indiana University Press, 1998.

Clark, John F., ed. *The African Stake in the Congo War.* New York/Basingstoke: Palgrave McMillan, 2002.

Clarke, Walter, and Jeffery Herbst, eds. *Learning from Somalia.* Boulder, CO: Westview Press, 1997.

Clayton, Anthony. *Frontiersmen: Warfare in Africa since 1950.* London: University College of London Press, 1999.

Cohen, Herman J. *Intervening in Africa: Superpower Peacemaking in a Troubled Continent.* Macmillan Studies in Diplomacy Series. Basingstoke (UK): Macmillan, and New York: St. Martin's Press, 2000.

Connell, Dan. *Against All Odds: A Chronicle of the Eritrean Revolution.* Lawrenceville, NJ: Red Sea Press, 1997.

Crocker, Chester A. *High Noon in Southern Africa: Making Peace in a Rough Neighborhood.* New York: W.W. Norton, 1993.

———. "Military Dependence: The Colonial Legacy in Africa." *Journal of Modern African Studies* 12, no. 2 (1974): 1–14.

De Spinola, Gen. Antonio. *Portugal and the Future.* Lisbon, n.p. 1974.

Deng, Francis, and I. William Zartman. *Conflict Resolution in Africa.* Washington, DC: Brookings Institution, 1991.

Durch, William, ed. *UN Peacekeeping, American Politics, and the Uncivil Wars of the 1990s.* New York: St. Martin's Press, 1997.

Echenberg, Myron. *Colonial Conscripts.* Portsmouth, NH: Heinemann, 1991.

Feil, Scott. *Could 5,000 Peacekeepers Have Saved 500,000 Rwandans?* Washington, DC: Institute for the Study of Diplomacy, Georgetown University, 1997.

Flower, Ken. *Serving Secretly: Rhodesia's CIO Chief on Record.* Alberton, South Africa: Galago Press, 1987.

Foltz, William J., and Henry Bienen, eds. *Arms and the African.* New Haven, CT: Yale University Press, 1985.

Foltz, William J. *Chad's Third Republic.* CSIS Africa Notes no. 77. Washington, DC: Center for Strategic and International Studies, October 30, 1987.

———. "Regional and Sub-Regional Peacekeeping in Africa." *African Journal of International Affairs and Development* 3, no. 1 (1998): 1–8.

Francis, Dana. *Peacekeeping or Peace Enforcement? Conflict Intervention in Africa.* Cambridge, MA: World Peace Foundation, 1998.

Frankel, Phillip H. *Pretoria's Praetorians: Civil-Military Relations in South Africa.* Cambridge: Cambridge University Press, 1984.

Glickson, Roger. "The Shaba Crises: Stumbling Toward Victory." *Small Wars and Insurgencies* 5, no. 2 (1994): 189–200.

Gourevitch, Phillip. *We wish to inform you that tomorrow we will be killed with our families.* New York: Farrar, Straus and Giroux, 1998.

Grundy, Kenneth W. *The Militarization of South African Politics.* Bloomington: Indiana University Press, 1986.

Hanlon, Joseph. *Beggar Your Neighbor: Apartheid Power in Southern Africa.* Bloomington: Indiana University Press, 1986.

———. *Mozambique: The Revolution under Fire.* London: Zed Books, 1984.

Hempstone, Smith. *Rogue Ambassador.* Sewanee, TN: University of the South Press, 1995.

Henk, Daniel. *Uncharted Paths, Uncertain Visions: U.S. Military Involvements in Sub-Saharan Africa in the Wake of the Cold War.* Colorado Springs, CO: Air Force Academy, 1998.

Herbst, Jeffrey. *Securing Peace in Africa.* Cambridge, MA: World Peace Foundation, 1998.

Howe, Herbert M. *Ambiguous Order: Military Forces in African States.* Boulder, CO: Lynne Rienner Publishers, 2001.

———. "Private Security and African Stability: The Case of Executive Outcomes." *Journal of Modern African Studies* 36, no. 2 (1998): 307–31.

Human Rights Watch. *Angola Unravels: The Rise and Fall of the Lusaka Peace Process.* New York: Human Rights Watch, 1999.

Jaster, Robert S. *South Africa's Narrowing Security Options.* Adelphi Paper No. 165. London: International Institute for Strategic Studies, 1980.

Kaplan, Robert. "The Coming Anarchy." *Atlantic Monthly* (February 1994): 44–76.

Khadiagala, Gilbert M. "Reflections on the Ethiopia Border Conflict." *Fletcher Forum of World Affairs* 32, no. 2 (1999): 1–9.

Kramer, Reid. "Liberia: Casualty of the Cold War's End." *CSIS Africa Notes* no. 174 (July 1995): 1–9.

Liddell-Hart, Basil H. *Strategy.* New York and Washington: Frederick Praeger, 1968.

Martin, David, and Phyllis Johnson. *The Struggle for Zimbabwe.* Harare: Zimbabwe Publishing House, 1981.

Magyar, Karl, and Earl Conteh-Morgan. *Peacekeeping in Africa.* New York: St. Martin's Press, 1997.

Mazrui, Ali. *The Warrior Tradition in Modern Africa.* Leiden: E.J. Brill, 1977.

Mills, Gregory. "How to Intervene in African Wars." Crimes of War Project, *War in Africa* Magazine (October 2004): 1–10.

Mank-Koefoed, Captain (French Army). "Routing the Libyans." *Marine Corps Gazette,* August 1987, p. 26.

Prendergast, John, and Colin Thomas-Jensen. "Blowing the Horn." *Foreign Affairs* 86, no. 2 (2007): 59–67.

Prunier, Gerald. *The Rwanda Crisis.* New York: Columbia University Press, 1995.

Reno, William. *War Lord Politics in African States.* Boulder, CO: Lynne Rienner Publishers, 1998.

———. "No Peace for Sierra Leone." *Review of African Political Economy* no. 84 (2000): 325–48.

Richburg, Keith. *Out of America: A Black Man Confronts Africa.* New York: Harcourt, Brace, 1998.

Romer-Heitmen, Helmold. *War in Angola,* Gibraltar: Ashanti Publishing, 1990.

Science Applications International Company. *Analytical Study of Irregular Warfare in Sierra Leone and Liberia.* September 30, 1998.

Snow, Donald M. *Uncivil Wars: International Security and the New Internal Conflicts.* Boulder, CO: Lynne Rienner Publishers, 1996.

Steenkamp, Willem. *Border Strike: South Africa into Angola*. Durban-Pretoria, South Africa: Butterworths, 1983.

Stockwell, John. *In Search of Enemies: A CIA Story*. New York: W. W. Norton, 1986.

St. Jorre, John. *The Brothers' War: Biafra and Nigeria*. New York: Houghton-Mifflin, 1972.

Thom, William G. "Angola's 1975–76 Civil War: A Military Analysis." *Low Intensity Conflict and Law Enforcement* 7, no. 2 (1998): 1–44.

———. "Congo-Zaire's 1996–97 Civil War." *Journal of Conflict Studies* 19, no. 2 (1999): 93–120.

———. "Sub-Saharan Africa's Changing Military Environment." *Armed Forces and Society* 11, no. 1 (1984): 32–58.

Van Creveld, Martin. *The Transformation of War*. New York: Free Press, 1991.

Vogt, Margaret, ed. *The Liberian Crisis and ECOMOG: A Bold Attempt at Regional Peacekeeping*. Lagos, Nigeria: Gabumo Publishing, 1982.

Welch, Claude, ed. "Praetorianism in West Africa." *Journal of Modern African Studies* 10, no. 2 (1992): 629–68.

Weller, Mark, ed. *Regional Peacekeeping and International Enforcement: The Liberian Crisis*. Cambridge International Document Service, vol. 6. Cambridge: Cambridge University Press, 1994.

Wolfers, Michael, and Jane Bergirol. *Angola in the First Line*. London: Zed Press, 1983.

Zartman, I. William, ed. *Collapsed States: The Disintegration and Restoration of Legitimate Authority*. Boulder, CO: Lynne Rienner Publishers, 1995.

Index

17; map, 71; MPLA (Popular Movement for the Liberation of Angola), 63–72, 74, 76, 79, 82–88, 95, 166, 236; oil and West Africa countries, 41; "Operation Final Assault" and, 81; Russian T-34/85 tank and, 116; three guerilla armies in, 50; UNITA (National Union for the Total Independence of Angola), 50, 63–69, 71–74, 76, 79, 81–88, 107, 122, 191, 234, 239

Angolan Armed Forces (FAA); 83, 85–88, 192, 234

apartheid, 54–55, 68–69, 72, 86, 91–92, 95–97, 102–4

Arlington Hall Station (AHS), 53, 65; "A Building" at, 90; military capabilities (mil cap) shop at, 28

Armaments Corporation of South Africa (ARMSCOR), 98–99

Armed Forces Movement (formerly "Captain's Movement"), 52

Armed Forces of Liberia (AFL), 199–202, 204–6, 231

Armed Forces Revolutionary Council (AFRC), 212–13, 231

Army's Foreign Area Officer program, 32

Aspin, Les, 151

Atwood, J. Brian, 158

Azores Islands, United States interests in, 47

B

"Bantustans," 91

Barclay Training Center, 202

Barlow, Eben, 86, 121

Barry, Marion, 43

Bassoon, Wouter, 102

Bendix, William, 11

Berlin Conference (1884–85), arbitrary collections of peoples into territorial units, 39

Bicesse Accords, 82–84

bin Laden, Osama, 160

Bishop, Jim, 138

Black Hawk Down, Somalia and, 150–52

Bloch, Johan, 11

BM–21 multiple rocket launcher (MRL), 117

Bolling Air Force Base, 103, 148; military capabilities (mil cap) shop at, 28

Botha, Pieter W., 96–97

Boutros-Ghali, Boutros, 147

Brinkley, David, 54

British South African Police (BSAP), 56

Brown, James, 18

Bull, Gerald, 99

Bureau of Intelligence and Research (INR), Department of State, 53; basic structure of intelligence community and, 1

Burundi: civil war and, 195–98; transition to peace and, 197; Tutsi conspiracy and, 196

Bush, George H. W., 72, 147

Bush, George W., 222, 227; Sudan and, 161

Butt, Victor, 193, 201

Buyoya, Pierre, 195

C

Cabora Bassa Dam, 51

Cabral, Amilcar, 52

Caetano, Marcelino, 48

Castro, Fidel, 70, 76–79, 129, 226

Central Intelligence Organization (CIO), 58

Chad: "Toyota Wars" and, 170–77; map, 173; war against terrorism and, 177

Cheney, Dick, and briefing on Somalia, 36–37

China: construction of the Tan-Zam Railway and, 94; Tanzanian People's Defense Force (TPDF) and, 131

CIA: Angola Intelligence Task Force and, 65–66; Turkish invasion and, 30

Clapper, James, 24, 114

Clark, Donald O., 53

Clinton, Bill, 183

Liberians United for Reconciliation and
Democracy (LURD), 207, 235

Libya: acquisition of MiG 25 FOXBAT jet
fighters, 17; Habre's counter–offensive
and, 174–75; "Toyota Wars" and,
170–77; U.S. air strike against, 176

Liddell-Hart, Basil, 12

Lisbon: counter–insurgency campaign and, 48;
Portuguese Guinea (Guinea Bissau)
and, 52

Lomé Peace Accord, Sierra Leone and, 215

Lord's Resistance Army (LRA), 220–21, 235

Lusaka Protocol, 87

M

Machel, Samora, 106

Mahele, Marc, 189

Mandela, Nelson, 94; and African National
Congress, 58

Marriott, Ronald, 24

Martin, David, 61

MASINT, intelligence cycle and, 2

Mavinga: battle for, 74–76; location of, 81–82

Mbumba, Nathaniel, 167

media as two–edged sword, 40

Mengistu, Haile Mariam: 17–18, 126–29,
136, 139–44, 153–54, 156, 233,
239; closing of Kagnew Station
and, 17; coup attempt and, 140; exile
in Zimbabwe and, 143; Marxist
mass army and, 142; racial identity
problems of, 18; "Red Star" offensives
and, 139

MiG 25 FOXBAT jet fighters: Libya's
acquisition of, 17

Military Intelligence Board, 2

military order of battle (OB) analysis, 90

missionaries as "passive collectors" of
information, 21

Momoh, J. S., 25, 210

Morgan, Mohamed Siad Hersi, 136–37

Movement for Democracy in Liberia
(MODEL), 207, 236

Mozambique: American attachés' plane
attacked in, 49; "Captain's Movement"
and, 52; Gersony Report and, 108;
growing problems in, 48; Operation
"Gordian Knot," 51; RENAMO
War in, 105–10, 123; Sant'Egidio
Community and, 109; winding
down of war in, 109–10; U.S. policy
and, 107–9; weak link in Portugal's
colonial chain, 51

Mozambique National Resistance (RENAMO),
59, 236; growing insurgency and,
105–10

MPLA (Popular Movement for the Liberation
of Angola), 63–72, 74, 76, 79, 82–88,
95, 166, 236

Mugabe, Robert, 60–61

Munson, Jeff, 122

Museveni, Yoweri, 180, 196

N

Nakasongola Airbase, 133

Nakfa as Eritrean Alamo, 154

Namibia, Caspir armored personnel carrier in,
118

National Front for the Liberation of Angola
(FNLA), 50

National Intelligence Council (NIC): Defense
Intelligence officers (DIOs) and, 4–5;
Angolan crisis and, 67

National Intelligence Daily, Turkish invasion
article, 30

National Intelligence Officer (NIO), and
Angolan crisis, 67

National Patriotic Front of Liberia (NPFL),
201–7, 209, 211–12, 235–36

National Security Agency (NSA), basic
structure of intelligence community
and, 1

National Security Council: 40 Committee
of, 66; Defense Intelligence officers
(DIOs) and, 5

National Union for the Total Independence of
Angola. *See* UNITA

NATO: and Ogaden War, 129; soft underbelly of, 19–20

Nigeria: civil war and, 220; Colin Powell's visit and, 25–26; OAU (Organization of African Unity) and, 220; oil and West African countries, 41; Operation Sandstorm and, 214

Nigerian-Biafran War, 220

Nkurunziza, Pierre, 198

Norman, Hinga, 217

NRM. *See* Mozambique National Resistance (RENAMO)

Nyerere, Julius, 61, 131–32, 226

O

OAU (Organization of African Unity), 220

Office of the Secretary of Defense (OSD), on oil and region's strategic importance, 41

Ogaden War: capture of Jijiga and, 127; from insurgency to invasion and, 126–28; overview of, 125; Soviet Union control of, 129. *See also* Somalia

oil and West African countries, statistics on, 41

ONUB (United Nations Operation in Burundi), 197

Operation Burn House, 214

Operation Desert Shield, 137, 214

Operation Desert Storm, 137, 210, 214

Operation "Gordian Knot," 51

Operation No Living Thing, 214–15

Operation Pay Yourself, 214

Operation Restore Hope, 147, 150, 183–84

Operation Sandstorm, 214

Operation Turquoise, 183–84

Operation United Shield and Somalia, 152

Organization of African Unity (OAU), 130, 237

Oueddei, Goukouni, 170

P

Palestine Liberation Organization (PLO), 132

Pan Africanist Congress (PAC), 94

Patch Barracks, 15–19

Peace Corps, 227

Perry, William, 183–84

Peters, Ralph, 215

Polana Hotel, 24

Policymakers and strategic intelligence, 5–6

Popular Movement for the Liberation of Angola (MPLA), revolt against Portuguese rule, 50

Portugal: Armed Forces Ruling Council and, 63; Bicesse Accords and, 82–84; collapse of African empire and, 48; counter-insurgency (COIN) program and, 49–52; and fighting nationalist insurgencies in Africa, 47; Portuguese Guinea (Guinea Bissau) and, 52

Portugal and the Future (de Spinola), 52

Powell, Colin, 25, 59, 210

Prendergast, John, 158–59

Pretoria: 32nd "Buffalo" Battalion of, 75; heading a delegation to, 103–4; influence throughout sub-Saharan Africa of, 91; and showdown with Havana, 75; UNITA's dependence on, 74; weapons of mass destruction (WMDs) and, 100–101

Q

Quick Reaction Force in Somalia, 151

R

Rawson, David, 182

Reagan Doctrine, 96

Reagan, Ronald, 72, 102

relief workers: as "passive collectors" of information, 21

RENAMO War, 105–10

Revolutionary United Front (RUF): economic insurgency and, 211–12; invasion of Guinea and, 216; Operation Burn House and, 214; Operation No Living Thing and, 214–15; Operation Pay Yourself and, 214; rise and fall of, 216–17

Revolutionary United Front (RUF), 209–17, 238. *See also* Sierra Leone

Rhodes, Cecil, 55, 60

Rhodesia: "C Squadron, Special Air Services (SAS) Regiment," 56; "Green Leader" raid and, 59; heart of Rhodesian military establishment, 56; Unilateral Declaration of Independence (UDI), 55, 56, 61, 239

Rhodesian African Rifles (RAR), 56

Rhodesian Air Force, Canberra Light Bombers and, 57; ZIPRA SA–7 shoulder-fired anti-aircraft missiles and, 58

Rhodesian Light Infantry (RLI), 56

Rhodesian war: two phases of, 57–60

Roberto, Holden, 50, 66

Roberts, Andy, 190

Roberts International Airport, 202

rocket-propelled grenades (RPGs), 64

Rumsfeld, Donald: briefing on Africa, 36

Rwanda: background to crisis in, 180; battles in, 183–84; civil war and genocide crisis, 179–86; and death of Habyarimana, 181; evacuation of U.S. Embassy Kigali in, 182; intelligence failures and, 181; spread of war over Rwandan border, 184–85; and Tutsi and, 179–85

Rwandan Patriotic Army (RPA), 180–81, 183–85, 187–93, 238

Rwanda Working Group, 182–83

S

SADF (South African Defense Force): 68–69, 72, 74–80, 90, 92–97, 99, 103–4, 238

Salisbury Show, 61

Sanders, Harland, 23

Sankoh, Foday, 209, 211, 213

Savimbi, Jonas, 50, 69, 72–74, 80, 82–88, 108

Seko, Mobutu Sese, 50, 165, 185, 187, 190

Selassie, Haile, 126–27

Selous Scouts, 57

Serving Secretly: Rhodesia's CIO Chief on Record (Flower), 61

Shaba One (Shaba I), in Zaire: 167–68; Katangan Gendarmes and, 17

Shaba II, in Zaire, 168–70

Siad Barre, Mohammed, 125–26, 129, 136–39

Sierra Leone: accidental coup in, 210; Armed Forces Revolutionary Council (AFRC), 212–13, 231; and civil war, 209–17; economic insurgency and, 211–12; ETFSL (ECOMOG Task Force Sierra Leone), 213–15, 234; and Johnny Paul Koroma, 212–13; Lomé Peace Accord and, 215; major armed forces in, 213; Pentagon and, 211; Revolutionary United Front (RUF), 209–17, 238; Sierra Leone Army (SLA), 210, 212–13, 217, 238; tragedy of, 217; UNAMSIL (UN Mission in Sierra Leone), 213, 215–16, 239

Sierra Leone Army (SLA), 210, 212–13, 217, 238

SIGINT, intelligence cycle and, 2

Smiley–Pickett billets, and Third World regional experts, 31

Smith, Ian, 55, 57

Somalia: after the Ogaden War, 136; and Black Hawk Down, 150–52; briefing Dick Cheney on, 36–37; capture of Jijiga and, 127; civil war and, 135–39; intelligence responds to crisis and, 147–48; lessons learned from, 152–53; and leveling of Hargeisa, 138; major events in, 150; Mohamed Farrah Aideed and, 137, 150–53, 240; Operation Eastern Exit and, 137–38; Operation Provide Relief and, 146; Operation United Shield and, 152; Quick Reaction Force and, 151; sending U.S. troops to, 28; Somali gunmen, 148–49; UN and U.S. intervention in, 145–53; UN efforts in Mogadishu, 146–47; UNITAF (Unified Task Force) and, 146–50, 239; United Somali Congress (USC), 137

Somalia Intelligence Task Force, 147

Somali Democratic Salvation Front (SDSF), 136–37

Somali National Army (SNA), 126–29, 136–37

Somali National Movement (SNM), 136–37

South Africa: "32nd Battalion" of, 70; 1961 Sharpeville massacre in, 93; 1976 Soweto riots in, 93; and apartheid, 91–93, 95–97, 102–4; Armaments Corporation of South Africa (ARMSCOR), 98–99; Citizen Force of, 92; construction of the Tan-Zam Railway and, 94; defense industry of, 97–102; and defense strategy, 89–94; and Israeli connection, 101–2; major weapons systems made in, 99; MPLA and, 68–69; Permanent Force of, 92; and surprise in Angola, 94–95; training black African forces by, 70; weapons of mass destruction (WMDs) and, 91, 100–102; and white threat perception, 93–94

South African Army Staff College, 23

South African Defense Force (SADF), 68, 92–95

South African Navy (SAN), 90

Southern Rhodesia, insurgency in, 55

South-West Africa People's Organization (SWAPO), 72, 78, 82, 94, 239

Soviet Union: airlift from Russia to Brazzaville, 70; Bicesse Accords and, 82–83; Cuban troop withdrawal (CTW) and, 78; Ethiopia's army and, 143; expelled from Somalia, 128; Mengistu Haile Mariam and, 139; nuclear weapons test sites in Kalahari Desert, 100; Ogaden War and, 129; and Russian T-34/85 tank, 116

SPLA (Sudanese People's Liberation Army), 160–64, 238

Stoakley, Bill, xiii–xiv, 121

Stockwell, John, 66, 70

Strasser, Valentine, 210–11

Strategy (Liddell–Hart), 12

The Struggle for Zimbabwe (Martin/Johnson), 61

sub-Saharan Africa (SSA): and Africa Hot Spots briefing, 20; cocktail circuit and, 21; crisis support and, 29; defense attaché offices (DAOs) in, 22; demise of the RUF in, 216–17; final observations on, 221–22; and the General Defense Intelligence Plan (GDIP), 27; global war on terrorism and, 223; illness and, 25; as legitimate focus for defense intelligence, 33; optimists versus pessimists on, 39–42

Sudan: Darfur and the oil, 162–64; George W. Bush's foreign policy team and, 161; modern history of, 164; and second civil war, 160; slow-motion war in the south of, 162; war in, 159–64

SWAPO. *See* South-West Africa People's Organization

Switzer, Barry, 9

T

T-55 tanks, 113, 162

Tanzania: "Farm 17 Nachingwea" in, 51; Kagera Salient in, 130–31; spread of Rwandan war over the border, 184–85; Tanzanian People's Defense Force (TPDF), 131–133

Tanzania-Uganda War: air war in, 133; counter-invasion, 132; Nyrere versus Amin, 130–32; TPDF march to Kampala, 133–34; overview of, 130

Taylor, Charles, 200–209, 211, 213, 235–36, 239

Tessema, Azaz Kebbede, Mengistu Haile Mariam and, 18

Thomas-Jensen, Colin, 159

Thom, George, 9

Thom, Henry, 9

Thom, Margaret, 9

Thom, Michael, 9, 11

Thom, William, 9

Thom, William Frederick, 9